Scapegoat of Shiloh

Scapegoat of Shiloh

*The Distortion of Lew Wallace's
Record by U.S. Grant*

KEVIN GETCHELL

Foreword by Stacy D. Allen

McFarland & Company, Inc., Publishers
Jefferson, North Carolina, and London

Library of Congress Cataloguing-in-Publication Data

Getchell, Kevin, 1951–
  Scapegoat of Shiloh : the distortion of Lew Wallace's
record by U.S. Grant / Kevin Getchell ; foreword by
Stacy D. Allen.
      p.   cm.
  Includes bibliographical references and index.

  ISBN 978-0-7864-7209-3
  softcover : acid free paper ∞

  1. Shiloh, Battle of, Tenn., 1862.   2. Wallace,
Lew, 1827–1905.   3. Grant, Ulysses S. (Ulysses
Simpson), 1822–1885.   I. Title.
  E473.54.G47 2013
  973.7'31—dc23   2013023739

British Library cataloguing data are available

On the cover: *insets, left to right* Ulysses S. Grant, Lew Wallace;
background Battle of Shiloh (all images from the Library of
Congress)

Manufactured in the United States of America

*McFarland & Company, Inc., Publishers
  Box 611, Jefferson, North Carolina 28640
  www.mcfarlandpub.com*

To Randy Getchell and my father John S. Getchell, who served and suffered. May they and all have the peace that comes with the true meaning of Shiloh.

"Future years will never know the seething hell and the black infernal background, the countless minor scenes and interiors of the secession war; and it is best they should not. The real war will never get in the books."

— Walt Whitman

Table of Contents

Acknowledgments

I wish to gratefully acknowledge persons who have been of critical importance to the production of this work.

Stacy D. Allen, historian and chief park ranger of Shiloh National Military Park, offered his time, encouragement, and friendship on visits to the battlefield where the matters in this book were played out 150 years ago. He recommended I submit the book proposal to McFarland. He has the highest respect and esteem for the public trust of anyone I have encountered. His scholarly and firm view of the way to approach Shiloh history has been an inspiration and enabled me to avoid certain pitfalls.

The officers and staff of the U.S. Grant Association at Mississippi State University were of great assistance. Dr. John Marszalek, director and managing editor of the Association, was supportive of my search through the files of unpublished materials. Dr. Mike Ballard, associate editor, also provided encouragement when he took time to discuss vagaries of the historical record available. Ryan Semmes, assistant archivist, was of great help and truly careful in his preservation of archival materials. Along with Ryan, Elizabeth Coggins, library associate, patiently and professionally provided the copies and procedures I needed to follow.

I am also grateful to the Newberry Research Library of Chicago, which possesses some of the lesser known resources of the Civil War.

My personal editor and wife, Janet Weeden, helped in the editing of my manuscript. Without her exceptional knowledge as an English teacher and belief in and support of my writing, I could not have completed this book.

I must not fail to acknowledge the part Lana Getchell played in my striving to be a writer. Though she did not directly participate in the production of this work, for 35 years she was my partner in life and always an encouragement. I owe her praise that is impossible to fully express.

Foreword

With the publication of *Scapegoat of Shiloh: The Distortion of Lew Wallace's Record by U.S. Grant*, Kevin Getchell delves deeply into one of the most controversial aspects of the Battle of Shiloh: General Lew Wallace's ill-fated forced march of 6 April 1862, in which the major portion of the division under his command moved overland from its encampments off the battlefield to successfully reinforce U.S. Grant's hard pressed army engaged on historic Shiloh Hill. To give a complete picture, Getchell draws heavily on official records, makes generous use of numerous memoirs, letters and reports gathered from widely scattered sources, and uncovers new sources yet used in other publications. With these sources, the rarest of them hastily scribbled during combat, Getchell has crafted a narrative of human complexity in the face of life and death difficulties, and attempts to seek firmer answers regarding the dynamics of leadership, decision making, logistics, and stress under combat conditions. His work sheds light on common human failings and emotions that often reflect the sum total of humanity when faced with and exposed to even remotely similar difficulties and decisions requiring performance and action. The study also reflects the role selective memory always plays in understanding past human events.

For twenty-four years it has been my great privilege to live and work on the actual ground where the momentous Battle of Pittsburg Landing or simply Shiloh was fought. As park historian and now chief ranger for Shiloh National Military Park, my primary professional responsibility has been stewardship of the story of the battle and of the battlefield — the crucial elements which give meaning to this battle's history and the important place this significant event of the Civil War occupies in the broad context of our national experience. In that capacity, I continually read, review, analyze, correlate, and interpret the evolving bibliography and historiography that deals with the brutal combat and awful carnage experienced by the tens of thousands of souls engaged in this battle. It is from examination of this body of knowledge all students of Shiloh eventually discover why, in the opinion of the late Lloyd Lewis, the guns of Shiloh still echo across the ages — they still roar.

In tackling the often confusing and misunderstood history of Lew Wallace's controversial experience and performance at Shiloh, Kevin Getchell offers the reader a well researched and thoroughly documented examination of what transpired before, during and after the battle that turned Wallace's Shiloh experience into the haunting nightmare of his war service. His uncovering of new evidence in the form of correspondence and records yet published or known to the common Shiloh bibliography provides the ability to reexamine the old traditional "tardy" and "lost" Lew Wallace scenario. It provides the opportunity to question what has been known and understood about the battle, and provides the rare opportunity to question old impressions and prejudices within the Shiloh historiography.

This is not the first time someone has accepted the challenge of tackling the Lew Wallace at Shiloh controversy. Many historians, including myself, have attempted to illustrate that what occurred at Shiloh was larger and far more complex and important than the historical perception that one individual failed to perform as expected by his superior. Often, the conclusions reached are that the battle turned or significant consequences befell one side or the other as a result of individual failure. One person, occupying a key leadership or decision making role, made a mistake. That one individual, in this case a volunteer general officer (Wallace), engaged in a Civil War battle, possessing command of more than 8,800 officers and men comprising an army division, made a crucial error and thereby significantly altered the course of events in the context of a battle documented to have been experienced and seriously affected by the collective conduct and performance of nearly 110,000 combatants, rank and file.

History, however, often holds military officers at a higher standard, particularly in regard to their performance under the stress and strain of combat, and thus in the examination of the course of events in any military undertaking, the personalities, behavior, decisions, and actions of the leaders in command are always grist for the historian's mill. The key for us is to remember the humanity of the subject matter and understand that battles the magnitude of Shiloh are fought by armies made up of tens of thousands. The performance of individuals or even a handful of individuals must always be examined against the whole.

In *Scapegoat of Shiloh,* Kevin Getchell probes the complex relationships of a cast of individuals caught up in the difficulties and strenuous pace of a divided nation at war, and raises new questions in our understanding of both

Lew Wallace and U.S. Grant. The study also illustrates the state of logistics, command and control, line of authority, and staff deficiencies at this early point in the war. On the issue of professional staff capabilities, skills, knowledge, and performance, Grant himself will acknowledge to his superior, Major General Henry W. Halleck, in correspondence sent from Oxford, Mississippi, in December 1862, "my individual labors [as commander of his department and army] have been harder," primarily "due to having an entire staff of inexperienced men in military matters."

Throughout history a standard military maxim has marked the performance of the most successful professional captains and students of warfare: "Amateurs study tactics, while professionals study logistics." In addition, the best modern war studies of what the late John Keegan termed the "face of battle" labor to probe the causes and effects of war and combat, moving beyond the popular "glory, glory hallelujah" approach marking earlier studies. Ultimately, Kevin Getchell's conclusions of what transpired before, during, and after two bloody and confusing days in early April 1862 will generate discussion and most likely — as published history most often does — provoke more questions and meaningful controversy. In this regard, Getchell's examination of the pivotal performances of U.S. Grant, the inexperienced officers comprising his military staff, and division commander Lew Wallace, in view of the momentous chaos that was Shiloh, illustrates the dynamic interactions of men engaged in an ultimate test of human endurance — the practice of war and individual performance under the strain of combat on a field of battle.

Chief park ranger at Shiloh National Military Park since 2002, Stacy D. Allen is a 24-year veteran of the National Park Service. He is the author of several articles and books on Civil War topics.

Preface

My great-uncle plopped a worn family album down on my lap when I was about ten years old. Staring out from one of the first pages was an ancient picture of a family, all with stricken faces. The father's and mother's faces looked very severe; the six children all had waning looks. I asked who they were and why they all looked so bad. He replied that the man and woman were my great-great-grandfather and -mother and turned the picture into a story. They were from Alabama, and the reason they all looked so bad was "they could hear the guns of Shiloh." That was not the only time I heard that expression, and it was not the only branch of the family that I learned had something to do with the Battle of Shiloh. My mother was raising me with what some called pacifist teaching and turned away from discussing war when I asked, but the expression "the guns of Shiloh" had planted seeds in me that have lasted all my life.

Over the years, with what facts I could find out, I determined to write a novel dealing with the effects of the Battle of Shiloh. In doing so I began looking for some physical artifact that could put me in a direct touch with the battle. I was particularly interested in the Southern side as my ancestor, a Rebel cavalryman, fought under Colonel Nathan Bedford Forrest. I acquired a number of items at auctions over the years, but then I came upon a phenomenal discovery that turned my focus more to the Northern side. Arguably the most controversial determination of the Northern side is the blame placed on Union general Lew Wallace, claiming that he failed the Federal forces by his late arrival on the first day of battle, thereby being responsible for the terrible casualties. Among the papers of a Wisconsin lieutenant were documents written while the battle raged. Among them were signatures of Captain Algernon Sydney Baxter. Baxter was chief quartermaster of General U.S. Grant and was the man who carried the message to General Lew Wallace to bring his division up to the battle. The written order was subsequently lost after delivery. For one hundred and fifty years Lew Wallace has been the object of scorn. The documents I discovered have proved to refocus the controversy. This book in large part explores the proposition that choosing the chief of supply and transportation, Captain A.S. Baxter, as the messenger to go to General Lew Wallace was one of the greatest mistakes of the Union side at the Battle of Shiloh, rather than the time of arrival of General Lew Wallace's troops. This is something that has never been explored before, though the fact was in plain sight. Neither have there been battlefield records to show the manner in which nor character of the way Captain Baxter discharged his responsibilities. The evidence presented in this book will show a concerted effort was made to turn attention away from General U.S. Grant's mistake and scapegoat General Lew Wallace.

When Sunday, April 6, 1862, dawned over the swollen Tennessee River at Pittsburgh Landing, the population along the wilderness bluffs had also swollen. Incredibly, it rivaled that of Chicago, the city noted for slaughter-houses. Unknown to the flood of Unionists that had pooled in those Hardin County fields, tens of thousands of Secessionists had streamed in from the South. Crisscrossed by ravines, the plateau was crowded with almost 100,000 inhabitants. The farm fields and forests around Shiloh meeting house were set to become the largest human slaughterhouse the continent had ever known.

To understand the impact of those three days in April requires going beyond claims of victory and defeat. The impact of the carnage so appalled both sides that scapegoats had to be found, and though there was plenty of blame to go around, in some cases the accusers were actually the most culpable. This was a battlefield of a different sort. Many of the officers in the armies were lawyers. The best lawyer would win the struggle of command ascension. Probably the best lawyer at Shiloh was Captain John Rawlins, General U.S. Grant's adjutant general. Rawlins was his main aide, but more than that, he was psychologically attached to Grant as a father figure. He was the best spin doctor of the war, but if it had not been for his legal skills, fierce personality and obsequious enabling of Grant, someone else would have gotten the laurels and claims of superiority of mind and action than U.S. Grant.

Grant had already gained a national following for his unconditional sur-render demands at Ft. Donelson, making his U.S. initials an acronym. Grant's staff grudgingly admitted that one of his subordinates, young General Lew Wallace of Indiana, assisted in making that resounding demand possible. At Shiloh, Grant was not the knowing, in-control commander his later biographers painted. After the battle Wallace nearly disappeared as a player in the national military drama. Benign documents of an obscure Wisconsin lieutenant at Shiloh now point to an engineered scapegoating of Lew Wallace, as he always maintained had happened. It is curious to note the lack of documents in regard to the critical orders transmitted to General Wallace by Rawlins through staff quartermaster Captain A.S. Baxter — curious because duplication of even the most minor of requisitions was law in the Quartermaster Corps. It is curious that Baxter subsequently disappeared from Grant's staff due to "illness." It is curious how the following year's excessive vilification by promoted-to-colonel John Rawlins has earmarks of the Shakespearian self-conviction of blame, since Rawlins "dost protest too much, methinks." This is also true of the lengths that were gone to in denying Grant's proclivity to drunkenness.

By a study of the timeline contained in Shiloh battle records in the archive of Lt. Richard P. Derickson, Company K, 16th Wisconsin, reasonable assertions can be made. These documents are a time capsule containing undoctored records of intersecting actions of U.S. Grant, his staff quartermaster A.S. Baxter, forgotten lieutenant colonel Enos P. Wood, Gen. Benjamin Prentiss, and a host of other uncelebrated junior officers and enlisted men.

These Derickson documents could have provided evidence in a court of inquiry that was denied to Wallace by General H.W. Halleck. Halleck was a kind of bottleneck. His desk in Missouri should have had a plaque like the one belonging to the later Missourian Harry Truman that said, "The buck stops here," but it did not; he passed the buck. Halleck's pompous and jealous military micromanagement as the architect of the Tennessee Expedition resulted in the ghastly body count at Shiloh; yet General Halleck deserves a second look for the wash-out history has given him. The irony of his culpability for slaughter by hamstringing his subordinates' efficacy has its flip side in his economy in spending human life while in direct command.

As to the Confederate States of America, it has been stated that it was a romantic lost cause from the beginning. Statisticians point to the overwhelming logistics on the part of the North as causing the doom of secession. A factor that is possibly more dooming to the rebels was its own internecine strife among clashing personalities of the political administration and military command structures. The self-mutilation of the Confederacy through the scapegoating of General G.T. Beauregard is a case in point of how the Confederate administration cut off its nose to spite its face.

It has been claimed that the Confederates surprised the Federals at Shiloh. The clandestine arrival of a massive rebel army was not the real surprise. It was the bursting of the national bubble of innocence. The confluence of two naïve human streams filled with a euphoric sweet water of vainglory turned like the Biblical plague into blood. Combatants on both sides were filled with ambition, visions of fame, and ideas of a quick war with minimal loss, but this battle was a sudden massive coronary in the heartland. Look at a map of the whole country and imagine Maine and Florida as outstretched arms of the nation, the rest as the fallen torso. Its geographical heart is Shiloh.

It has been said that Shiloh is a Hebrew word that means "place of peace." The Hebrew is not translated that way; rather, this mythology is part of the postwar ruminations of the combatants and their descendants who have tried to reconcile what happened there with attempts at making poetry out of the horror that took place around that church and meeting house.

Shiloh was not only the pivotal battle in the War Between the States, but it remains a trauma that affects the descendants of the participants, generations after the events. With occasional information coming out of attics, Internet uploads of records by historical societies, and the ever-increasing data available through Google, the insights on this event will never end. After all, the 100,000 and more humans who were there each had a multitude of anecdotes and episodes that influenced the battle. Each and every individual and incident was a horseshoe nail that held the horseshoe to the horse that carried a rider who fought the battle that supported a "kingdom." The loss or preservation of a single one of those horseshoe nails could have changed everything.

What follows is largely a telling of certain events reconstructed from never-before-published documents and letters, especially of Prentiss's 6th Division. It is not intended as a comprehensive study of the whole battle. Remarkable works have done that, such as Wiley Sword's *Shiloh: Bloody April* and Larry Daniel's *Shiloh: The Battle That Changed the Civil War* and the long-hidden, now-published, authoritative manuscript by O. Edward Cunningham, *Shiloh and the Western Campaign*. It is hoped that this book will add to the understanding and scholarship of this particular battle. It is also intended as reflections of a militant pacifist. You may have had an ancestor there. The participants came from the far reaches of the continent. The search for an ancestor led this author to write down these accounts. These are only a fraction of the number of accounts that could be related. The many what-ifs of the battle define it more than any other battle of the Civil War. If taken collectively as a warning, they add up to the biggest what-if of all. What if it had not happened?

1

Before the Fame Came

The evidence was found floating in the river. The soggy mass of records was rescued just before the Ohio River merged with the Mississippi and carried them southward to oblivion. What they contained was proof of mass corruption in the supply and transportation department, the quartermaster corps of General U.S. Grant.[1]

Grant's staff quartermaster was Captain Rueben B. Hatch. He was not someone to deal with easily. Brigadier General Grant inherited Hatch from General John C. Frémont's military administration. Hatch had friends and relatives in high places. The quartermaster's brother was Secretary of State of Illinois, and he also knew President Abraham Lincoln personally. For months Hatch had a kind of free reign in the disheveled Department of the West. This came about after one of the biggest ironies of the Civil War. General Frémont, who had been in charge of military administration of the Western departments, was fired for emancipating slaves under his jurisdiction, by none other than the later Great Emancipator, Abraham Lincoln.

Major General Henry Wager Halleck succeeded Frémont. In the flux that happened because of Frémont's sacking, every ambitious Union man was waging his own strategies for advancement and fame. Captain Hatch seemed more concerned with fortune. He purchased cheap prairie grass and sold it to the government as prime forage at high bid price; he gave government contracts to friends who could benefit him. Until an ordnance officer was assigned, Hatch had even been in charge of the ammunition depot. He bought substandard ammunition and artillery shells and rockets, probably lining his pockets substantially with ill-gotten gain that could cost untold lives.[2] Whether it was part of a corrupt strategy or not, Hatch had apparently allowed a steamboat full of good ordnance to capsize at Cairo, losing its stores. Only a small amount was retrieved by dangerously tossing it into the mud onshore. It had caused no end of misery to General Grant. Captain Hatch had become

CAPTAIN CLARK B. LAGOW.

DR. JAMES SIMONS

WINNING HIS SPURS AT CAIRO.

Few will recognize in this early and unusual photograph the man who at Appomattox, wore plain fatigue dress in striking contrast with the fully uniformed Lee. Here Grant appears in his full-dress Brigadier-General's uniform as he came to Cairo to assume command of a military district including southern Illinois, September 4, 1861. Grasping at once the problems of his new post he began the work of reorganization, assisted by a well-chosen staff. Without waiting for permission from Frémont, his immediate superior, Commander of the Department of the West, Grant pushed forward a

BRIGADIER-GENERAL U. S. GRANT.

force and occupied Paducah, Kentucky, before the Confederates, approaching with the same purpose, could arrive. Grant was impatient to drive back the Confederate lines in Kentucky and Tennessee and began early to importune. Washington to be allowed to carry out maneuvers. His keen judgment convinced him that these must quickly be made in order to secure the advantage in this outlying arena of the war. Captain Rawlins was made Assistant Adjutant-General by Grant, and lifted from his shoulders much of the routine of the post. Captain Lagow and Captain Hillyer were two of the General's aides-de-camp. Dr. James Simons was Medical Director of the District.

CAPTAIN WILLIAM S. HILLYER.

CAPTAIN JOHN A. RAWLINS.

General U.S. Grant and staff at Cairo, before fame came (*Review of Reviews*, 1911).

a nightmare, but Grant still had to deal with him during a transition awaiting a court of inquiry to decide the outcome of charges against him. Hatch was under a kind of roaming arrest, while the mass corruption charges waited a scheduling in Washington. Due to the fact that protocol had to be kept, and there were ambitious enemies within the command structure, General Grant approached Hatch's ouster and prosecution with caution. He could not simply replace him. His strategy was to ease someone else in as quartermaster as he eased Hatch out and slam the cell door shut on Hatch.

Although he was now a brigadier general, Grant was far from notable in the growing sea of men seeking military prominence at the outbreak of the Civil War. Recognition and fame would not come to him until a victory at Ft. Donelson, Tennessee, where his initials U.S. would play a huge part in rescuing him from obscurity. This current paperwork mess in the river did not bode well for his career and something had to be done. Since his re-entry into the army, Grant had been trying to assemble a staff that would enable him to spend his time fighting the rebels rather than dealing with paperwork. Before he could rid himself of Hatch he needed to line up a quartermaster with solid qualifications. That man was Captain Algernon S. Baxter.[3]

Grant took counsel with his mentor and friend General C.F. Smith. Grant [to] Smith on January 9, 1862:

> I had made application for a Quartermaster to take at least part of Capt. Hatch's duties off his hands during Gen. Fremont's Administration, and also since Gen. Halleck took command. After an investigation of the lumber purchases in Chicago, and getting no Qr. Mr. from St. Louis, I ordered Captain Baxter down [from Paducah, where he was serving as regular army Post Quartermaster] and required him to make all purchases until such time as something [illegible] may be done at Head Quarters for our relief.[4]

Relief was pressed upon the attentions of General Halleck in a January 12, 1862, correspondence. Grant informed Halleck he had

> placed Capt. Hatch A.Q.M in arrest and directed him to turn over all public property to Capt. A.S. Baxter. This was done on notice from Washington that charges would be preferred against the former, and if not already in arrest he should be so placed at once. Every day develops further evidence of corruption in the Quartermaster's Department, and that Mr. Dunton, Chief Clerk, if not a co-conspirator is at least an accomplice. I have ordered his arrest and confinement.[5]

This same day, Captain A.S. Baxter was appointed by Grant in General Orders No. 2 as District Quartermaster of Cairo with instructions to

> make, or properly provide for making, all contracts, and purchases, within the District, including contracts for water Transport, and everything pertaining to

the Quartermaster Department. All contracts, estimates for funds and requisition within this District, will be sent to the Chief of the Department, here, for approval, before passing to higher authority, and no contract, within the District, will be regarded as valid without this or higher authority.[6]

Grant had to do something of a waltz to get things done in his department. Despite the implications of corruption, Hatch was in the good graces of Frémont's successor General Henry Wager Halleck in St. Louis. Grant needed friends in high places in order to deal with the problem. He set out in a purposeful way to achieve that goal, but it would not make his immediate superior Halleck happy. No commander likes to be bypassed. Grant already had one patron in Washington: Illinois Congressman Elihu Washburne. Washburne had helped him get his first army commission at the outbreak of the war. He sent Baxter to Washburne in Washington with this letter in his pocket:

> Headquarters, Dist. Of Cairo.
> Cairo, Jan.y 23d 1862
>
> Hon. E. B. Washburn
> Washington D.C.
> Sir:
>
> The bearer, Captain Baxter who goes to Washington, by my order, in hopes of doing something for the relief of this much distressed portion of our Army is at present my District Quartermaster.
>
> I am at last satisfied that I have an efficient and faithful servant of the Government in Captain Baxter and anything you can do to further the object of his mission will not only be regarded as a personal favor to myself but will serve to advance the cause you and I both have so much at heart.
>
> Captain Baxter can tell you of the great abuses in his Department, here and efforts I have put forth to correct them, and consequently the number of secret enemies necessarily made.
>
> I am desirous of retaining Capt. Baxter in his present position and if promotion to a higher grade is necessary to enable me to do so I would very much desire that the promotion be given.
>
> Very respectfully
> Your Obt. Svt.
> U.S. Grant
> Brigadier Genl[7]

Grant had become acquainted with Baxter in St. Louis before the war during the period Grant was transitioning from a failed farming effort. In St. Louis he tried working in real estate and then applied for an engineering job. During that period Grant's friend Augustus Chetlain described Grant as "a man of considerable talk, with his friends he was a great talker, talked well too. He had not a wide command of words, but he was vivid."[8] With that personality, Grant walked the streets of St. Louis trying to stir up business and ran across the business of Baxter & Co. Breadstuffs and Provisions.[9] It was not just a corner store, since St. Louis was the Gateway to the West. It was an outstanding supplier of all kinds of provisions in that metropolis on the upper Mississippi. Baxter and Co. was a place pioneers sought to outfit their covered wagons and fill them with needed foodstuffs and other provisions. This kind of business also had a connection to leather goods, a business Grant's father and brother ran in Galena, Illinois.

Algernon Sydney Baxter came from a family of considerable reputation. His father was a Vermont Supreme Court judge. Business success ran in the Baxter family. Algernon's brother Horace Henry Baxter was one of the wealthiest men in America. He owned the largest marble quarry in Vermont, was a successful Wall Street broker in New York, he built his own bank, and he was building a railroad empire that would soon put him in partnership with Commodore Vanderbilt. Living in that kind of shadow, however, Algernon Baxter had set out to make his own mark out west in St. Louis.[10]

With the outbreak of the war Baxter was as filled with military fervor as the next man. Furthermore, his older brother Horace became adjutant general of Vermont. It was something else Algernon now had to live up to. His brother raised and outfitted, with his own money, the first militia in Vermont, and then became responsible for raising regiments for the Union cause there. Algernon S. Baxter decided to use his business acumen in the supply and transportation corps of the regular U.S. volunteers. He was appointed post quartermaster at Paducah, Kentucky, through Grant. Their acquaintance grew, and because they were both about 41 years old, their age peerage promoted camaraderie. He would be a perfect addition as a staff member for Grant, but Hatch already had that position.

Protocol had to be dealt with and Grant had to be clever about it. One of the cleverest men on his staff was Captain John A. Rawlins, his adjutant general. Rawlins had been Grant's father's lawyer in Galena, Illinois, where he was also the town's lawyer. Rawlins's job provided that he be Grant's close assistant, but Rawlins had developed a father-figure relationship with Grant. He had begun to insulate Grant from just about everyone.

Rawlins was not without his own desires to rise in rank. The request that Baxter receive a promotion to higher grade had to have been noted by Captain Rawlins. Baxter was already Rawlins's senior in date of appointment; a promotion would place Baxter above him in rank. It also put Baxter, a man of Grant's age, in a more intimate interaction with Grant. Captain was the army prescribed rank for assistant quartermaster on a general's staff, but Hatch held a rank of brevet major. That gave Hatch a bit more clout. As it is with most careers, he was not all bad. He had proved of honorable service in Missouri at the Battle Belmont.[11] He had exerted himself rigorously at many tasks asked of him. Maybe the temptation of so much merchandise and money proved too much after such hard service with too little reward. A quartermaster's life was much more rigorous than that of the average general. Until things could be proved against him, Hatch still had to remain the quartermaster at Cairo until appointment of Baxter to Grant's staff by the War Department.

All this was not well and good with General Halleck, and the enemies in secret places came out of the woodwork to thwart Captain Baxter's appointment. But until something happened to revoke his appointment, he went about performing all kinds of strenuous activities. He supplied cavalry units with equipage and horses, he had barracks built and hired the carpenters, he set up General U.S. Grant's personal cavalry bodyguard, for the first time affording Grant more protection in war and on the streets of the towns. The tasks he performed were legion.[12]

Then came the bad news. He was relieved of duty.[13] In the massive corruption investigation of the Department of the West, that very trip to Washington on which Grant had sent him backfired on Grant. While there, Baxter succeeded in obtaining $150,000 to operate within his district. Baxter's judicial father and influential brother would have influence that helped get that money, if in fact they had not donated some of it themselves. But when Captain Baxter returned to the District of Cairo he was forced to hand the money over to the corrupt parties being investigated by military protocol during his interim status. When that happened, the money just disappeared into thin air. He was held responsible, though it could not have been in his power to stop it. If the money had been acquired with the aid of Baxter's own family, he was more than chagrined. Baxter had come west to establish his own fortune, but now his New England Brahmin family could not approve of the way things were going for him.

Grant, Rawlins and Baxter tightened up their procedures and practices. In company with coarse men of unscrupulous designs, it was imperative that there be careful duplicates of everything; written records had to be kept of every transaction and order.

Captain Baxter had barely gotten back from Washington when Grant decided to seize the initiative and move on Halleck's military plans against Ft. Henry. The fort proved to be a piece of cake for the gunboats. Having taken the fort so easily, Grant then moved quickly on Ft. Donelson, without permission from Halleck. For General Halleck this move by Grant was a bit like the nursery rhyme in which Little Jack Horner, carrying his boss's pie, "stuck in his thumb and pulled out a plum ... and said what a good boy am I!"

The actual battle for Ft. Donelson was Captain Baxter's baptism of fire. As a key member of General Grant's personal staff, Baxter found that his work at the Battle of Ft. Donelson required vigorous effort. Just back from Washington, he was behind the curve. Grant's aggressiveness had not allowed for careful planning of supply and transportation. There were problems keeping up at Ft. Donelson. That was the main emphasis of General Halleck: preparation first. Going after the work was no problem for a strapping New Englander like Baxter. He had been a sculling champion in school rowing contests back in Boston. As with many of his background, horsemanship was looked upon with pride. The Baxters of Vermont were known for their work ethic.

Baxter performed his duties admirably, but was for the first time also introduced to the war's grim cost in human life. Alarmed at one appalling discovery of dead bodies in a storage vault, he had to investigate as to whether an atrocity had been committed. The aftermath of Donelson was even more taxing than the battle. Captain Baxter was charged with processing some 15,000 prisoners of war, thousands of horses, mules, wagons, artillery pieces, thousands of captured muskets and side arms, coffins and burials. It was a staggering amount of work, but General Grant could not have had picked a more capable man for the job.[14]

The victory at Ft. Donelson was the biggest breakthrough of Ulysses S. Grant's life. His serendipitous initials U.S. triggered a feeding frenzy for a victory-hungry public and a sensationalist press. His terms for the Confederates were "unconditional surrender," so his initials came to stand for Unconditional Surrender Grant; others called him Uncle Sam Grant, or United States Grant. All of this belied the fact that at the most critical time of the battle he was miles away and a young colonel from Indiana, Lew Wallace, saved that day for Grant. With victory, that did not matter. The victory left everyone in a rosy spotlight.

General Halleck, having had his thunder stolen, was not quite as happy. His careful nature has led to his being criticized as nothing more than a glorified clerk, but what happened at Ft. Donelson, with little emphasis on preparedness, would be repeated horrifically at Shiloh and would kill and maim more than twelve thousand Union men. It is one thing to sit tall in the saddle and give the orders; it is another to carry the logistics of the battle. A look at Baxter's further record up until April 6, 1862, reveals much about his tremendous work responsibility and also the "black infernal background" of the command struggle going on about him.

2

The Hard Foot of Uncle Sam in Hardin County, Tennessee

O'Neill was some kind of kin to Private Sam Garrett, who was with Wirt Adams's cavalry, a distant relative from a distant place. Whether all his stories were true or not, it was the news that O'Neill brought that riled Samuel Asbury Garrett. The invasion of the Deep South by the Union Army, concentrated in Hardin County, Tennessee, caused him to join the rebel cause.[1] The Union effort was headed by a General U.S. Grant.

The family trusted that O'Neill was blood somehow. "O'Neill" was what everybody called him; nobody could ever get a first name out of him. He was a traveling man and an enigma who just showed up every couple of years to visit Sam, but he seemed to have been everywhere and witnessed just about everything. He took a special interest in Sam's oldest son, Joseph. O'Neill always had news and tales to tell. One story was that the Garretts were related to the Indian Princess Pocahontas. It seemed believable, for somebody had named the town of Pocahontas, Tennessee, and there were kin there. There were some dark-skinned Garretts, too. O'Neill didn't seem to care about proof; he just liked to tell stories, be the bearer of news, have a meal and a bed, and then be on his way. The name O'Neill was absorbed into the Garrett family for four generations.

Four generations. That was significant to the deep religiosity of the South. The period called the Great Awakening had peaked, but Bible verses like Exodus 20:5 were still continuously thumped. A preacher's voice from a log meeting house like Shiloh near Pittsburgh Landing might be heard for a great distance intoning: "Thou shalt not bow down thyself to them: for I the LORD thy God am a jealous God, visiting the iniquity of the fathers upon the children to the third and fourth generation of them that hate me."[2]

Verses like this were subject to varying applications by ministers. It would not have been unusual to hear "Thou shalt not bow down thyself to them" being applied in theological twists to the Yankee regiments that were invading the South. This type of theology was also used in regard to slavery, using Bible verses of early Christianity steeped in Greco-Roman culture, to justify the existence and tolerance of that peculiar institution. But for many trying to make a hardscrabble living, Unionists' talk of abolition just represented a threat to the economy of the South and a chance at upward mobility. They were about four generations from the Revolutionary War, and they were not about to bow down to a god that threatened their understanding of the constitutional right of "life, liberty and the pursuit of happiness."

On March 8, 1862, the first foot regiment of Union troops showed up in Savannah, Tennessee, on the east side of the Tennessee River. The river cut Hardin County in half, Savannah about ten miles below the small farming community around Pittsburg Landing. Hardin County had not voted in favor of secession, and there were pro–Union sentiments in the eastern half especially.[3] The 46th Ohio Regiment set ashore and through callous behavior began effectively to change the minds of many about preserving the Union. The idiocy of many Union soldiers demonstrated that they had other things on their minds than noble causes. They acted like pirates.

The occupation of Savannah took place during the flux when U.S. Grant was replaced by General Halleck in favor of General C.F. Smith. When the 46th Ohio debarked at Savannah, Grant was still in limbo at Ft. Henry and Ft. Smith. After a spectacular victory at Ft. Henry and Ft. Donelson that gained him national fame and acclaim, he was confined by Halleck to post duty at inundated Ft. Henry, under virtual arrest on a steamboat. Halleck considered him insubordinate. Major General C.F. Smith replaced U.S. Grant as head of Halleck's Tennessee River Expedition to cut the Southern Confederacy in half at the significant rail crossroads of Corinth, Mississippi. Grant got the command back when General Halleck became supreme commander of all the western departments. His restoration was also facilitated by an unfortunate accident that befell General C.F. Smith. He had a mishap jumping from steamboat to rowboat, scraping his shin badly from ankle to knee. What should have been a superficial wound opened Smith up to infection, probably septic blood poisoning or tetanus (lockjaw).

On this Tennessee Expedition, the 46th Ohio was part of the 5th Division of the Army of West Tennessee. Brigadier General William Tecumseh Sherman commanded it. It was totally unacceptable to him the way that the 46th Ohio behaved when it arrived in Savannah, but he had been beaten to Savannah, outmaneuvered by another West Point graduate in one of his brigades, the 46th Ohio's Colonel Thomas Worthington.[4]

Worthington graduated West Point in 1827 at twenty, a peer of General

C.F. Smith. He, like most of the West Pointers, was a veteran of the Mexican War, but came home from that war with an ax to grind. He claimed to have lost 1,800 acres of land that should have been protected by his government service. The issue of literal axes as a concern of Worthington would come into play with General Sherman one month later. Worthington in that case was possibly the only officer at Shiloh insistent on cutting trees and building breastworks. He kept up a continual barrage of requests for axes until Sherman told him he had already acquired all of the axes in Kentucky. In fact the reason Worthington was not getting the axes he wanted was that 5th Division General Sherman had forbidden his quartermaster to receive anything and "Baxter will only answer requisitions of the Division Quartermasters."[5] This was as should have been, but it showed General U.S. Grant himself had little concern for building breastworks.

When boats were being secured for the Tennessee Expedition, Worthington set out to prove a personal point. He embarked, told the captain of the vessel to full steam, passed all of the other steamers, and arrived at Savannah before everyone else. He promptly allowed his troops to do just about anything they wanted. This included taking over homes of the town's residents. They only had to perceive someone was a secessionist to seize his property. Fifty-five years old, Worthington was respected by his own troops, but looked upon somewhat as an old coot for his eccentric ways. One of his oddities, as other steamers with regiments arrived, was to dress in civilian clothes and high boots and walk about giving orders as if he were the general-in-chief.

It was the worst possible scenario for General W.T. Sherman when he arrived to find one of his regiments carrying out such travesties. Sherman knew the people of the South. He had served as the first president of a Louisiana military academy that later became Louisiana State University. He liked the Southern people, but when their agitation for war boiled over, he prophesied their downfall, not yet knowing he would become the most major force in their demise. Sherman was a colonel at the Battle of Bull Run and was disgusted there by the behavior of an army not under control. He wrote to his wife about the Union debacle and the reason for it:

> It was as disgraceful as words can convey, but I doubt volunteers from any quar-
> ter could do any better. Each private thinks for himself. If he wants to go for
> water, he asks leave of no one. If he thinks right, he takes the oats and corn, and
> even burns the house of his enemy. As we could not prevent these disorders on
> the way out [from Washington, D.C.], I always feared the result, for everywhere
> we found the people against us. No curse could be greater than the invasion of a
> volunteer army. No Goths or Vandals ever had less respect for the lives and
> property of friends and foes, and henceforth we ought never to hope for any
> friends in Virginia.[6]

The same could be said of all the states affected by the Tennessee Expedition. Although a number of men in Savannah volunteered to fight for the Union when it arrived, the affect it had on many residents was devastating. Small communities like Savannah, Purdy, and even Corinth would never prosper the way others did, largely because of the iron foot of the Union in Hardin County. Private Sam Garrett, who had removed to Corinth, thought the volunteer Union Army was like the Giant in "Jack and the Beanstalk." He had come down out of the clouds and was stomping around on everything good and lovable. Like Sherman himself said, there was no greater curse than this volunteer army. Many more went over to the Southern side as result of it.

An example of the attitude and actions of the 46th Ohio when it arrived is found in the letter of Sergeant Waldo T. Davis. He and a group of other soldiers took over the residence of J.D. Martin, which sat on the bluff over-

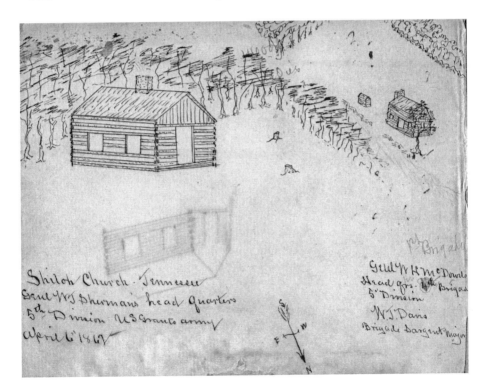

Waldo T. Davis of Colonel Worthington's Regiment, evicted from housing in Savannah, was moved with McDowell's Brigade by General Sherman to the far right of the Union Army. Waldo T. Davis sketched his impression of nearby Shiloh Church (author's collection).

looking the Tennessee River and was next to the Cherry Mansion of William Cherry. J.D. Martin was the town constable and a judge. These men seized his property under an assumption. They were given permission to inhabit the house by Mr. Martin's brother-in law. Sergeant Davis wrote:

Savannah Tennessee March 11, 1862

Dear Mother,

Once more I happily occupy a few moments in writing to you. I wrote a letter to you the evening we arrived which you will no doubt receive the same time you receive this letter. I am now sitting in a home formerly occupied by a rank cecessionist [sic], who is now in the rebel army, his name is J.D. Martin, and was Justice of the Peace, and Judge of the County.

I captured a cessession [sic] flag the first taken by our Regiment. The Colonel was very anxious that I should let him take care of it, but I concluded that it was but small matter for me to take care of it myself. I have also in my possession several little trinkets which I have collected together and will distribute among my friends as rellicks [sic] of Tennessee.

There has been twenty-two boat loads of soldiers come up the River within the last two hours their destination at this place. There is to be 62 boats in all. 5 more are coming around the bend of the river. I have an excellent view of the Congregation of steamers with men, as they arrive into port, as the home I am in is on the left bank of the river and on quite a bluff, and commands a view of quite a portion of the River both ways.

The weather is delightful, such as we generally have in Ohio in the month of May or June, the leaves are putting forth and the blossoms are coming to life on the trees, the meadows are covered with green Sward, and the wild flowers are gaily nodding to the soft zephyrs of Spring. My health is exceeding well, I am heavier now than before, the last time I weighed my weight was 187 and that was about 2 weeks ago now. I presume me way [sic] about 195, and you may be assured that I feel fine and saucy. I am getting $24 dollars a month for writing in the Adjutants Office, or in other words for Clerking it suits me very much as I have no other duty to perform, unless I wish to, and in fact I cannot some times even then. I wanted to go out on scout last night, and the old Colonel would not admit of it, and I as usual became quite wrathy [sic], but no go. With them I believe the old Colonel is nothing else but Contrary for his own delight; this letter is written as you will notice on Tennessee blank Summons orders, (or the paper that they are on) this was found in the house the Esq. J.D. Martin. I send you a few flowers which I have just picked from the garden, and a small bunch of honey suckles buds with rose leaves.

Also a certificate of marriage, which I hope may come through safe with this letter. A letter too written on Cesesh [sic] paper. I would like to send more but my opportunity is limited.

Give my regards to all. Tell Nettie She must try and dream something that then may be some prospects of coming true. Receive the regards and love of your Affectionate Son,

Waldo to Mother Write Soon, Direct your letter to Paducah Ky. Ie[7]

From this letter, it is easy to conclude that if Judge J.D. Martin was not a secessionist at the time Waldo Davis and the others took over his home, comparable to the Cherry Mansion, he was surely a secessionist afterward.

When General Sherman arrived on the scene, he turned out all of Worthington's men occupying these houses. It was too late to mollify some of the respectable citizens who had been wronged. Even as Sherman ordered the men out of the residences in extreme anger, Colonel Worthington tried to shush the General, saying, "There, there ... they have already been told."[8] It enraged Sherman, and he and Worthington never had a good relationship afterward. General Sherman put Worthington and the 46th Ohio Regiment as far to the right of his Division at Camp Shiloh as he could arrange. The 46th guarded the way to Owl Creek Bridge. It was a fateful road. The road to Owl Creek would haunt General Lew Wallace.

Today most Americans do not know how this road to the fields of Shiloh has affected them. The Battle of Shiloh booms down through time and its effects have been felt to the fourth generation.

3

Steaming Situations
That Shaped the Battle

"Mark Twain!" was a critical cry for the leadsmen on the steamboat *Iatan*, the first week in April 1862. The river in spring flood heading up to Pittsburgh Landing was running much deeper than the twelve-foot declaration of safe clearance required for navigation, but eddies and sand bars hiding below the flooded Tennessee lurked. The man who took the pseudonym Mark Twain was no longer a steamboat pilot. As war broke out, Samuel L. Clemens abandoned his steamboat pilot's license after an artillery shell burst in front of his pilothouse near St. Louis.[1] He later stated, "I could have become a soldier if I had wanted.... I knew more about retreating than the man who invented retreating."[2]

Captain Albert Pearce of the steamboat side-wheeler *Iatan* did not retreat, nor had Captain Bart Able, who frequently piloted this same steamer.[3] These and other master pilots were trading routes and shifts in the pilothouses on western rivers, like normal, only now all were subject to government retainer and contract. Commercial trade was severely curtailed on the rivers because of the Confederate blockades of the Mississippi at New Orleans and Vicksburg. The pilots of the *Iatan* were in Federal service since the very first altercations of the war in the western theater.

The Sources of Grant's Staff at Shiloh

Near St. Louis at Camp Jackson, Captain Able on the *Iatan* participated in one of the first Civil War altercations in the West. Days after the firing on Ft. Sumter, Captain Nathaniel Lyon thwarted a clandestine pro-secessionist operation by Missouri governor Claiborne Jackson and northern-born, West Point–educated General Daniel M. Frost. Their objective was to take over the St. Louis arsenal. Dressed as a woman, Lyon had a free black coachman

Pittsburg Landing, a few days after the battle. The steamboat second from the right has been identified as General U.S. Grant's *Tigress* (***Review of Reviews***, 1911).

drive him through the camp. He discovered smuggled howitzers and siege cannons seized by the Confederacy at another Federal arsenal at Baton Rouge, Louisiana. They had come disguised in boxes labeled as raw marble aboard the steamer *J.C. Swon.*[4] Enlisting a huge number of immigrant Germans, Lyon surrounded the camp and forced General Frost to surrender. A battle-riot burst forth on the streets of St. Louis as General Frost and his men were marched to detention by Captain Lyon. At least 28 were killed, including women and children. Civilian William Tecumseh Sherman, witnessing the march with his son Willie, pulled his son to cover in a ditch to avoid the hail of gunfire.[5] Subsequently, Captain Bart Able used the *Iatan* to tow the confiscated *J.C. Swon* into Federal custody.

About that time in St. Louis, besides private citizen W.T. Sherman, were other people who would become significant in the Battle of Shiloh. *Kennedy's 1860 St. Louis City Directory* shows U.S Grant lived on the side street of Martha behind the business of Menard and Buel. William S. Hillyer was in a real estate partnership at 221 Locust. Algernon S. Baxter was a successful businessman of Baxter & Co. Breadstuffs and Provisions on Main Street. U.S. Grant developed relationships with these men while trying to earn a living in a number of ways, then soon moved to Galena, Illinois, to work in his father's leather goods store. There he developed relationships with his father's lawyer, John A. Rawlins, also town attorney, and William R. Rowley, chief court clerk. Another friend of Grant's was Clark B. Lagow. There was business, political and social camaraderie among these men before the war. As the *Iatan* steamed toward Pittsburgh Landing, all were now on Major General U.S. Grant's staff, commanding the military Department of West Tennessee.

Seeds of Disparagement: Prentiss vs. Peabody and Grant vs. Prentiss

The steamboat *Iatan* may have ferried the few escapees from the Confederate siege of Lexington, Missouri, where Colonel Everett Peabody was captured with most of his command by a force of 15,000 to 20,000 rebels. Brig. General Benjamin Prentiss came to the aid of the escaped remnants of the siege of Lexington, including a friend of Peabody's, Lieutenant O.P. Newberry. While praising the Union garrison at Lexington in his report, Prentiss may have felt disdain for Peabody's 13th Missouri Militia, which had surrendered there.[6] It was best he should not feel that way, for as the proverb says, "Pride goes before destruction, and a haughty spirit before the fall." Peabody's surrender actually gave Prentiss an edge from which he benefited at Shiloh.

While the *Iatan* steamed toward Pittsburgh landing on April 1, 1862, General Prentiss there was resisting counsel from Colonel Peabody, who was now Prentiss's 6th Division, 1st Brigade commander. Prentiss's camp was southernmost at Shiloh and somewhat isolated from the others there. As an acting brigadier general, Peabody also created a rivalry situation for Benjamin M. Prentiss, who was rank sensitive.

So was General U.S. Grant. He and Prentiss had tussles over command in Missouri because they had been appointed brigadier generals the same day.[7] Grant won the fight, though both had served in the Mexican War. Regular Army service and West Point training trumped Benjamin M. Prentiss. Prentiss was now trying his best at Camp Shiloh to perform like a regular army man. The rise to the military top ranks was not over. There were many rivalries between men on the Tennessee Expedition, marshaled to crush the rebels at the critical railroad center at Corinth, Mississippi. The internal command and personality wars would be as significant to the outcome as sanguinary battle. Prentiss was now under Grant.

The Zouave Affair and Its Ramifications

Early on in the war, Lew Wallace, who was now Grant's 3rd Division commander, was arguably as good at battle as Grant. Grant had had some successes in Missouri, particularly at Belmont, but the engagements were small compared to what Shiloh would bring. Both men had received national press acclaim. Wallace had seasoned himself in battles in the East, with his Zouave 11th Indiana Volunteers, acrobatically trained, colorfully dressed fighters patterned after French fighting units. This early style of fighting fit Wallace's well-read personality, which was also romantic and adventuresome. Some disdained this outlook as the "Walter Scott disease," a plague of knight crusaders of the type that defined that author's books. It was an epidemic personality disease with many ambitious men, North and South.[8] It may have been a sticking point, clashing with the dogged style of generalship that Grant practiced. Before Shiloh, a thirty-two-year-old Lew Wallace from Indiana was already a major general, the youngest in the Union army at the time. It probably generated ill-willed jealousy and aspersions from the young bucks close to Wallace's age who surrounded General U.S. Grant as aides. This was especially true of Grant's thirty-two-year-old adjutant general Captain John A. Rawlins.

The pot was boiling in the command structure. For West Point–trained and phlegmatic General U.S. Grant, erratic command communications were just part of his job as a professional soldier. However, a conspiratorial relationship between General Grant and a volatile Captain John Rawlins becomes apparent in an unusual correspondence that foreshadows the plotting against young General Wallace by Captain Rawlins. Sorting out these clues requires some going back and forth in examination of various correspondences:

Head Quarters Dist. W. Tenn.
Savanna March 31, 1862

Maj Genl. L. Wallace,
Crump's landing,
I am directed by Major General *Grant* comdg. to acknowledge the receipt of your communication of the 30th inst, and in reply to say that *he* is command of this District and Army in the field; that certificates of disability returned to you by Asst Adjt General <u>Newsham</u> were received at these Headquarters and sent to Surgeon Hewitt acting Medical Director of the District for his approval to be returned when acted upon to these Headquarters. Enclosed find General Orders in regard to leaves of absence, furloughs, and passes.

John A. Rawlin

Asst. Adjt. Genl.[9]

Rawlins was normally exacting about protocol in communications. In behalf of Grant, he had the power of military attorney to sign Grant's name. He did not do it in the above correspondence. The lack of typical protocol etiquette in the signing of this correspondence exhibits a psychological quality. Animosity is exhibited on the part of Rawlins toward Lew Wallace in underlining emphasis on Grant and Newsham.

This previously unpublished correspondence reveals the ill will between Rawlins and General Wallace, which goes to the heart of contentions about the famous order sent to Wallace on the first morning of battle. In no uncertain terms, Rawlins was putting Wallace on notice as to the need for written orders. Rawlins made sure that Wallace understood that his movements were tentative to proper written communications, yet Rawlins himself is deficient in assigning attribution to Grant. The lack of proper signing in the above communication helps in understanding the problems of communication the morning of April 6, 1862. Was the communication given by Rawlins to Wallace on the first morning of battle a properly signed one, or was it more like this one above?

Notice that he also underlines the name of adjutant general Newsham. There shows one of the roots of his strong feeling. The personal interrelationships of all these officers had a tangled history. Untangling the ramifications of this March 31 letter helps much in understanding the events of Shiloh's first day.

Captain Newsham was adjutant general to Major General C.F. Smith. General Smith was West Point mentor and friend of General U.S. Grant. When Rawlins wrote the above to General Lew Wallace, General Smith was lying sick at the Cherry Mansion from the accident sustained just after a meeting with General Lew Wallace. Previously, at Paducah, Kentucky, all of these men had come together for the Union cause and a reorganization to better fight the Confederacy. However, Kentucky was officially a neutral state when Colonel Lew Wallace arrived with his Zouave regiment, the 11th Indiana. Colorfully dressed, using acrobatic tactics in battle, they were fresh from successes in the eastern theater of the war. They seized and occupied a local residence for quarters because the home was flying a Confederate flag. As they were tearing the banner down and replacing it with a U.S. flag, General C.F. Smith's adjutant general Captain Newsham arrived to interfere, with word from General Smith that they had taken the home unconstitutionally. The reaction from Wallace's Zouaves was explosive. Lew Wallace's adjutant general Captain Frederick Kneffler got into a fistfight with Smith's adjutant general Captain Newsham over the matter.

The whole incident was incendiary. It was similar to the matter involving high-spirited young Zouave Colonel Elmer Ellsworth, who had dashed with his New York Fire Zouaves out of Washington, D.C., to Alexandria, Virginia, to pull down the Confederate flag that flew over the tavern home of a man named Marshall. Marshall killed Ellsworth, and then was killed himself. Ellsworth had worked in the law offices of Abraham Lincoln and was a dear friend to the president. He was the first Union officer killed in the civil conflict. With the colorful French uniforms they wore, the Ellsworth incident became, like the French phrase, a *cause célèbre,* a national patriotic revenge furor. Now in Kentucky, local politicians and newspapers picked up this Zouave altercation. They quickly went after General C.F. Smith, calling him a Confederate sympathizer who should be relieved of duty. The Secretary of the Treasury urged President Lincoln to oust Smith. The Union West Point officers in the army, including U.S. Grant, rallied round Smith.[10] The matter died down after Lincoln refused to fire Smith.

Feathers ruffled need time to smooth out. It had been a national news story, and public opinion dies hard. As it did, Lew Wallace briefly bunked in the same quarters with General Grant, and they became somewhat better acquainted. Just then, Captain John Rawlins arrived to finally be of service to Grant. He had just returned from burying his wife in Goshen, New York, leaving his two young children with his wife's parents. Bereaved, he entered his first military situation as Grant's new adjutant general. Finding his own father figure Grant ruffled about what had happened to good friend General C.F. Smith, he probably commiserated with Grant about the Wallace/11th Indiana affair. The perceptions of Rawlins about Lew Wallace had just begun to simmer. There would be other events to come that would leave Rawlins and the other young aides miffed about Lew Wallace. All were protective of their General Grant.

Just after Rawlins's arrival and reporting for duty, an all-night Officers Club–style meeting ensued. Someone spread rumors that an "orgy of drinking" had occurred, and with the Zouave affair still in the air, Grant's aides laid the blame on then–Colonel Wallace for spreading slander. There may have been a grain of truth. Wallace was not very guarded with his opinions. A ravenous press created more controversy. The grain of truth was also present with Grant. He was not a man who could hold his liquor well.

Slow to Move

On April 1, 1862, Major General U.S. Grant was comfortably ensconced with his staff at the mansion owned by slave-owning Southern Union man Mr. William Cherry. The mansion was very close to the landing berths, and it seemed to offer a brief commute to the real scene of army operations almost ten miles upriver at Pittsburg Landing. Grant felt no urgency to implement a move to Pittsburg Landing, though General Order No. 30, issued by himself, stated that the Headquarters of the Army of the Tennessee was already changed to Pittsburg Landing as of March 31.[11] The lack of swift implementation of General Order No. 30 proved to be a catastrophic error affecting the Union outcome of the first day of the Battle of Shiloh. This is how the order read:

GENERAL ORDERS No 30
HEADQUARTERS DISTRICT OF WEST TENNESSEE
Savannah, March 31, 1862.

Headquarters of the District of West Tennessee is hereby changed to Pittsburg Landing. An office will be continued at Savannah, where all official communications may be sent by troops having easier access with that point than Pittsburg Landing.

By command of Major-General Grant:

JNo. A. RAWLINS,
Assistant Adjutant-General. —

General Grant was not at the scene when the Confederates attacked early in the morning of April 6, 1862. No efforts were seriously being put forward to move Headquarters. The claim that only an office was being continued at Savannah was simply untrue. It was nice at the mansion. Chicanery about this order would occur a year later when General Lew Wallace asked for a court of inquiry as to why he had been effectively shunned and accused of causing the Union disaster at Shiloh the first day of the battle. It is of note to point out who was strongly engineering things at the Cherry Mansion in Savannah. In his own words, John A. Rawlins stated: *"I was in charge of the office at Savanah, Tenn.,* with instructions to make out all the necessary orders, and send forward to Pittsburg Landing all troops arriving from below."[12] Lew Wallace would provide a convenient target to turn away attention from this Grant mistake.

A Medical Matter Creates Friction

In those first few days of April 1862, there seemed no prejudicial intent against General Lew Wallace by General U.S. Grant himself. Wallace had been vigilant, his troops spread out across a broad area west of Crump's Landing, by river about four miles south of Savannah in an elbow of the Tennessee waterway. There had been rebel activity in General Lew Wallace's sector, which he dutifully reported to Grant. General Grant was very concerned that Wallace's 3rd Division was the most vulnerable and likely place of attack from Confederates. He also considered Wallace to be of such high personal integrity that he designated him president of courts-martial. He was carrying out just such duty when Grant swung in for consultation on April 6.[13]

If there was any animosity brewing toward Wallace in Grant's command, it was because of a no-win situation precipitated by large numbers of sick and dying men. It was swampy and unsanitary, especially in Lew Wallace's sector of military operations. The rest of the army had the same problem. The post hospitals in Savannah were filled. Pittsburgh Landing divisions were sending men there and farther north to Cairo, Mound City and even St. Louis. When Lew Wallace tried to bring his men to Savannah for care, they were turned away, leaving him with a humanitarian crisis. Unable to get cooperation through lower command channels to save his men, he acted on his own and sent his disabled north. Grant's superior, General Henry Halleck in St. Louis, got wind of these men being sent north.[14] Not understanding the gravity of the situation, he reprimanded General Grant. In turn Grant demanded from General Wallace an accounting as to why he had not been informed. Wallace replied, always through Grant's adjutant general Captain Rawlins, that he knew Grant's nature would not have objected to an urgent life-threatening situation. It looks as if Rawlins considered Wallace's tone overly familiar with Grant. Wallace may have felt comfortable with Grant, but he was not part of the cadre of the young men with whom Grant had surrounded himself as aides. Especially sensitive was Captain John A. Rawlins. The exchanges between General Grant and General Wallace, through adjutant general Rawlins, transpired as follows:

> Head Quarters, District of West Tennessee
> Savanah, March 21, 1862
>
> Brigadier Gen. L. Wallace
> Commanding 3rd Division
> Genl:
>
> Your attention is called to the note of the 19th inst[ant] asking for information, as to the authority for sending the sick of your command out of this Dist[rict] has received no answer. Yesterday more sick of your command were sent to Cincinnati by Col. Stedman, with your apparent knowledge. An explanation is required.
>
> I am Genl. Very Respectfully,
> Your Obt. Servant,
> General U.S. Grant
> Major General[15]

On the same day, March 21, Lew Wallace promptly replied, writing to Capt. John A. Rawlins, through whom all correspondence filtered. There had been a delay of delivery of the message to Wallace. It was a harbinger of worse courier problems to come. Wallace wrote back:

This morning I received a note from Gen. Grant dated March 21, 1862 enclosing an order of mine, directed to Capt. John Godman of the Steamer "Telegraph," and instructing him to "Fire up and proceed with his boat to Evansville Ind. as fast as possible, stopping at no intermediate point; and to land the sick there, and return to Paducah for orders." In this note the Gen. asks me–"By what authority do you send sick of your Division to Evansville or out of the District at all? By what authority do you direct steamers from the course they were ordered to take by higher authority?" I beg you [Rawlins] submit to the General the following explanation.

I. Special Order No. 27 directs the troops of the 3rd Division not yet debarked and at Pittsburg to return to the lower Landing [Crump's] and report to Genl Wallace, and concludes by saying Genl. Wallace "will cause their debarkation and discharge of the steamers with as little delay as possible." The General will understand, at a glance, how easily the language of that order [Order No. 27] might be construed as authority for my discharge of the Steamer Telegraph. A mistake growing out of it I am satisfied he will pardon.

II. In addition to that order I will say, in justification, that the sending of the steamer to Evansville was, in my opinion, a military necessity. It had on board about two hundred and sixty sick men from my command, some of them in dying condition. On Monday last, I think, in charge of my Staff officer, Dr. Fry, I sent the boat to Savanah to land the sick there for lodgement in the Hospital. They were sent back to me the same day. On Tuesday I again sent the *Telegraph* to Savanah for the same purpose. Again the crowd of suffering men were sent back to me, one of them having died while the boat was at the town. Upon the return of the Steamer I boarded her, and having no hesitation in saying that I never saw such a scene of disease and misery. *Believing* that, under Order No. 27 I could discharge the *Telegraph*; that, from the fact of sending her sick back to me, there was no Hospital accommodations at Savanah; and *knowing* that I had none here, not even medicines, not even lumber for coffins for the dead; that, in one instance, the planking of a berth in a steamboat state-room was taken and used for burial purpose; I supposed the intention of the medical authorities was to leave me to my own judgment to do the best I could. Under the circumstances, I never for a moment doubted that the General, when he became informed of the facts, would, as he has done, justify my proceeding. It may be further said, that the dying condition of so many soldiers on board the Steamer, would not allow time for correspondence with Head Quarters on the subject. It is but an honest expression of my opinion on my part that when I say, the General's character of tender solicitude for his sick soldiers not only would sustain me in my action in the premises, but even gain me his hearty commendation. I knew his humanity could be depended upon; and it makes me inexpressibly glad to know I was not mistaken. In conclusion, Captain [Rawlins], pardon me in the way of observing, in the way of assurance, that you need not fear or expect that at any time, I will march my Division without orders....

P.S. Herewith I append the report of Dr. Fry. I should have added to the above that I sent the sick to *Evansville*, because I had been informed, the Hospitals at Mound City, Paducah and Cairo, were already crowded. A letter, addressed to the Mayor of Evansville, accompanied the boat, earnestly asking him and his citizens to receive the unfortunate sufferers. [Usual signing with typical correspondence etiquette.][16]

Notice that Wallace was keen to acknowledge command structure in this matter. In no uncertain terms, Wallace saw what was being emphasized by Grant through Rawlins's lens. Wallace stated, "That you need not fear or expect at any time, I will March my Division without orders."

The tension that this correspondence exhibits between the command structure of Major General U.S. Grant and his 3rd Division commander, a younger Major General Lew Wallace, transpired in part from problems of perception regarding the passage of time. Individual minds either exaggerated or minimized the time passage between official correspondences. Even with the technological development of the telegraph (ironic, insofar as the steamer involved was the *Telegraph*), perception of time was shaped by each individual's need to receive a satisfactory answer within a time-frame that was not physically possible.

The tension was exacerbated further by other orders that crossed in opposite directions at the same time. No sooner had Lew Wallace made his decision to send his sick men away, than General Grant independently saw the necessity to remedy the medical crisis with requisitions to higher command. On March 22, 1862, Grant requested of his superior Halleck medical supplies sufficient for 10,000 men and two hospital boats to be sent to him.[17] This issue of time perception and allowance for receipt of messages was compounded when Grant received from his superior, Major General Henry Wager Halleck, a message that had crossed his, dated March 24, 1862. In it Halleck criticized Grant for not having a properly appointed medical officer and was told to discharge the one he had. General Halleck's communication lines were more propitious than General Grant's, way down south in enemy territory. Halleck had received word of General Lew Wallace's actions with the sick, while they were already being dealt with by Grant. Imagine U.S. Grant's chagrin when he received these words:

I call your attention to gross irregularities in your district in regard to the sick and wounded. A telegram from New Albany today says that 200 sick & wounded of Genl Wallace's division had just been landed at that place & there were no hospital arrangements there. By whose order were these sent to New Albany? I have made orders for them to be sent to Cincinnati....[18]

If that was not enough, General Halleck pounced on General Grant about abuses:

It is impossible for me to have proper requisitions made for the sick and wounded where no regard is paid to my orders and where each one assumes to act on his own authority. Again colonels of regiments in your command have been giving furloughs on surgeons certificates for 60 and 90 days, and many cases not sick at all! ... there seems to be collusion between officers & men to give well & healthy men sick leaves who wish to visit their homes. This should be immediately stopped....[19]

General U.S. Grant was faithful to execute the corrections on these matters. By the first day of the Battle of Shiloh, up until an undetermined hour, important officers were under arrest.

Colonel David Moore, 21st Missouri, was one of the first of those court-martialed. He was charged with allowing his men to fire recklessly into civilian homes from their transport boat on the way to Pittsburg Landing. General Lew Wallace presided over this court-martial, and Moore was acquitted, later to become the first Union colonel wounded at Shiloh, sacrificing a leg.[20] Other high-ranking officers in this Halleck-driven purge were Brigadier General John McArthur, second in command to General W.H.L. Wallace; Lt. Colonel A.S. Chetlain, 12th Illinois; Lt. Col. Morgan, 25th Indiana; Col. Reed, Cruft's or Cruff's Brigade; and Col. Gaddis, 8th Iowa. Affirmatively known to be under arrest also was Major Thomas Reynolds of the 16th Wisconsin volunteers.[21] Grant played no favorites with these arrests, as Lt. Col. Chetlain was a close friend who had aided him in getting his first military command.[22]

Leading Up to the Battle of Shiloh

All these situations were being generated while the steamboats were pressed into government service. Marching from Arkansas, a few months away from the Battle of Shiloh, was a private in the Confederate 6th Arkansas. A young man with an inquisitive mind, he had not seen combat yet, but from above the Battle of Belmont, Missouri, Henry Morton Stanley witnessed the *Iatan* and other boats bringing U.S. Grant into action. From high bluffs above Columbus (across from Belmont), Stanley watched "a fleet of vessels ... descending, a few miles above Belmont."[23]

Like most riverboats, the *Iatan* was in constant motion on the western rivers, carrying whatever cargo the U.S. government ordered, participating in combat situations at government behest. On March 29, 1862, the *Iatan* was carrying a load of ordnance, comprised of 200 24-pounder solid shot with pound weight of 4800, 200 32-pounder solid shot with pound weight of 6400, 100 8-inch Columbiad shells with pound weight of 5000, 45 barrels of explosive powder with pound weight of 4680, 43 boxes more of gunpowder with pound weight of 6361, and still another separate 2 boxes of powder at pound weight of 386, amounting to a total of 27,627 pounds. That is a fraction of what she carried to a multitude of river landings. Thousands of men had already been carried by the *Iatan* and a vast fleet of other steamers to Savannah and Pittsburgh Landings, Tennessee.[24]

The *Iatan* stopped at the captured forts of Heiman and Henry on April 1, 1862. There she picked up Lt. Richard P. Derickson of the 16th Wisconsin Volunteers, retrieving his men from hospitals because of serious winter sicknesses. He had two other members of the 16th Wisconsin with him.[25] There was also an army officer who traveled from Paducah to Savannah, 225 river-miles. It was 165 river-miles from Ft. Henry/Heiman to Pittsburg Landing. It cost the Federal government one cent per river-mile to transport an officer. It cost a cent per mile for each of the two privates with Lt. Derickson. Captain Albert Pearce, the master pilot, received a voucher for the owners to collect $5.55 from the government.[26] In other situations a retained steamer might receive a flat rate. The *Iatan* churned water going up the Tennessee River against the strong spring run-off current. It made a normal stop at Savannah, Tennessee, unloading supplies and personnel. It took on cargo, couriers and other personnel for delivery to Pittsburg Landing about nine miles up river. Lt. Derickson and the *Iatan* were about to play an important role at the Battle of Shiloh. Brigadier General Benjamin Prentiss's new 6th Division was still forming and was in the keenest need of supplies and ammunition of all troops on the fields at Camp Shiloh. Lt. Derickson was of that division, and as he returned, he was being selected by Prentiss as a key member of his staff. For now, these men on board looked up in wonder and probable envy at the grand white mansion on the river bluff at Savannah.

The average soldier knew little of intrigues in the interiors; they only saw the official surface courteousness of the generals. All of the earlier mentioned orders and correspondences had transpired by the time Lt. Richard P. Derickson arrived with his two men of the 16th Wisconsin on the *Iatan* at Savannah on April 1, 1862. Shortly, the *Iatan* debarked from Savannah Landing and curved up the river toward Crump's Landing.

Chance Encounters Plant Seeds of Religious Metaphor for Lew Wallace

If the *Iatan* made a stop at Crump's Landing on April 1, it is not known. It is known that a very interesting man did stop at Crump's Landing with orders to report to Major General Lew Wallace. That man later became the greatest orator and antireligionist of the 19th century. He was Robert Ingersoll.[27] On April 1, 1862, the future celebrity infidel was a colonel commanding two battalions of cavalry that he had raised himself, the 11th Illinois Cavalry.

Here at their meeting at Crump's Landing, a seed was planted in Lew Wallace's mind which would not germinate until a chance reunion on a night train years later. The former cavalry officer and agnostic, Ingersoll, would be a cavalry lance to the side of Lew Wallace, gutting him to examine his religious beliefs. The festering bloody boil of Shiloh's effects would burst out of Wallace in the record-shattering novel *Ben-Hur: A Tale of the Christ*. It requires a literary and metaphorical bent to get the connections to cavalryman Ingersoll. Metaphorical allusions and other literary devices are the stock in trade of writers, such as the play on words, Calvary and cavalry. At the end of the novel, after a long search for vindication, Ben-Hur finds himself below an impaled man on a hill. The hill was called *Calvary*. There an infidel Roman soldier pierced the side of an impaled Christ. Blood of salvation poured out of Jesus' broken and ruptured heart, covering in effect all that Judah Ben-Hur had labored in vain to correct.

Eyes and Ears of an Army

In the days before and after Shiloh, Robert Ingersoll was no match for another cavalry officer. That horseman ended Ingersoll's military career a year later when Col. Nathan Bedford Forrest captured him. On April 1, 1862, while Ingersoll was meeting with Lew Wallace at Crump's Landing, Forrest was the eyes and ears of the Confederate army. On the approach to Shiloh, Forrest's patrols were clandestinely operating, especially in the area of Hamburg in coordination with Wirt Adams's cavalry. There were also partisan members of his cavalry spread out Pony Express–style all the way to Nashville, monitoring the movements of the Army of the Ohio commanded by General Don Carlos Buell. In one of the few times Forrest was ever fooled, a Union feint movement toward Alabama caused him to deduce Hamburg was the way Buell would cross the Tennessee River and join Grant's Army of West Tennessee. That corridor along the river was the far left of the Union encampments. It was the key to General Albert Sidney Johnston's strategy to push the Federals away from the landing. Johnston would spend personal attention to make sure his strategy went as planned.[28] Eyes and ears do not always reveal the truth.

Grant's Headquarters at Savannah in the Week Before Shiloh

While Captain John Rawlins was managing paperwork, General Lew Wallace was rushing brigades to Adamsville in the middle of the night on March 31 to thwart a suspected attack by Confederate general Cheatham's division.[29] Wallace and Rawlins were about the same age. If they had encountered one another under different circumstances, they may well have become friends. Had they sought commonality gained through their respective life sojourns, Wallace would have learned of Rawlins's struggle with his father's drunkenness. Rawlins would have learned of Wallace's intolerant mother, who in her ragged inability to cope with a rambunctious boy, resorted to dressing Lew up like a girl.[30] Such forces shaped the drive of these two. Instead, while Rawlins admired West Pointer U.S. Grant to the point of saying he loved him like a father, Rawlins probably had no inkling that Lew Wallace had a West Point father that he loved.

On April 2, 1862, there is a dearth of record as related to the goings-on about the Army of West Tennessee, except for one order involving General Lew Wallace. Wallace is directed by General Grant to have his division "in readiness for review on April the 4th instant at 10:00 A.M. Noted as Official" and signed simply John A. Rawlins, Asst. Adjt. Genl. It again lacks courtesy, but it was co-signed by a different aide, "*Yours Respectfully,* Clark B. Lagow, Aide-de-camp."[31]

It seems a full review never happened. If it did, it was only a partial review of those troops guarding supplies at Crump's Landing. It was really an unreasonable expectation to review the whole division. Wallace's 3rd Division was spread out for upwards of ten miles in the direction of Purdy. Grant's other five divisions were easily reviewed, being concentrated within a few mere acres of space, in their respective places on the fields around Shiloh Methodist meeting house. Grant was not eager about reviews anyway. There is no indication that Grant ever traveled on horseback with his 3rd Division commander Lew Wallace away and west from Crump's Landing where Wallace carefully placed his brigades. For that matter, at Pittsburg Landing there is no record that Grant even looked beyond the Snake Creek Bridge on the Savannah-Hamburg road. It was the so-called *river road*, a flood-inundated, unimproved lane, that was later emphasized as the correct road Grant had instructed Lew Wallace to take. Major General U.S. Grant never understood the ground that his 3rd Division was charged with protecting and traversing. Grant preferred traveling by riverboat. There had been some sort of an examination by Colonel James McPherson, an engineer who was actually on staff with General Halleck, but who quickly became a favorite of Grant. The only allusion to his "study" of the river road comes a year later, and after the facts of the Battle of Shiloh, it now seems disingenuous.

On April 3 the Confederate Army was on the verge of its massive march to drive the Union Army to annihilation. It was into the swampy ground, away from the Pittsburg Landing that Lew Wallace was forced to cross, that the supreme Confederate commander intended to drive the Union Army. That is how bad the ground was. Second in command General Beauregard spoke for himself and supreme commander General Albert Sidney Johnston: "We expected to back the Federals against Owl and Snake Creeks — the two narrow and rickety bridges of which could not have withstood heavy pressure — early in the day without incurring much risk from the gunboats."

This is the ground Lew Wallace coped with between his division and the rest of the army. If the Confederates could cut the Federals off from the landing before reinforcements from General Don Carlos Buell's Army of the Ohio, they felt they could annihilate them on that ground.[32]

Running Out of Time and Steam

Little things mean a lot. On April 3, "Ulys" Grant found time to write to his wife Julia. In the letter he tells her he is sending home his timepiece. He sent for a plain watch of silver for himself, saying, "There would be no great danger in keeping the other but should it be lost I never could forgive myself. I want to preserve it to the last day of my life, and want the children to do the same thing, in remembrance of poor Simp. Who carried it in his lifetime."[33] So Major General Ulysses S. Grant was without a watch. He could not personally keep track of the time on the battlefield now. Ever-present adjutant general Captain John A. Rawlins was now in complete control to state times when things happened at the Battle of Shiloh for the official record.

However, a not-so-small thing needed attention; on April 3, Grant dashed off an order himself: "We are entirely out of coal here. Please send some at once." Rawlins did not write this order. Rather, Chief of Staff Col. Joseph D. Webster stepped up to handle the paperwork in this instance. Webster addressed the quartermaster or master of transport at Paducah this way: "Please forward a supply of Coal as the supply is exhausted, and the want is, of course urgent. Send at once as much as you can by one tow boat."[34]

Coal was of extreme importance to the operation of the steamers. Grant's steamer, the *Tigress*, was perilously low on coal on April 3, "entirely out of coal." They would have to be conservative with what fuel was available to fire the steamboat boilers. Just to deliver that order was two hundred twenty-five river-miles to Paducah. Realistically, it would consume April 3. April 4 would involve paperwork, accounting and physically filling the order for "as much [coal] as you can" at Paducah, then steaming back against the dangerous currents of a river in flood stages to Savannah. That pushes the issue of a coal crisis at Savannah up through April 5, 1862, to transport. If the coal barge arrived, it was likely during the night of April 5–6. That cuts things very close to having proper coal supplies on the morning the battle broke out. It is in complete opposition to what Rawlins said a year later. He stated that Grant's boat, the *Tigress*, had steam continuously kept up. He did not state that in the most critical hours before the Battle of Shiloh, there was a coal crisis making the continuous keeping up of steam unlikely.

Considering that "Grant had not the faintest idea of attack," as stated in correspondence to General Halleck on April 5, it seems likely coal conservation seemed tolerable until it arrived. However, this becomes a potent issue as to when Grant actually left Savannah on board his transport on April 6, 1862. A year later, a promoted Rawlins, Lt. Col. John Rawlins, disingenuously omits effects of the coal problem. In his report Rawlins composed April 1, 1863, and sent to Washington against Wallace he states: "Up to the 5th day of April, 1862 ... you [Grant] had run up to Pittsburg Landing, and returned at night on the steamer Tigress, used for your headquarters, and on which steam was continuously kept up."[35] Rawlins's statement does not comport with the coal shortage.

This is where another coal-related issue arises. There was interference with the quartermaster corps commanded by Captain A.S. Baxter. The issue of coal supply would normally have been handled by Grant's staff quartermaster. Instead, The quartermaster headquarters was in turmoil. This is revealed in the subsection II of Order No. 44, April 3. Grant had put the state of supply and transportation in flux. Rawlins was apparently supervising that. It made him either harried or addled in the process; he again did not sign an order properly, even with his own name, only his title. It is a sloppy, slurred communication, reading as follows:

> Head Quarters Dist of West Tenn
> Savanna April 3rd, 1862
>
> {Special Order No. 44}
>   The District Quarter Master [Baxter] will vacate the Black Smith shops belonging to Wm. H. Cherry, removing all Government property, and occupy shops owned by Mr. J.J. Williams. was in possession of Post Quarter Master permitting Post Quarter Master if there is; sufficient room to occupy & use so much of said last mention shop as will be necessary for his department.
>
> By command of Genl U.S. Grant
> A. A. Genl.[36]

Beyond a shadow of doubt, there was still no plan to move headquarters to Pittsburg Landing; rather, the sense of this order is for staying at Savannah. The composition of Order No. 44 is another crude example of the normal handling of directions from Grant through Rawlins. Something was amiss at the Cherry Mansion. This unpublished order is part of the body of facts show-

Cherry Mansion was the headquarters of the United States Army. It was here while General Grant was at breakfast that he heard the first cannon that opened the battle on Sunday morning; it was here that both General C.F Smith and General W.H.L. Wallace died. Those grouped before the fence are the officers of the Shiloh Battlefield Association (beginning on the left) as follows: Commodore H.M. Sweetser, Major Julian Gracey, Major J.R. Ross, Captain G.R. Brown, General John A. McClernand, General Lew Wallace, General J.R. Chalmers, Captain R.C. McMechan, Colonel E.T. Lee, Dr. J.W. Coleman, Colonel W.T. Shaw, Colonel A.C. Waterhouse, Captain I.P. Rumsey, General George F. McGinnis, and Captain J.W. Irwin; members and relatives of the Cherry family, and the Monticello Band (*The Graphic Chicago*, an illustrated weekly newspaper, May 5, 1894).

ing the real cause of the late arrival of General Grant to the scene of the Battle of Shiloh on April 6, 1862, while thousands were falling dead and wounded on the fields of Shiloh. As late as April 3 there were still no plans to move to a combat-ready headquarters at Pittsburg Landing. The excuse given later was that he wanted to wait for General Buell. If the quartermaster headquarters were staying at Savannah as Order No. 44 states, then it looks like Grant wanted to stay comfortable as long as possible in the Cherry Mansion. The contents of Order No. 44, together with the problem of the lack of coal, are only two facts that needed manipulation after the Battle of Shiloh.

The next item of seeming insignificance has to do with obscure Lieutenant Richard P. Derickson of the 16th Wisconsin Volunteers, who was making his way back to Pittsburgh Landing and Prentiss's 6th Division on April 1. He preserved records before, during and after the Battle of Shiloh. They start on April 3.

General Grant assigned the *Iatan* as the quartermaster boat for all supply stores of General Benjamin Prentiss's 6th Division. Lt. Richard P. Derickson was appointed as Brigadier General Benjamin M. Prentiss's staff quartermaster to operate from the *Iatan*, responsible for supplying and transporting to his headquarters. This headquarters was off the Eastern Corinth Road near a field owned by a man named Spain. (See Appendix 1.1, 1.2.)

Derickson, in his capacity as a Prentiss's staff quartermaster, was also responsible to General U.S. Grant's chief quartermaster, Captain A.S. Baxter, executive supply and transportation officer of the whole Army of West Tennessee. Lt. Derickson's documents contain names, places and events of the Battle of Shiloh, giving insights never recognized. They do not stand alone, but like General Order No. 30, the documents become an arrow that points to the serious errors of Grant's command at Shiloh.[37] They crack the wall, stripping away obfuscation about facts strangely evident in plain sight without the Derickson documents. Had Grant through Rawlins not succeeded with this artful cover-up, clearly he would have never achieved his later iconic status.

The "wrong road taken" controversy with regard to Grant and Wallace at Shiloh is well known to all with Civil War interest. The road taken by Wallace has always been the issue relevant to casualties and outcome of the first day of the Battle of Shiloh. That overwhelming slant has favored Grant. Emphasis on the road taken by General Lew Wallace to get to the battlefield deflects attention away from the fact that Grant and his army were disabled not by the road taken by Wallace, but by *the choice of the messenger* sent to Wallace. The messenger was Captain Algernon Sydney Baxter, district quartermaster of the whole army of West Tennessee, *head of the supply and transportation corps.*

After Captain Baxter delivered the message to General Lew Wallace, Baxter virtually disappears from all records. Evidence shows he was expunged from the record; but Captain A.S. Baxter is present in the uncovered documents of Lt. Derickson. By dissecting their contents, and all the other available records they point to, the truth can be confirmed. That truth is: In the aftermath of the Battle of Shiloh, the legitimate prepared battlefield operations of General Lew Wallace were misrepresented and accentuated as inept so as to turn attention away from General U.S. Grant's responsibility for a Union debacle on April 6, 1862.

Leaving him baffled for the rest of his life, the convoluted insinuations against him compelled Lew Wallace to write one of the most popular novels of the late 19th and early 20th centuries — Ben-Hur. In that novel is the veiled personage of General U.S. Grant, the Roman procurator Gratus. There is an also an evil protector of Gratus, Messala. Ben-Hur, slapped into slavery by these men, is the literary version of General Lew Wallace and how he felt forever after Shiloh and about Grant.[38]

4

The Problem with Napoleon

The push of the Union into the Deep South happened after the Confederate loss at Ft. Donelson. In quick succession Clarksville and Nashville, Tennessee, fell. The loss of the huge garrison at Ft. Donelson thinned the Confederate Army commanded by General Albert Sidney Johnston, a personal friend of Confederate President Jefferson Davis. Without the strength to cover a vast front in northern Tennessee, the loss turned Johnston from a hero to a goat. His new strategy was to concentrate the army on the critical railroad hub at Corinth, Mississippi. There, he came together with General Pierre Gustave Toutant Beauregard, the hero of Ft. Sumter. Johnston offered Beauregard the command position, but Beauregard wisely refused it. He would become the commander anyway when Johnston was killed.

The white aristocracy's "one-drop" rule, that a person with one drop of Negro blood was a Negro, disqualified such a person from most privileges in Southern culture. Beauregard was a Creole of French descent. Creoles were known to have mixed with those of African descent. It has never been stated outright, but as the war wore on, some began to suspect Beauregard had "one drop." It did not help that Beauregard had an elegant "high yellow" (light-skinned) slave who waited on him hand and foot. Whatever the case, after Bull Run, President Jefferson gave Beauregard a "promotion," sending him to the western theater of the war. Robert E. Lee was given Beauregard's command in Virginia.

Beauregard was aware of this subtle bigotry, but never let it show in public. As a West Point student, he dropped the P from the signing of his name P.G.T. Beauregard. When the war broke out, he dropped the use of Pierre entirely after the Confederate Congress in Montgomery, Alabama, sent a letter to him addressed as "Peter." He loved his French aristocratic roots, but was a shrewd enough man to see it could work against him.[1] He may have let his name Gustave come to the fore because it sounded more Teutonic. Like Indians who could be romanticized one moment, then called savages the next, some Creoles could be considered suave one moment then "a nigger" in the next. The hypocrisy of it all was underscored by the prevalence of so many light-skinned slaves at the plantations across the country. The book *Uncle Tom's Cabin* veiled more than physical cruelty against blacks. Sexual bondage in slavery was reality, probably more prevalent than the use of the whip. People just went on and pretended that such things did not exist. In Mississippi there was an exception: a family of racially unprejudiced whites had intermarried with blacks. Declaring Jones County, Mississippi, a free state, a "kingdom of Jones," they waged a small war of their own against the Confederacy.[2]

Creole P.G.T. Beauregard shown about the time of his brief stint as commander of West Point. A Napoleon mystique surrounded him until he fell out of favor with Confederate president Jefferson Davis.

Then there was the matter of that Napoleon fellow. In 19th-century America it seemed sometimes that every important person pretended to be Napoleon Bonaparte in photographs. It did not matter that Bonaparte was a ruthless conqueror and a demanding dictator. The popular perception of Bonaparte was for many a romantic, dashing genius who had seen his demise too soon. A look at pictures of the time exhibits the favorite stance for men in photographs of tintype, daguerreotype, ambrotype and salt prints. Though there was practical purpose in the stance for the photographer, everywhere people were stuffing their hands in their shirts and mimicking the Emperor. West Pointer General George McClellan did this overmuch. He was called "Little Napoleon" and had written a book on bayonet tactics that was used as a standard in the Union Army he was commanding. It was not very original material. He had basically adapted it from European military tactics, which Napoleon's army had used quite effectively in its heyday. No one knew that the technology of rifled muskets and cannons had made the bayonet charge nearly obsolete. McClellan was small in stature, and his troops took to calling him Napoleon in Blue. Although his physical size was diminutive, his ego was not. He took the imperial comparisons seriously, and when photographed, he struck the Napoleon pose. General Henry Wager Halleck, a friend of McClellan, also exhibited the pose.

Union commander Henry Wager Halleck of the Western Department of the Union Army displays the tendency to "play Napoleon."

If anyone was truly the American heir to the Napoleonic mystique, it was General G.T. Beauregard. After all, he was French by ethnicity. He had actually been tutored by two of Napoleon's officers at a private school in New York City. He was quite studied in the Napoleonic art of war. When he went to Charleston, South Carolina, as the first Confederate brigadier general in March of 1861, he seemed exotically Gallic to the citizens of that city.

By the standards of settlement of the New World, Beauregard should have been considered as American as one could get. New England had its *Mayflower* blue-bloods. On the southeastern seaboard, Charleston had its corresponding "Three Boats" aristocracy. In the deepest of the South,

Beauregard was descended from the French Imperialists who had taken over much of the continent long before the Revolutionary War. They became an ethnic group known as Creoles, French-speaking colonizers of America. The upper-class egalitarians among them were the original movers and shakers in an ever-changing political landscape, and all were both liberators and enslavers at various points of the continent at various times.

When Napoleon sold off his claims to a third of the land on the continent in the Louisiana Purchase, the Creoles were left in a more peculiar class of their own. As Anglo-Saxon Protestants flooded the middle of continent that had been ruled by the French and Spanish Catholics, the colonizers got colonized themselves. With the advent of the Confederacy, another power struggle ensued. It may be argued that if ethnic distrust had not been directed toward Beauregard, the Confederacy might have seen a better fate. Jefferson Davis developed a scorn for the French General that was definitely personality-based, but it had indications of more than one basis in ethnic hatred.

Pierre Gustave Toutant Beauregard rose to fame because of Ft. Sumter. He spoke not only French but Spanish as well. He did not want to appear *too* French, though he was very proud of his ancestry. Among family and friends he went by the shortened form of his second name, Guste. He, of course, spoke fluent French, and his family still had direct connections in France, but he considered himself thoroughly American. He could lapse into the coarser idiomatic speech of the Western frontier without a thought. He enjoyed the allusions to Napoleon for military purposes, but the Revolutionary War hero Marquis de Lafayette would be more in line with his national mindset.

Along with a bevy of young engineering-oriented West Point graduates that included Robert E. Lee and U.S. Grant, he proved the worth of that relatively new academy during the Mexican War. With the end of that war, any who wished to stay in the regular army had few chances for promotion. Only a congressionally approved number at each rank could be employed. He emerged from that war with a regular army promotion to captain and a brevet promotion to major. The brevetted title of major gave him recognition and seniority status to jump a position to colonel if that opened up, but he languished for twelve years as a true captain.

He spent those years as an engineer, strengthening the fortifications along the country's coastline and along the Mississippi River. That is what got him in charge at Charleston. He knew the architecture and strength of the island forts. In his frustration at lack of promotion, he briefly considered the pirate President William Walker's offer to head the Nicaraguan army. He was talked out of it by General Winfield Scott, whom he had served under in the Mexican War. Beauregard had taken a military education, and he wanted to use it. He saw secession coming before it happened and positioned himself shrewdly for promotion. With the help of his brother-in-law, a senator of the State of Louisiana, he maneuvered to be appointed as the new superintendent of West Point. That position gave him a full colonelcy, as it was the official rank required to run that school. He officially held the position for only a few days, but it was enough for him to secure irremediable rank for further promotion to general. The Confederacy was full of West Pointers, and despite the secession, the military structure was duplicated in the South, and previous rank and seniority in the Union army remained valid for defecting officers to the Southern cause. He had no intention of seeing that promotion through with the Union army. His loyalties were to Louisiana, and he had thought himself a shoo-in for the position of brigadier general of its state forces.

His shrewdness did not protect him from white Anglo-Saxon Protestant bias. General Braxton Bragg, who outranked Beauregard, upstaged him. Bragg, who had just moved to Louisiana, pulled maneuvers of his own for high rank. Bragg became brigadier general of Louisiana's state troops. Bragg offered Beauregard the colonelcy. He was a true colonel now because of the West Point commission, but Beauregard demurred and continued applying his engineering talents to strengthening fortifications in New Orleans. He knew what he was doing. In what was probably a mock show of humility, with a view to being elevated general in the Confederate military, he enlisted as private in the Orleans Guard, which was an elite battalion of the New Orleans Creole population.

Beauregard was thoroughly familiar with the defenses of Charleston Harbor. That had the attention of the Confederate administration. President Jefferson Davis summoned him to the first Confederate Congress at the first Confederate capital at Montgomery, Alabama, to discuss the matter. Beauregard suspected he would be offered a promotion to brigadier general of the Confederacy because of the potent brew of militancy in Charleston, South Carolina, if he could give a good presentation. He did, but could have seen the signs of future command hamstringing, despite promotion, coming in the invitation addressed to him. At the bottom of the letter, Confederate Secretary of War Hon. L.P. Walker made a faux pas. He addressed P.G.T. Beauregard by a variant form of the name he had dropped: he addressed it to "Peter" Beauregard. The downside of the Napoleonic mystique was just under the surface, but he was appointed brigadier general of the new nation, not just a state militia. He would command the first shot fired at Fort Sumpter.

Beauregard did not return to New Orleans for four years. In Charleston, he charmed the population of the city. A lock of his hair if procured was priceless to a belle. He had with him from New Orleans his extremely light-skinned butler, a personal manservant with the air of an aristocrat. Newspapers said Beauregard had the servant just as a coiffure for his mustache. The servant spoke well and intrigued Charlestonians as to whether he was really a Negro.

Beauregard sent for his two sons, who were then enrolled in the military academy in Charleston. Their mother was dead, but General Beauregard had a new young wife back in New Orleans. He also never saw her alive again. Ecstasy erupted in Charleston when Beauregard commanded troops to fire on Ft. Sumter, and the news spread across the secessionist states. The rockets' red glare, the bombs bursting in air over the fort, transferred their glory to the Creole. It looked as if the light of his reputation would never dim.

Next he was declared "the hero of Manassas," or Bull Run, as the North called the battle. President Jefferson Davis, a West Point man, was watching when the Federals ran away in utter confusion. Seized with military ardor and some jealousy, he rode to the field in military regalia to stake a claim for some of the glory. Beauregard, out of respect, said he thought it inappropriate to his position as president. What happened next became a subject of controversy. Davis interfered with the commanders on the field. Beauregard claims in his military memoirs he wanted to follow the enemy to Washington, D.C., but Jefferson Davis's presence inhibited that. On the field Beauregard had primarily expressed to the president that he did not think it wise to risk the "Light of the Confederacy" (Davis) on the field of battle, meaning if Davis was lost, the Cause was in danger. It was a fair statement, but if there was not a rift on the battlefield at Manassas, it became so after the president read the newspaper articles. He began to stew and then seek to subjugate Beauregard. Davis became impossibly parted with Beauregard, unofficially, when newspapers suggested the president of the Confederacy was a dilettante. From then on Davis thwarted the previous darling of the Confederacy, favoring Anglo-Saxon generals and members of the white Protestant aristocracy.

Jefferson Davis saw to it that Beauregard was put out of his sight in the East after that. He offered Beauregard a promotion that was really a demotion. He was removed from command of the Virginia armies and placed second in command to Jefferson Davis's closest friend, General Albert Sidney Johnston. Johnston was the highest-ranking Confederate officer, but he had problems of his own. When the Union Army of the West broke the Confederate defensive line at its northern and middle tier by the victories at Ft. Henry, Ft. Donelson, Clarksville and Nashville, the Confederate newspapers nearly broke Johnston. He offered his resignation to his friend Jefferson Davis. Davis refused, decrying the media and stating, "If Sydney Johnston is not General ... then the Confederacy has none to give you."[3]

That vote of confidence from the President bolstered the fifty-nine-year-old Johnston, but behind his large-bodied charismatic appearance, he was a deeply sensitive man. As the Confederate armies were concentrated at Corinth to defend the rail lifelines, Johnston offered the whole operation to Beauregard and said he would become second in command. Johnston was the best ally the Creole could have had in the Confederacy. But accepting the offer was a dilemma of sorts, one which Beauregard had to turn down. It showed Johnston's confidence in the Creole, but had he taken the position, it is predictable how Jefferson Davis would have reacted. Beauregard continued to be a kind of odd-man-out in the West Point alumni club of the Confederacy.

Success in reaching a goal depends on strategy. Johnston, Beauregard and the rest of the Confederate command agreed on the goal: attack the Union Army at Pittsburg Landing before it could get reinforcements. General Johnston left the full implementation of the strategy in the care of Beauregard, who would dispense troops from behind, while Johnston would lead from the front. The battle plan was to concentrate on the Union right, push the Federals away from the Tennessee River and reinforcements at the landing, and then drive them into the swampy wetlands. This was the same place where Lew Wallace was crafting a reinforcement strategy with the other General [W.H.L.] Wallace. In that swampland the Federals would be forced to surrender, and the Confederacy would regain control of Tennessee.

The deployment of Johnston's strategy as implemented by the Creole was one that had been tried before. It had been tried on a European battlefield in Belgium, but everything had to go exactly as planned. It would not. General Beauregard first saw the battle plan go awry in the streets of Corinth. One command structure blocked the priority status of another getting out of town. On the three roads taken to Pittsburgh Landing, more confusion ensued, with blockage by conflicting commands, miserable weather, absent rations, and as much sickness as existed in the Union Camps. Beauregard himself was suffering a raging throat infection that had plagued him since leaving Virginia. He slept in an ambulance the night before the attack to stay off the unhealthy ground; but it was not his personal health that caused him twice to recommend aborting the whole operation. It was the fact that the Confederate battle plan had already gone somewhat sideways.

Beauregard did not realize it, but he would become the Southern counterpart of Lew Wallace in the matter of blame for the tremendous casualty count. Elements were all in place for his scapegoating. As with Lew Wallace ten miles away, nobody was yet conspiring to make that happen. It was just the way it was. The dice were in the hands of General Albert Sidney Johnston at sunrise on April 6. He cast them, and they rattled on the table with the first rattling of musketry in Wood's Field. Johnston was only several hundred yards behind the scene. Having been given a last warning by Beauregard against follow-through, Johnston stated: "The battle has opened, gentlemen. It is too late to change our dispositions." Turning to mount his horse, he proclaimed: "Tonight we will water our horses in the Tennessee River." Trailed by his staff, Johnston rode through the early morning mist toward the sun. As the morning sun rose over the Tennessee and the massive rebel onslaught began, a Confederate officer called to mind the halcyon days of Napoleonic triumph. Such a sun had risen over Napoleon at Austerlitz; this must be another "sun of Austerlitz."[4]

Soon Beauregard described the early clashes with another Napoleonic reference. He said the movement of Albert Sidney Johnston's army was like the crashing down upon the enemy of "an Alpine avalanche." However, if Johnston was a kind of Napoleon on April 6, he was not going to see "the sun of Austerlitz" set. General Johnston had but hours to live. The problem with Napoleon this Sabbath morning was that the battle strategy was not based on the one at Austerlitz. Incredibly, it was based on the famous final failure of Napoleon at Waterloo.

5

Precursors and Premonitions

Simple things can have far-reaching effects. Personal acquaintances acquired in one's early career can in later life influence the outcomes of battles and the fate of nations. Such was the case with H.W. Halleck, U.S. Grant, W.T. Sherman and a young man named Oliver Perry Newberry.[1] All of these men had things happen to them in the new Territory of California in the late 1840s that affected the Battle of Shiloh. Halleck worked with W.T. Sherman there, securing for Sherman a good standing from then on. The opposite was true of Halleck and U.S. Grant. He secured with Halleck a lasting impression of a drunkard based on the California experience. The relationships between these three men, all West Pointers, influenced what happened at Shiloh.

Relationships between men and alcohol in California followed O.P. Newberry as much as U.S. Grant, but the happenstance of bullets at Shiloh robbed Newberry of a relationship with Colonel Everett Peabody at Shiloh, a relationship that might have rocketed him to high command on a general's staff.

When gold was discovered in California in 1849, Newberry, no more than a boy of 19 years, had gone there like so many others, sure of making a fortune as a 49er in the gold fields. When that failed in 1853, he joined the filibustering expedition of young William Walker in an effort to seize the Mexican peninsula of Baja and create a new country.[2]

This buccaneering incident was part of "Manifest Destiny" thinking. Every white man seemed to have it. But by the end of the Mexican War, the public had had their fill of expansion for awhile. For veteran William Walker, half a continent was not enough. With the victory in the Mexican War, he felt that that whole country of Mexico was wide open for the taking. Walker and his band of forty-five men, including O.P. Newberry, seized a couple of villages in Baja and Sonora, declared "independence," and then were promptly repulsed by the Mexican army. In the process Newberry sustained a wound, was left for dead and abandoned by Walker's expedition, but somehow dragged

49

himself back home to a less than heroic reception from his family and friends. Even if making a new country seemed a silly idea, Walker went on to take over Nicaragua, and no less than brevet Major P.G.T. Beauregard came within a hair's breadth of accepting his offer to be head of his army.[3]

St. Joseph, like Independence, Missouri, was a "jumping-off point" for those headed west, but Newberry chose it as his point to return east after the shambles of the Walker Expedition. He had had enough of the west. There in Missouri, he attempted farming in nearby Cameron, and a friendship with alcohol grew. He married Lizzie McCorkle and fathered Walter Franklin, whom he named after his brother.

Then, remarkably, he had a real career breakthrough. He acquired a new job in an engineer's office and a better friend than booze, the man for whom he worked. This was the golden period of his life, employment as an engineer under the auspices of Harvard-educated Everett Peabody at St. Joseph, Missouri. Peabody was the best in the west, a superior engineer and pioneering railroad man of Missouri.[4]

Colonel Everett Peabody (WICR 30677 in the collection of the Wilson's Creek National Battlefield; courtesy National Park Service).

When secession came, Newberry tried not to remember himself as a twenty-two-year-old, when he had pretended to be a captain under a man who was not just interested in Manifest Destiny, but was a vigorously proslavery expansionist. William Walker had made the laws of Louisiana the laws of that professed country of Lower California. O.P. Newberry could see the value of owning slaves on his farm in Missouri, but he also remembered how he had been left for dead in the desert. Things had changed. O. P. Newberry was now allied with

Everett Peabody, a real man, a fair man who counted Perry Newberry his friend. Perry Newberry, as his family called him, was not about to let a good life, a good country, slip away to the kind of men who had views like William Walker anymore. While Newberry had shown some proslavery leanings because he was labor-poor on his farm, Everett Peabody changed his mind. Peabody was fiery when he wanted to be and worked Perry up about these things. Now as a colonel, Peabody was the same age as Perry Newberry, and he urged Perry to save the Union. "The rebs were bushwhackers all ... Damned Sesesh!"

Major O.P. Newberry (WICR 11781 in the collection of the Wilson's Creek National Battlefield; courtesy National Park Service).

When hostilities broke out in Missouri, the state did not secede, but the elected maverick Governor Claiborne Jackson went over to the Confederate side. He was driven out of power by Congressman Francis P. Blair and Captain Nathaniel Lyon. This schism of authority left Missouri without a Union governor for a year and chaos resulted. Jackson became a Confederate governor, while Union loyalists recruited unofficial militias to prevent Missouri from seceding.[5]

With the rank of major, Everett Peabody and R.T. Van Horn merged separate battalions into the 13th Missouri regimental militia. O.P. Newberry was a lieutenant of Company I. He composed a letter to his mother in New York, filled with excitement and exuberant hopes of renewed fame through military exploits. Asking his family to purchase two sets of rank-designating shoulder straps, he ordered one set with the single bar of lieutenant and the other with two bars for the expected future promotion of captain. Colonel Peabody had taken him under his wing.[6]

When the Battle of Lexington, Missouri, resulted in a victory by Confederates because of overwhelming numbers, Peabody was disabled by a spent ball to the chest, and when he was carried from the field, he was shot in the foot and captured along with the majority of the 13th. Newberry somehow escaped, coincidentally with the help of General Benjamin Prentiss.[7] As

Peabody recovered from his wounds in captivity, Newberry went home to Cameron, Missouri, like the whipped pup he had been after the Walker expedition. Newberry's escape made him feel ashamed. Abandoned by Walker so long ago, he now felt he had abandoned Peabody. He found some solace in Walter, the three-year-old son he called "his pet," but renewed his friendship with the bottle. No matter; better men than he were familiar with drink, like General Grant, and it did not hurt their professional performance. He could do that, too.

By the time Colonel Peabody was paroled, the number 13 was given to a different regiment, with Missouri now under a Federally approved Union governor. After what had happened at Lexington, the number 13 was not a providential one anyway for Peabody. There was a new 13th Missouri at Shiloh, including Birge's buckskin-clad, bobtail-capped sharpshooters, but Peabody now commanded the 25th Missouri.[8] Superstitious ruminations were common in the 1800s, and even the highly educated Everett Peabody was not immune. He had premonitions. Nonetheless, fate was not his master, so Peabody upon his parole recruited new men and re-recruited the men he knew before capture. He found Perry Newberry and arranged for him to be 1st lieutenant again, in same Company I, but now in the 25th Missouri. Peabody did not cast any aspersions on Perry about his escape at the siege of Lexington.

Peabody was a gentleman and a true friend to those who were true with him. He loved to talk things out with western men, so different from his Puritan background in Boston, Massachusetts. At 6'2" he felt at home with rough-and-tumble men, but when alone, he meditated in wilderness settings while surveying new railroads. He wrote home to his family in Massachusetts about staring up at the stars on railroad cars with men of calloused hands, and he counted them excellent.[9]

The 25th Missouri was formed after the excitement at Ft. Henry and Donelson, and Peabody was not about to miss what many thought would be the final blow to the Confederacy expected at Corinth. After his release in a parole exchange for officers captured at Ft. Donelson, on crutches Peabody supervised the drilling of his regiment. He would confidently slap Newberry on the back and encourage all with shouts to remember the siege of Lexington. Newberry drilled and redrilled with his fellow junior officers under Peabody. Superior discipline and drill would overcome the fluke success and wild dash of the secesh at Lexington. This coming battle would also give Newberry the chance to display sanctioned heroics. He vowed to finally get family approval.[10]

The four hundred men in the 25th Missouri regiment were assigned to the division of Brigadier General Benjamin M. Prentiss, a lawyer in civilian life, who had experienced success in military actions in Missouri. Engineers like Peabody and lawyers like Prentiss did not look at things in quite the same way. Engineers got things done, sometimes literally paving the way, as with railroads. Out front on the perimeter, Peabody acted like an engineer, carefully studying the situation in front. It did not feel right. He sensed something he had felt at Lexington. Premonitions are sometimes just the sense of chance favoring a well-prepared mind.

At Pittsburg Landing, Lieutenant Oliver P. Newberry was in his prime, in his early thirties like Peabody. He left while his wife was pregnant and had never seen his baby girl Ella Perry. On the campground of Peabody's 1st Brigade, 25th Missouri, he was a line officer. But in Newberry's mind, something was different about himself. He did not feel like other people even if they were in the same army. He felt Colonel Peabody was the only man who understood him. The 25th proved to be the most alert regiment of the Union Army. While keeping alert like his mentor Peabody, Newberry's mind went to his family. He wished his brother were there in Tennessee. Prentiss's division was full of brothers fighting in the same regiments, even side by side in the same companies, like the Goforths. Perry Newberry loved his brother dearly, but felt withered under praise that seemed to always be directed to Walter. Perry subconsciously felt he lived in the shadow of his brother Walter, named for his rich uncle in Chicago. It was hard for him to understand why people he knew did not also respect his youthful military efforts back when he was younger. He went back and forth about this in his mind but did not necessarily speak of it to anyone. After the trauma on the Baja Peninsula, Newberry was subject to confusion spells. It fed his drinking inclination. He understood now, with the secession, why they had looked down on him about the Walker Expedition, but it was puzzling. It was so different back when he and his brother grew up together in Oneida County, New York, reading Horace Greeley's words: "Go west, young man!" He, O.P. Newberry, had actually done it. Greeley had urged the taking of the continent from the Indians and the Spanish and the Mexicans. The Louisiana Purchase was filling up. Go west, young man? Then the country put on the brakes when he got to California. Henry Wager Halleck and others had become wealthy with the land grab of half a continent, but it seemed everybody wanted to look down on his youthful aspirations for wanting to take a mere finger of land and a sliver of desert down in Baja with William Walker.[11] How was that different from Halleck in California? Halleck was now head of this army.

When his brother Walter Cass Newberry joined the Union Army as a private in the 81st New York regiment, Perry wrote that Walter should come out west where he was in the Army of Tennessee. Here Walter could not fail to advance, because he was "as brave a man there is alive." Perry Newberry also wished his father, who was born during the American Revolution, were still alive to see what was happening with him. Memory surges of the Walker Expedition pummeled him with the disappointment he had been to his father. This time fighting for a cause was going to be different.

The excitement in camp this spring of '62 bode better than his previous adventurous spurts. He would show them this time. Yes, friendship with Colonel Peabody would see him through his hopes for recognition. Peabody kept Newberry close even after the shame Perry had felt after his capture at Lexington. The whole 25th was looking for revenge when they offloaded at Pittsburgh Landing from their steamer *Continental*, flying a giant banner to remember Lexington.[12] Colonel Peabody was pleased to be in front of the army perimeter in Prentiss's 6th Division.

Personality Clashes Rifle the 6th Division

Col. Peabody was self-deprecating about the title of acting brigadier general. His charisma had attracted some and rankled others unfamiliar with him. There were strong rivalries and ambitions among officers throughout the whole Union Army here at Camp Pittsburg, as some called it; others knew it as Camp Shiloh. Peabody found himself disgusted with Prentiss's reticence to acknowledge serious enemy movement in front on the evening of April 5. But Prentiss, unlike Peabody, had not experienced the rapid envelopment of Lexington by 25,000 Confederates swelling to 40,000 with irregulars by time of the Union surrender there.[13] There are premonitions, and then there is a feel that comes on the air with the movement of large bodies of troops. Peabody felt the Confederates in the air. There were tens of thousands of Confederates nearby, as there had been advancing at Lexington.

It was getting near dark, and had been raining at times throughout the day of April 5. The roads were sloppy. General Grant had canceled a review of Prentiss's division. He may not have been on the fields at Pittsburg Landing that day because of his ankle injury. He kept in touch with division commanders through his aides. Based on information he received from General Sherman, artillery fire that afternoon against Buckland's Brigade in a place of fallen timbers was not a true threat. The particulars in conversations on these matters between Prentiss and Grant would never be officially reported, but they apparently hardened Prentiss toward Peabody and against the idea of major attack. Prentiss's headquarters resided on a hill difficult to approach from the east, and at his west in the woods, he had stationed two camps of artillery. Prentiss's headquarters tent was situated such as to probably give him personally a false sense of security. It buffered him from the urgency of Colonel Peabody, whose camp was more exposed and over half a mile to the west.

One of the regimental colonels under Peabody's command, David Moore of the 21st Missouri, was deferential to Prentiss's outlook. When Prentiss seemed to satisfy Peabody's concerns by ordering a reconnaissance, a rubber stamp of Prentiss's opinion was ensured by the choice of Moore to head the party. They set out about dusk on Saturday, April 5, with five companies of his own 21st Missouri and five companies of Peabody's 25th Missouri. Moore was gone only about an hour, but claimed he had traveled three miles in the dark with what amounted to a full regiment of ten companies from two Missouri regiments.[14] Returning prematurely at 7:00 P.M., Moore watched Major Powell of the 25th Missouri fall out of the patrol with his five companies at their place on the far right of the 6th Division camps. Peabody met them and found that Major Powell disagreed with Colonel Moore's view that there was no cause for alarm. The little major did not have a blunt-force way of insisting, but he was regular army and older than the two young colonels, Peabody and Moore.[15] There was a gray giant out there in the dark. Colonel Peabody's engineering mind turned more furiously now.

This kind of infighting ran all the way to the top. Perhaps Prentiss could not be blamed for his chafing at Peabody. He was only imitating what he had been taught as the way to rise in rank. As the war began, Prentiss and Grant were appointed as brigadier generals the same day. A rift resulted from two occasions when they struggled with one another for control. Both of them had Mexican War experience, but Grant won with better political influence and his "regular army" status gave him seniority over volunteers.[16] The galling hypocrisy was that army regulars continuously made the claim that volunteers only got high rank through political influence.

Prentiss toed the line after that, now resigned that the way to further success in this man's army was strict adherence to military protocol. As for Prentiss's adherence to excessive caution, he was scrupulously obeying Grant. But therein lay another perfidy in the chain of command. Commander Major General Henry Wager Halleck had been sabotaging Grant. He had jealously yanked command out from under Grant after the public acclaim about Grant's initials U.S. meaning Unconditional Surrender at Ft. Donelson. Halleck had hoped to court-martial him. Lincoln quashed his hopes, and then Halleck disingenuously praised Grant, restoring him to command at Savannah and Pittsburg Landing.[17]

Grant was intent on obeying Halleck's orders to the letter now. Those orders stated that by no means should the army be drawn into engagement with the enemy. The Army of the Tennessee was to wait for "Ol' Brains" Halleck to arrive from St. Louis for that. He had literally written a book on war: *Halleck's Elements of Military Art and Science*. Grant claimed he liked Halleck, despite the shelving he had received.

Military art and science in a book is one thing, but Lt. Newberry and others picked up rumors of war from Major Powell's half of the reconnoitering patrol and the scattered interactions with other regiments and quartermasters and commissary. On Saturday, April 5, someone had seen rebel artillery in the trees behind a house; others claimed to have seen long lines of campfires stretching into the distant south. Some loitering soldiers around a mess fire chuckled and said those alarmists were all just "seein' things," but at dusk General Prentiss assented to sending out a reconnaissance party led by Colonel Moore of the 21st Missouri. Grant had finished up late and limping on Friday night, April 4, at Pittsburg Landing; apparently he never came to Pittsburg Landing on April 5.[18] Official headquarters was supposed to be at the log house at the top of Pittsburgh Landing. It was supposed to have been that way for a week. How different things might have been at the Battle of Shiloh if U.S. Grant had bunked in an officer's tent at Pittsburgh Landing the night of April 5, 1862. Instead he was in an ornate bedroom in the Cherry Mansion in Savannah.

Colonel Peabody paid special attention to the observation of his own Major Powell, who was part of the patrol General Prentiss had ordered out to mollify the 1st Brigade commander Peabody. Major Powell was someone to whom attention should be paid. An old army regular of small physical stature, he had not only long experience, but had a special concern since his 12-year-old son was in camp at the time.[19] This probably meant the boy was a drummer. Powell urged Prentiss to vigilance. When General Prentiss said that everything was all right and the idea of the bulk of Johnston's army being closer than Corinth was laughable, the major went immediately to Peabody's tent, who did respond with strengthening pickets of his own brigade. This did not set Peabody at ease. Peabody stalked his camp, and at midnight poked his head into the officers' tents of some of his key men. Captain Evans of Company E was tenting with Major Powell. Orderly sergeant James M. Newhard was with them. Newhard was about to get a field promotion as the colonel woke them up and asked if they would consider it an intrusion if they all talked. First he made the sergeant an acting lieutenant, since both lieutenants of the company were away in St. Louis. They took cigars and talked in the lamplight from midnight to 3 A.M.[20]

Col. Peabody told them he sensed they were lying in the face of a powerful enemy, in a very careless and unguarded position, liable to be surprised and overwhelmed at any time. These veterans of the siege of Lexington needed no convincing, hearing it from Colonel Peabody. He was uncomfortable lying idle and wanted to put his brigade into some kind of condition to resist attack by Johnston, which was likely at any time. He wished for artillery and had asked Prentiss for one of the batteries that were in park so he could position it in front of his regiment. It was not granted. Prentiss had hooted at the idea Johnston was any nearer than Corinth and said everything was all right.[21]

Prentiss may have been overburdened at the time. His division was still forming. The 18th Wisconsin had just arrived at the division. He was expecting the 15th Michigan at any time, as well as the 23rd Missouri and the 14th Wisconsin. There were two battalions of Major Robert Ingersoll's 11th Illinois cavalry behind his camp that were loosely responsible to him. There were five batteries of artillery looking for a home in his division. One of them, Silversparre's, didn't even have enough horses and limbers to get out on the field. Prentiss had just begun to get his supply and commissary straightened out by assigning a very capable Lt. Richard Derickson of the 16th Wisconsin's company K as acting quartermaster on the division headquarters boat, the *Iatan*.[22]

There was also the rivalry factor. Prentiss was not fond of dealing with Peabody as an acting brigadier general. This is where he had started with U.S. Grant: two brigadier generals vying for control. Now, with Grant's comeuppance over Prentiss, Grant was up there in Savannah, living in style and operating a "flagship," as Grant had called the *Tigress*. Grant got that rank by what Prentiss considered a technicality. Prentiss would not risk causing himself a technical disqualification again.

The sensationalist newspapers of the time claimed there were no pickets at Shiloh guarding the perimeters to avoid surprise attack, but there were in fact pickets in front of the Union army. They were assigned according to regulations, too. In the 6th Division, the 16th Wisconsin sent out three companies as pickets. They were thrown out to front and west of their camp according to regulation. They were lying in the woods and clearings close to a nameless wagon road.[23]

Because of General Prentiss's reticence, Peabody implemented what amounted to a bloody sacrifice to prevent the Union Army from being surprised. He acted under his own responsibility. He sent out Major Powell and three companies from the 25th Missouri and also obtained two companies of the 12th Michigan which were conveniently located next to the 25th Missouri. This was no picnic to obtain, either. In the 12th Michigan there existed a schism between its Colonel Francis Quinn and Lt. Colonel Graves that made getting things done difficult. Each had his own quartermaster.[24] Ammunition had to be acquired. Further east the 2nd Brigade of Colonel Madison Miller was an embryo still forming, and it was set directly in front of General Prentiss's tent. In order to follow through with his instincts about a terrible force in their front, Peabody had to quietly send out as many men as he could judiciously at 3 A.M. April 6, without raising the ire of Prentiss and senior men in the division cleaving to General Prentiss's inaction and opposition. It was impractical to involve the 2nd Brigade this early in the morning. The newest of the regiments included the 61st Illinois and Miller's home regiment, the 18th Missouri. The night before, the 18th Wisconsin had also shown up, and they had not even set up their tents yet. If the 15th Michigan came in the middle of the night, their newly mustered troops might get carried away with this action and spoil it. Peabody told those who went out that he would accept all responsibility; he expected to die, but he would not allow the Union army to be caught totally by surprise. He would sound the alarm this way at risk to his rank and life.

A little over an hour and a half later, the reconnoitering party led by Major Powell of the 25th Missouri later struck cavalry vedettes that were part of the Confederate advance in Wood's Field. The vedettes fired at the reconnoitering party, but it was more to warn the companies of rebel infantry that were gathered along the edge of the field in the trees. In a normal reconnoitering tactic, the procedure of troops in the advance of the army was to "develop the enemy." This meant to get them to demonstrate by their firing just how heavy was the presence of the enemy. When the returning Confederate cavalry vedettes reached their own lines, this was accomplished. The Confederates in advance fired along a long line in the trees. Major Powell's Union men met the challenge with fire of their own.

While still early morning, the 16th Wisconsin pickets began to see wounded men being brought back to the 25th Regiment, right of their brigade up the reconnoitering road. Excitement perked up among the youngest men. An older Wisconsin backwoodsman claimed he could feel movement in the ground. After tamping the earth with his rifle butt and putting his ear to the ground, he said could hear the rumbling of artillery and what could be none other than movement of large numbers of men forming with stamping feet.[25] The crackling and popping sounds of gunfire soon confirmed something big was happening in the near distance. It was a precursor. The Battle of Shiloh had begun.

6

Forrest's Movements

Off to the far left of the Union 6th Division lay the southern stretch of the Savannah-Hamburg road. A few miles down that road in the near-dawn dark was a large group of Confederate cavalry, comprising Colonel Nathan Bedford Forrest's Tennessee and Colonel Wirt Adams's Mississippi cavalry. Along with them were five companies of the 1st Tennessee Confederate Regiment, Colonel Maney's Brigade, and the 19th Tennessee Regiment of Colonel D.H. Cummings. They were guarding the approach to Hamburg on land the Greer family owned at Lick Creek. The bridge there had been constructed by the Greers and was known locally and appropriately as Greer's Ford. A contingent of troops this size at this spot could inhibit approach from Hamburg Landing. Confederate intelligence reports had understood the Army of the Ohio might soon be ferried across at Hamburg. Nathan Bedford Forrest had obtained this information through his own mounted infantry. They had gathered it when the Federals had broken the midsection of the Confederate defensive line across Northern Tennessee. Cavalry screened the Rebel withdrawal from Nashville and squads of Forrest's men on horseback watched through trees all across West Tennessee.[1]

Nathan Bedford Forrest, here at Greer's Ford, was reaching the summit of a learning curve. He concluded that much of the Confederate high command were inept, "pompous sons of bitches." For those who knew Nathan Bedford Forrest, the fierce countenance he could demonstrate belied a humility that originated in poverty and the love of his mother. He was somewhat of a legend already in Mississippi and Western Tennessee because he had killed two men in Hernando, Mississippi, when he was only seventeen years old. Those not informed thought this had been a cold-blooded execution, but relatives of the victims who were on the scene later related that Forrest had, in fact, put the men on notice as they approached the small mercantile he owned with his uncle. He pleaded with them to come back another time. His uncle was suffering diminished mental capacity. Forrest himself had been shocked to find that the business he had just inherited an interest in was already bankrupt, and his uncle was deep in debt. He told the armed men in their heated debt-collecting state of mind that if they forced the issue, he would have to protect kin no matter the rightness or wrongness of the issue. Before Forrest realized what was happening, his uncle emerged from the building behind him, brandishing a shotgun and leveled it at the face of one of his creditors. The man raised his own weapon, Bedford drew his; one man shot Forrest's uncle dead, and in the ensuing shootout, Nathan Bedford Forrest sealed his first reputation as a killer when there was cause.[2]

He had not prided himself in this, but his nature and personality went before him from then on. His family was part of the early poor Scotch-Irish immigration from the old Cherokee lands in Georgia and the Carolinas. The Gaelic that was still spoken among many of them described a genetic disposition peculiar to them as Celts. It was translated as "warp-spasm." This was an almost supernatural change in appearance that occurred in the physiques of the ancient Celtic heroes. These normally calm, beneficent men could turn into a fierce, terrifying, powerful force of nature in battle. Of course, the Celts were given to hyperbolic descriptions of warriors of their race, but Nathan Bedford Forrest, guarding Greer's Ford, had such a "warp-spasm" reputation with his men, and it was justified. It had not dawned on the aristocratic Confederate officers at Shiloh that they were treating a giant with dismissal.

At Shiloh, Scotch-Irish Nathan Bedford Forrest displayed the capability of mythical Celts to transform a quiet countenance into a "warp-spasm" of a mighty warrior.

Forrest's father died when he was only a boy, and he became the surrogate father to the family. He had no childhood to speak of and had developed a pragmatic, no-excuses work ethic that was required in a Southwestern wilderness still filled with bears, panthers and lawless men. He abhorred liquor after an experiment getting drunk in the woods. He had no use for it thereafter. After the fatal incident in Hernando, his mother found someone to marry, and young Nathan felt a freedom of movement that he had been deprived of while taking care of his mother and siblings. When the Mexican War broke out, he was stirred to fight the Spanish-speakers, partly out of patriotism and partly out of the recognition that changes were in the offing for the acquisition of territory. He knew from several obvious waves of immigration that "he that got there first would get the most." The Spaniards had explored nearly half the continent and put Spanish names all over it, like the town Hernando in Desoto County, Mississippi, at the expense of the natives. The French laid claim after the Spanish to the middle third of the continent and set up a Creole culture that was subjugated in turn by the whites of the eastern U.S. upon the abstract sale of the Louisiana Purchase. For the United States, the conflict with Mexico allowed time to take the rest of the continent from the Spanish dons and Catholics that held sway. Forrest had no substantial monetary means at that point, but was hoping to overcome the colloquial expression: "Them that's already gots, gits."

Forrest arrived in the Republic of Texas only in time for the Treaty of Guadalupe Hidalgo to rob him of a chance to build stature by military exploits. He had to split fence rails for several months in order to make enough money to get back to Mississippi. On the journey home, he formulated a plan to put him in league with the big plantation owners. The plan involved selling slaves, the most lucrative commodity in the South. Unlike types of the region, he was not a true hater of commonly called "niggers." The culture was what it was. Forrest would learn that his peculiar chosen profession produced a glass ceiling, preventing entry into the social hierarchy of wealthy Southern aristocrats. It would not matter that he became a millionaire; the elite would not let him in. They would do that to the demise of their cause. At Shiloh they discounted Forrest again.

This assignment at a creek known for its salty sulfurous deer licks, Lick Creek, by the corps commander was a waste. The classic rules of European warfare stated battles could not be won by cavalry; cavalry were only to serve as the eyes and ears of the army. What the Confederate high command had not come to appreciate about Forrest was he had created lightning innovations to mounted soldiering. His men were really infantry on horseback, ready to jump to the ground and carry the momentum forward with surprising swiftness. He had modified the expression "he that gets there first gets the most" into "he that gets there first with the most [men] wins the battle." Or, as he put it, "Get there firstest with the mostest." He, like W.T. Sherman, revealed himself to be a "genius born of battle." That genius acknowledged that "war is hell." If you are going to engage in its horror, do it with a machine-like attitude and an abrogation of the conscience inherent in normal people. Forrest simplified it this way to his men: "War means killin'." "If you're here for war, get on with the killing, it's what you signed on for."[3]

On that approach to Hamburg and among those mounted on horseback with Forrest's command sat Samuel Asbury Garrett of Senatobia, Mississippi.[4] He wanted to be near Forrest because the man had once been a neighbor in Hernando, Mississippi, less than fifteen miles away from Senatobia, and Sam, like Forrest, was also a common man with nothing handed to him. The fact that a man like Forrest could become a millionaire gave him hope he could rise financially, though he was just sharecropping part of a sizable plantation deeded to a young twenty-year-old wedded couple related to General Featherston of Holly Springs, Mississippi. He was not able to ride off with Bedford Forrest when he came recruiting earlier, but when Wirt Adams came through, he started making preparations to join up like some of the other kin had already done. Adams was no Forrest, but he had turned down the prestigious job of postmaster general of the whole Confederacy to recruit a body of troops that would be the eyes of the army in constant movement about the foe. Adams was real people, not just some pretending potentate.[5]

Sam Garrett's kin were salted all across northern Mississippi when General Albert Sidney Johnston and General Beauregard rapidly concentrated Confederate armies at Corinth. The excitement was running as high as the Mississippi at flood stage in the whole region. Although there was still cotton in need of harvest on Sam's and his brother Joe's part of the Featherston estate, valuable share money at stake, Samuel Asbury Garrett took the stand with Nathan Bedford Forrest. It would not matter the issues bandied about in newspapers, such as abolition and secession; he would side with kin because there was kin within walking distance of Pittsburgh Landing. He caught up with Wirt Adams's men and offered his services. He expected short work. There would be time to finish off the Yankees and then finish off the cotton crop at home.

Sam Garrett brought his most valued property with him, his horse. Confederate cavalrymen did not have the luxury of government-supplied horses, like the Union did, but the men were better on their own personally acclimated mounts, and they would get compensation later, or so was the promise. Forrest was proof of what to expect. He was sacrificing his own personal fortune to equip the men who were with him. Word trust was the true Southern man's way, but Sam did not take everything totally for granted. Like most cavalrymen he had less property to lose than the moneyed officers, but because of that, what little he did have, he felt stronger about than those elitists. They could lose a lot and still have a lot. If men like Sam lost, they lost it all.

Promises of aristocrats like the Featherstons had worn thin. Hopes that he and his brother, Joseph Martin Garrett, had while farming bottom land with their two large families were beginning to fade. They seemed one step closer to the slaves who were working the Featherstons' land. Sometimes slaves worked side by side with his family in the cotton fields. Most white folks in these parts came out to these lands from Georgia and the Carolinas. Most folks who came were Scotch-Irish, but much of the good land had been snapped up by already rich Carolinians, and they were only getting richer. "Ain't that the way?" was how hardscrabble folks resigned themselves.

When that government census man came by in 1860, Sam saw what the clerk wrote down about those two Featherstone kids who had never worked a hard day in their lives. Those little braggarts had shown tens of thousands of dollars' of worth on that good-for-nothing census form. Sam and his brother weren't about to let those rich kids show them up on a public paper anybody could get at. It wasn't proper to brag like that. Sam and Martin kept silent about what they owned and told the men how many household members they had and then told that government man to get on his way.

Repentance comes of powerlessness. Soon Sam Garrett and his brother Joe hunkered back down in dealings with the young Featherstons. The chance they could parlay their share of cotton crops into the purchase of their own land was something to hold onto. Also, the concentration of Confederate forces at Corinth and the worries about the Garrett womenfolk, up near Shiloh Church, supplanted the feelings of injustice the Garrett brothers had to stomach about their landlords. "Yankees! Damned Abolitionists! Hypocrites!" They had built their world up North on the backs of blacks, too. Now, the rules had changed after they all got rich and industrialized. Now, they were looking down their noses at the South. It was hard for Sam to figure why these Northern men, men he had never met, were coming down here to take away what they had built up. He surely would never have gone up North to do that to them. This giant blue army that had formed around Pittsburgh Landing seemed like the giant that lived above the beanstalk, only he did not stay up there in the clouds; the giant came down and was stomping around on all that was good and lovable, just like General Johnston had said in the letter read to every regiment.

What did they want from Sam Garrett? He did not even have a nice white rain slicker like that Tennessee boy, William Butler, in Maney's infantry over there in the woods. It had been raining on and off, and Sam was soaked to the bone. "Well, God bless Will Butler, anyhow! God bless the child that's got his own. We gotta keep what's ours. God bless Jeff Davis! Goddam the Yankees! We will send 'em to hell where they belong! Lick Creek will be more than salt lick today. Those Federals, we will lick 'em before dark and water our horses in the Tennessee next to Albert Sidney Johnston himself."

These were fast thoughts just now for Sam Garrett. He was exhausted from the constant movement of the last couple of weeks. Unattached to any specific brigade as yet, he knew the weak side of the Union encampments. It was just down the Hamburg–Savannah road, past McCuller's field, on up through Noah Cantrell's farm, on through Sarah Bell's cotton field, up through Cloud's land. That was Johnston's thrust. They could circumvent trouble with the big ravine in front of Pitt's log cabin by going around through the old Indian mounds. General Johnston had it right. Cut them off from the landing and drive them into the swamps past Owl and Snake Creeks. Samuel Asbury Garrett allowed himself to close his eyes since others around him were doing so. He lapsed into sleep in his saddle and slipped into a half-dream. He dreamed of the good bottom land he was working near the Mississippi river; he dreamed he saw his wife Nancy waving to him while his ten-year-old son Joseph Martin, daughters Jane and Ruth, whom the family called "Duck," and little Sam picked white balls of cotton. In his dream they all turned and waved to him, too.

7

While Waiting for Grant

On April 6, 1862, steamboat captain Bart Able had a beautiful view at the Tennessee River boat landing of Pittsburg. In his *Iatan* officer's quarters, the Texas, on the hurricane deck, Captain Able sat high off the water. At dawn a pink pastel glow fringed the vast oak wilderness on the east side of the river. The river running north was rising and falling because of winter snow melt and periodic heavy thunderstorms on the vast watershed that comprised the Tennessee River and its tributaries. Several other rear- and side-wheel steamboats were berthed. Many of the boats were set up as commissaries, and reorganization was taking place for rations of the army.

On April 5, John Rawlins scrawled off a note to General Prentiss. The *Iatan* was to supply the 16th Iowa, 18th Wisconsin, and 23rd Missouri with Captain Morton in charge. The *Hiawatha* was to supply the 21st Missouri, 18th Missouri and 61st Illinois under Captain Leland's oversight. The *Chancellor* was to supply the 25th Missouri, 16th Wisconsin and 12th Michigan with Captain Simmons. This was done, as stated, "to obviate the necessity of hiring additional boats for Commissary purposes as the commissaries now doing the issuing are sufficient for the entire army." When this order was given, at last it seemed some efforts were being made to remove operations from Savannah. The boats contained equipage for the regiments as well and, no doubt, some remedial supplies of ammunition.[1]

In the efforts for organization the *John J. Roe* was apparently a mother-boat to the others. Rawlins had issued the above arrangement with that in view. Other orders that dovetailed with commissary boat instructions were sent out by aide-de-camp W.R. Rowley. The 4th Division's General Stephen A. Hurlbut was "to furnish a detail of fifty men daily for five days fatigue duty, to report to Quartermaster *Baxter* on the steamer *John J. Roe*.[2] The order to Prentiss was only signed "Rawlins," no title, no authority given, though in the journal recordings of Rawlins's Special Order No. 45, it did

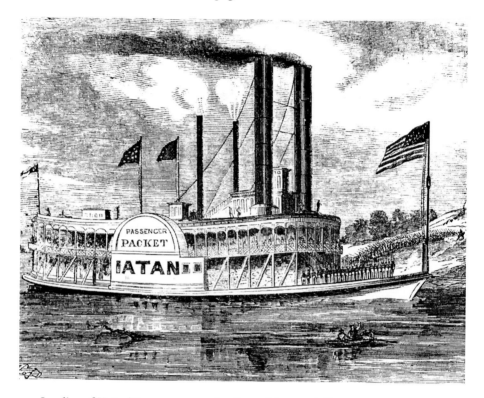

Landing of United States troops under General Lyon at Jefferson City, Missouri. The *Iatan* became headquarters for General Prentiss's 6th Division at Shiloh under the control of quartermaster Lt. Richard P. Derickson of the 16th Wisconsin Infantry (sketch by Orlando C. Richardson for *Harper's Weekly*, July 1, 1961).

receive a neat writing protocol treatment. As with his previous orders to Lew Wallace about the sick and of the movement of Baxter out of the Cherry Mansion blacksmith shop, there was an apparent lack of scrupulousness in Rawlins's communications to the intended parties. This imperfect writing protocol could have characterized a slipshod manner for the dictation and signing of the famous order to General Lew Wallace on April 6.

However, all this proves strenuous work was taking place by the district quartermaster on Grant's staff, Captain A.S. Baxter, though he had received no promotion. While many about him were receiving their new shoulder straps with changed insignias because of Ft. Donelson, Baxter was still wearing only two bars. It is not what General Grant had asked of Congressman Washburne. Grant had asked for higher rank for Baxter. Many senior officers of the battle at Ft. Donelson had received promotion, and Grant's aides were in line for promotion as well. Halleck had promoted Brigadier Generals Smith,

McClernand and Lew Wallace as major generals, becoming official on April 5, 1862.

General B.M. Prentiss was instructed by Captain Clark B. Lagow to furnish ten men for six days to fatigue duty aboard the propeller-driven ammunition ordnance steamer *Rocket* with Grant's Staff Ordnance Officer Brinck in charge of that boat. General U.S. Grant would be steaming up in his flagship *Tigress* later to join the covey of vessels.[3]

Two steamboats at the landings were loaded with two regiments that had not offloaded as of yet. The men were extremely frustrated at their confinement and lack of a camping ground. Colonel Chambers's 16th Iowa was chafing aboard the *Crescent City*. His badly needed artillery under the command of Captain Bouton would have been a great help to Colonel Peabody at that very moment. Instead it was sitting idle, and General Prentiss had insulated himself behind two camps of artillery, Munch's and Hickenlooper's. Still another, the battery of Captain Silversparre, was proving useless without horses and equipage and was sitting on the slope of the landing. The steamer *Planet* with Colonel Jacob Tindall's 23rd Missouri was coming up from Savannah. All these men had been ordered on April 4 to report to General Benjamin Prentiss and his 6th Division to be brigaded. On this morning, April 6, 1862, they could not figure the reason nothing was happening. Grant and his staff were nowhere to be seen. There was only an office at the top of the hill and no main headquarters at which to report.[4]

A few other vessels were due at the landing this day. The *Minnehaha* was returning from delivering sick soldiers to Northern hospitals and another regiment was returning on it. On board, somewhere below Savannah, the vessel was carrying someone General Grant would prefer not to see: Mrs. W.H.L Wallace, wife of the 2nd Division commander. Grant had prepared an order to prevent wives from visiting their husbands in camp. For Mrs. Wallace it was fortunate timing in more ways than one. Their spring-summer marriage would end at Shiloh by W.H.L. Wallace's mortal wounding, but she would be able to spend his last hours with him. The presence of Mrs. Wallace allowed something else. It was the disappearance of the record of arrangements for the road to be used in case reinforcement was needed.[5] On April 5, General W.H.L. Wallace and General Lew Wallace, both division commanders, were preparing the best road to and from Shiloh, in case of emergency reinforcement for either portion of the Army of the Tennessee. They had cooperated to make the Hamburg-Purdy road over Owl Creek Bridge and thence to Adamsville the road of choice. The communication disappeared mysteriously in the personal effects of the dead general after the battle. The lack of it allowed incrimination of Lew Wallace as inept. The real incrimination is that General Grant was later mute about whether he knew of these preparations.

At least two other steamboats were berthed at the landings on April 6 in the early morning. One was the *John Warner*, the other was the *Galena*. The 15th Michigan was ashore and ready to tramp out to Prentiss's camp, while their regimental quartermaster tried to sort out the supply and transport organization. Passing from officer to officer in the quartermaster corps, each would have given him the normal procedural responses: "The District Quartermaster is not with us yet this morning ... Baxter will only answer the requisitions of the Division Quartermasters.... You will need to wait for his approval through your Brigade quartermaster."[6] The 15th Michigan had no brigade yet, no brigade quartermaster, and Grant's headquarters was truly not yet at Pittsburg Landing. District quartermaster Captain A.S. Baxter was not there because he depended on Grant to be there. He could not tend to his supply and transportation corps. The 15th Michigan therefore reported without ammunition to General Prentiss just as the Confederates began slamming into the 6th Division.

Baxter would normally be at a staff meeting with General Grant. Breakfast was often utilized for this. In fact, members of Grant's staff were with him that morning as the first booming sounds of artillery traveled down the ravines onto the Tennessee River and bounced back and forth off the buffs. The records of that morning were being kept by Captain John Rawlins. There is no mention of Captain Baxter's being present when Grant came down for breakfast.

Before the attack became evident to the body of the army, there were close to a dozen boats at the landings at Pittsburg, there was relative relief from the boiling cacophony and clamor of the multitude of steam transports that had lined up four deep to offload close to forty thousand men in the last few weeks. There were the normal maintenance routines, no graveyard atmosphere, though it was still dawning. Roustabouts called out to one another in low tones of early morning; deck hands swept up and tidied loose ends. Cooks prepared meals for Captain Able and the other officers, as well as for Lt. Derickson and the other captains.

Lt. Derickson struck a match and lit candles in his quarters off the main deck and arranged his stationery; stashes of requisitions, passes, vouchers, etc. They had embossed quartermaster seals of locomotives and steamboats, indicating the critical role the transportation corps had in the army. There were pads of the ubiquitous foolscap, common lined pulp paper used for sundry communications, though some of this also had embossed seals as well.

District quartermaster Captain Baxter and newly appointed 6th Division quartermaster Lt. Derickson were men in their early forties, both with successful business backgrounds. It was a good fit for them to be working together. Both made exceptional dispersion officers. On staff with General Grant, Baxter carried side arms and if necessary could be called on to act as a field officer. Lt. Derickson was himself an officer of the line as 1st lieutenant of Company K, 16th Wisconsin, second to Captain Williams. Now, as General Prentiss's staff quartermaster, he would also be called on to act as an aide in any capacity the general might require. In Derickson's absence, 2nd Lieutenant David Vail was serving in Derickson's place. The 6th Division was more in need than the others, and Baxter and Derickson could facilitate a rapid satisfaction of the needs of General Benjamin Prentiss's regiments, but Captain Baxter was not there early. Lt. Derickson used the idle time to compose a beautiful cursive handwritten request to Brigadier Benjamin M. Prentiss, asking to assign Corporal O.J. Valentine as his assistant noncommissioned officer.

The previous problems with Captain Hatch in the Quartermaster Department demonstrated that Baxter needed solid professionals. Grant had picked Baxter for that very reason. Baxter was now battle-hardened, making him all the more valuable for service. The experience that Baxter had been through presiding as chief quartermaster of transportation and supply corps in the last few months was invaluable to operating under combat conditions. He had survived the Battle of Ft. Donelson. The expectation would be that he would be indispensable during coming battles.

Derickson was well suited to his quartermaster job as well, having operated a lumber business near Port Washington, Wisconsin, owning or controlling thousands of acres of timber.[7] He was used to overseeing teams of animals and hauling heavy merchandise. Some of the men who were in his Company K had worked closely with him in the private sector. This was a common thing in both armies. Officers were most often men of some means or reputation, and as such, recruited people they knew. 1st Lt. Derickson had worked with 2nd Lt. David F. Vail and his family in civilian life. Vail was a wagon maker and lumberjack. Corporal O.J. Valentine was a good friend of 2nd Lt. David Vail, and it was for these reasons that Derickson knew Valentine would make a good assistant. He began composing the request for General Prentiss to get the corporal assigned.

The Reconnoitering Party Returns

Out in the far fields, Colonel Moore with five companies of his regiment was in a mood. Due to the firing, the 6th Division had been aroused. Peabody prevailed on a resistant Moore to come to the assistance of the reconnoitering party. Just after dawn, men of the 16th Wisconsin witnessed Colonel David Moore rebuking Major Powell as he retreated from Wood's Field, denouncing him and his men as cowards for running from an inferior force, despite the obvious injuries.[8] Perhaps it was lack of sleep that made Moore so testy in those early hours. He had come back from the previous reconnaissance only hours earlier to confirm Prentiss's assessment that there was no significant enemy presence. But Lt. Colonel Graves of the 12th Michigan and Major Powell of the 25th Missouri had not agreed with 21st Missouri Col. Moore about that previous evening's reconnaissance. Some of the men in the patrol had seen long lines of fires, and had heard abbreviated bugle notes and tapping of drums in the darkness to the south where no Union camps existed, yet Moore said there was nothing to worry about. He aborted the mission after only an hour and a half and reported to Prentiss they had traveled three miles without any sign of enemy presence.[9] Three miles was an exaggeration; at worst it was a falsification spurred by disdain toward his superior, Colonel Peabody. Moore commanded Powell to enjoin what able men were with him to turn around and finish up this troublesome "skirmish," although Major Powell had described long columns of rebels emerging from the forest across the field where he had been fighting for some time. Moore continued to deride the idea that there was anything more than a skirmish in force, and became downright acrimonious and "cast a slur" to the men of the 16th Wisconsin who came "rushing up like a lot of school boys," according to one of their number.[10]

Lt. Derickson did not know all this was happening as he wrote in flowery script, requesting Corporal Valentine. Beyond his perception, the four companies of his 16th Wisconsin regiment were coming together at about 6 A.M. after picket duty to join Colonel Moore in a steady escalation of fighting. Companies A, B, C and D had been deployed over a wide area in front of the 6th Division camps during the night. In normal picket procedure each company was divided into thirds. Two of the thirds were broken up into squads of three and thrown out at regular distribution of intervals of width and depth, while the remaining third of the company acted as reserve for the others to fall back on. With the men spread out over several hundred yards this way, certain individuals among the pickets of the 16th Wisconsin passed hushed communications about unknown men they were hearing, not their own, coughing in the night. Then the soldiers heard gunfire at the first light. It increased from periodic pops to the substantial repetitive concussions of hundreds of rifles and muskets off to the west at dawn.[11]

As Company A came enthusiastically forward upon seeing the reinforcement party of Colonel Moore, titillated conversation among the 16th Wisconsin boys was picked up by Colonel Moore. An even uglier side of David Moore's personality surfaced here. Indications were Moore was chafing as a subordinate under brigade commander Peabody, who had just ordered him out on this reinforcement of Major Powell's reconnoitering patrol. Moore tossed out some sort of insult involving state rivalry and derision of "green" Wisconsin troops. The previous evening Moore had buttered his bread on the side of General Prentiss's assessment that there were no significant numbers of rebels in the vicinity. Prentiss, Peabody and Moore were all Missouri men. Prentiss and Moore were showing the undesirable side of the Missouri "show me" attitude. In these moments it was an unfortunate obstacle. What was needed was camaraderie and mutual enthusiasm as to the cause all were claiming to serve. Still considering this a military fool's errand, Colonel Moore demonstrated it in his disdain for Peabody's mother regiment, the 25th Missouri, its Major Powell and the Wisconsin companies.

The 16th Wisconsin's Company A under Captain Saxe was nonplussed and asked where Moore wanted them to fall in. When Moore gave a choice of right or left, Saxe seized the moment to demonstrate Moore was wrong. "We will show them we are not afraid ... we will lead them," he said, and led his men to the front of the column, and to his death minutes later. Captain Saxe of Company A became the first officer to die, along with 1st Sergeant Williams and sixteen other casualties. They dropped dead when Confederates rose from behind a split rail fence edging a field owned by a man named Seay and fired into the faces of the whole contingent. Colonel Moore took the bitter pill of a Minié ball that shattered one leg below the knee, requiring amputation of the limb and a doctoring in his report of what happened. The Battle of Shiloh was now in earnest as approximately three thousand Confederates emerged from across that field.[12]

An Acoustic Cloud

During those early couple of hours Sunday morning, no gunpowder concussions were heard at the landings. Bucolic smells of manure and forage ruled the air. As the post baker fired up his ovens in front of all the steamboats being used as commissaries, smoke curled from the chimney of the temporary wooden building at the landing. Thin bread cooking, called hardtack, smelled better than it ever would around the camp mess. Captain Baxter was responsible for this building, working in cooperation with the commissary officers. The consolidation of the commissary steamboats was also working. Horses neighed and snuffled, mules hawed and harnesses clinked as teamsters readied mule-wagons for the day's hauling. Some animals contentedly grazed in their feedbags. Men coughed and hacked as they struggled to get more awake for the day's tasks, clumping about on wooden floors.

There was a pleasant new atmosphere on board with *Iatan*'s most recent large load of passengers, the 3rd Iowa Regiment: 775 men, with all of their horses, mules, wagons and camp followers. They were picked up in St. Louis on March 4 and arrived on the *Iatan* at Pittsburgh Landing on March 17.[13] The quarters of this confined regiment, along with all the horses, mules and slaughter animals, had turned the *Iatan* into a pesthole. The men were stricken with diarrhea and fevers. After they debarked, the captain worked hard to clean up his ship. This was not true of the boats new regiments were arriving upon. The 16th Iowa volunteers were still pent up on their vessel. The 15th Michigan was still offloading, the men weary but enthusiastic to get to camping grounds.

The woods above the three landing berths, below Mr. Pitt's tavern, the little burgh that was a byway to Corinth, had been denuded in staging operations of this military city. Brigadier General John McArthur had excavated a second steeper landing south of the original Pittsburg Landing; another was needed for easy access and debarkation by the gunboats *Tyler* and *Lexington*, and it was put in, too, during the period of teeming gridlock and offloading of most regiments. Soldiers at campsites amid teepee-style Sibley tents had thinned more forest, but farther south along the river bluffs and bordering the deep ravines on this plateau between Lick and Owl Creeks there still was thickly forested terrain. These stands of woods in spring leaf buffered the repetitive firecracker sound, the popping of skirmishers as dawn broke into day.

The *Iatan* had been in service since 1842, and for Bart Able, being a pilot was not only a grand job, but a critical one. The river bottoms were strewn with hulks of sunken vessels that had grounded or had sunk due to boiler explosions. In 1842 the *Iatan* was next to a steamer at St. Louis, full of German immigrants. Its boilers exploded and its stacks collapsed. The *Iatan* became a hospital ship that day. It would happen again today. Still, the life of a pilot was an enviable profession. A steamboat captain made more money than the vice-president of the United States.

Coincidentally, the 14th vice-president of the United States, John C. Breckinridge, who had run against Abraham Lincoln and lost, was just four miles away. Now a Confederate general, Breckinridge commanded a full reserve corps of rebels backing three other corps, comprising over 40,000 men. The front corps was commanded by General William J. Hardee, a tactician whose manual was being used by both sides. The Confederate second corps was commanded by aptly named General Braxton Bragg. Third corps

of the Confederates was commanded by an anomaly: General Leonidas Polk, Episcopalian bishop of New Orleans, "a man of the cloth," was about to soak it in blood in a worldly conflict.

The Confederate battle formation was inspired by Napoleon's tactics. Its wave-after-wave columns would make U.S. Grant think there were 100,000 rebels; however, it was a battle formation that did not take into consideration the shape of the ground. European battlefields were often open plains where alignment of troops could be maintained. Not here between Lick and Owl Creeks. The plateau was criss-crossed by ravines and wetlands. There was a temporary brilliance as rank after rank poured forth out of the woods, first overwhelming the most exposed 6th Division, then pressing forth in fine ordered style into the outward-lying regiments of General W.T. Sherman's 5th Division.

Technically, it was Union troops who started the heavy volleys of musket fire in Fraley Field. Colonel Peabody had sent a patrol of five companies of his 25th Missouri regiment and two companies of the 12th Michigan, encountering cavalry vedettes that fired almost in darkness. The Federals responded with a heavy volley that was returned by the troops of General S.A.M. Wood, becoming a significant engagement of rattling musketry.

The Battle of Shiloh was begun though most of the Federals still did not know it. The battle's significant noise was still obscured on board the *Iatan*. Even regiments less than a mile away from the warm firing in Fraley Field could not discern what was happening. The phenomenon of not being able to hear a close battle has been described as an acoustic cloud. No doubt the rolling terrain, with its deep ravines and forest, created muffling, but the common practice of discharging of stale rounds by returning pickets also contributed to an "all's well" sense of security when hearing the repetitive popping noises. In this early hour, the firing was further masked at the landings because of the bluff. On board the boats, the risen river also brought debris that banged against the hulls of the steamboats. There was periodic release of steam pressure from some of the boats as well, which has been compared to grand exchanges of musket fire.

No Concern Yet at the Landings

Bart Able could sit contented up in the pilothouse, sipping coffee and enjoying his kingdom. Today Bart's last name was extremely appropriate. He was an able pilot, but the Biblical sound of his name Able was a harbinger of brother-against-brother killings already begun in the far fields.

There was the fragrant mealy smell of hard corn and oats that had just been put up in gunny bags on the quartermaster and commissary boat. Captain Baxter had filled one requisition of General Prentiss's 6th Division with the delivery of 145,600 pounds of corn, in addition to huge amounts of oats. Colonel Madison Miller, commanding its 2nd Brigade, had no forage for his 140 horses and mules, and there was nobody to fill the order previous to Derickson's appointment.

From the perspective of Lt. Richard P. Derickson, a wondrous Sabbath was in store. April 3 had brought a change in his status, a promotion to field officer. Prentiss selected Lt. Richard P. Derickson for the job of division quartermaster. Prentiss's adjutant general Captain Henry Binmore presented Derickson with his promotion on April 3. Understaffed was not a good situation, so his request for Corporal Valentine was important. Derickson was aware of the problems with which Captain Baxter had previously had to deal. Records of everything were important. His current assistant was a young John Ryan, but he needed more, an NCO. He needed Corporal Valentine, so he readied himself to ride out to the headquarters of the 6th Division to speak with General Prentiss about it. Until he got the matter resolved, he would have to depend on young John Ryan.

Surprisingly, the Irish name Ryan was not very common in the army at Shiloh. This John Ryan may have had the middle name Michael. If so, a story is in order. Major Thomas Reynolds was then under arrest at the provost marshal's tent with several other important regimental officers. When recruiting for the 16th Wisconsin, he had enlisted a young Michael Ryan. It had not been easy. Ever the Irish storyteller, he related the gist of what happened with this teen recruit, and it went like this:

> So I went to the boy's mother and said what a fine lad he was and what a fine soldier he would make. And his ma says to me ... "Will you promise to keep me boy with ye?" So's I tells her ... "Yes I promise to keep the boy with me." ... And so his ma says to me, "You won't be lettin' him outta yer site now? ... you will keep me boy with ye?" ... and I says ... "Yes mum ... I will not let the boy outta me site ... I will keep the boy with me!" ... and so's she says to me ... "Ya won't be lettin' the rebs get to me boy will ye? Will ye keep me boy with ye?" ... and I says noooo, I will not be lettin' the rebs git yer boy ... I WILL KEEP THE BOY WITH ME! ... and she still keeps sayin' it over and over and over and over and I keeps sayin' it over and over and over and over ... I WILL KEEP THE BOY WITH ME!!! ... the boy had to drag me corpse away from that faughing home-place ... there is only one thing worse than a reb ... it's an Irish mother![14]

There is, however, one other possibility as to the identity of John Ryan. There was a private John W. Ryan in Company E of the 21st Missouri.[15] There had been a request issued to General Prentiss to provide a squad of men to go to the steamer *Rocket*, so it may well be possible that this John Ryan was selected from Peabody's brigade. Lt Richard P. Derickson was part of Peabody's brigade as well.[16]

Black freedmen, sleeping in the belly of the boiler room, grunted and coughed with the wake-up calls barked down to them by the white mud clerk. Some boats had taken advantage of the shortage of coal as the right time to clean out the fireboxes. Clanking doors and shovels hitting metal caused reverberating sounds as non-burnable coal clinkers were shoveled out. There was not as much pressure to work today; for free blacks it was the best job available. Down in those environs, they could be open with opinions among friends. Some of them had seen a young educated free black, James Milton Turner, with Colonel Madison Miller, 2nd Brigade commander of the 6th Division, checking on forage for his brigade animals. Request for forage is included in the Derickson documents, giving clear answer to the number of horses and mules in one brigade alone. These men were now in the black belt of the South and some of their families had been sold away on this river. A few blacks milled about the landing, smoking pipes, performing common labor, some acting as teamsters. Some runaway slaves, called contrabands because they were still viewed as someone's property, had got work in these camps as well and were transmitting local information among the subculture few white men cared much about. The slave church called Shake-A-Rag was some four miles south off the river. In fact, it was just across Locust Ravine from the 6th Division camps. Wishful thinking may have caused some to entertain thoughts about praising God this Sabbath in the African-influenced style that shaking a rag indicated. If they could get there, while the singing and worshiping were underway, maybe they could get a clue as to where a loved one had been sold. It was never easy to follow through with this kind of plan. Even with many Northern white men, a freedman's expressions had to be tempered with a "yassuh!" or an averted gaze.

Twenty-one-year-old educated free black James Milton Turner and these unseen black men who lived below deck, powering the steamboats that transported these thousands of white men with guns, were among the first to contribute to the liberation of their people.[17] Word to them was that a whole new army was on the way from Nashville to be ferried up from Savannah, and they would have a part in that. James Milton Turner's service as Miller's body servant was not out of the ordinary at Shiloh, just officially unnoted. Many Confederate officers had black servants. Many Union regiments had "colored" cooks who were on the government payroll and later gained recognition as veterans of the Battle of Shiloh. Some servants were killed in the battle. James Milton Turner was actually college-educated through the clandestine assistance of abolitionist whites. He was likely the Negro coachman who trotted through

Camp Jackson with the disguised, cross-dressing Captain Nathaniel Lyon. Unable to actually enlist, James Turner was present at early battles in Missouri, including the Battle of Pea Ridge, and witnessed the death of General Nathaniel Lyon. Associated with some of the most racially progressive whites in Missouri, James Milton Turner's father was known as "the horse doctor," skilled enough as a folk veterinarian to earn enough to buy his family's freedom. James's father was also nephew of the infamous Nat Turner, who had led a slave rebellion in Virginia. If the Confederates had known of his presence with Colonel Miller, their rage would have been even greater as they took over Colonel Miller's 2nd Brigade Camp near Prentiss's headquarters.[18]

As master of his domain, Bart Able in the pilothouse could also survey comings of the new regiments. Noticeable commotion began to occur as the 15th Michigan volunteers acted on their orders to get to their assignment area with Prentiss's Division. It was likely about this same time that Lt. Derickson headed out to report to General Prentiss at the headquarters of that division. He may have led them to the location.

The First Long Roll

Lt. Derickson was concerned about all the boys in the 16th Wisconsin regiment of Peabody's Brigade.[19] It is very likely that while Major Thomas Reynolds was under arrest at the Landing, he "kept the boy close" by putting him to work down at landing on the *Iatan*. From his own handwriting, John Ryan is shown to be a very competent boy. Some of the individuals in camp were truly boys. In Peabody's Brigade, says one account, there were three very small drummer boys, and only one survived the battle. It is known for certain that Major Powell of Peabody's Brigade had his own young son with him when the battle broke out early that morning. He did not go on the patrol to Fraley Field with his father, but he may have been the very first to sound the long roll at the Battle of Shiloh. His father would be killed that day. Lt. Oliver P. Newberry described the major's boy as "the idol of the regiment."[20]

Headed for Destiny Without Ammunition

Derickson may have led the 15th Michigan to the field since he had to report each morning to General Prentiss's headquarters just east of the Eastern Corinth Road. Their historical marker places them immediately south of General Prentiss's headquarters tent when they arrived and almost immediately were faced with oncoming Confederate forces. An unbelievably fresh regiment, they had only been mustered two weeks earlier. Though that was the case, it must not be inferred they were inept. They are praised by General McCook for their actions on the second day.[21]

What happened to this regiment in the early hours of April 6, 1862, is one of the most atrocious injustices of the Union command. It is logical that they would have gone first to the quartermaster boat *Iatan* and the *Rocket* for critical supplies and ammunition. They did not receive any. Lt. Derickson needed authorization from Captain Baxter. In those moments nobody at the landing suspected what was coming.

Marching to the field without cartridges, like sheep to the slaughter, the 15th Michigan were taunted by General Hurlbut's men for their apprehension, being told the firing was just men shooting squirrels. This shows that the men of the 4th Division were not yet aware that the firing was significant. Lt. Derickson and the 15th Michigan appear to have arrived just as the attacks were spreading east from the reconnoitering road through the 6th Division camps. The 15th Michigan wound up directly in front of Prentiss's headquarters, standing at right shoulder rest, with no way to fire at the oncoming rebels. They just stood there looking at them. This incident has been related as a kind of self-inflicted blunder — that it was their own fault they were not supplied.[22] The fact is Captain Baxter was not there, and probably not the ordnance officer Captain Brinck either, who was also on the staff of General Grant. They were still yet to make their appearance at Pittsburg Landing. There was no way for the 15th Michigan to get approved supply. All Lt. Derickson could do would be to say he would see to it that they were supplied when Captain Baxter arrived.

The 16th Wisconsin was well-drilled, though not veterans. As they first marched forty rods in front of the camp, they could not ascertain which direction the rebels were advancing. Prentiss rode into the camp urgently and gave the news to Colonel Benjamin Allen that they were being attacked from the southwest. He was late in getting the word, as there was nobody in Peabody's Brigade that could carry the news to him. Peabody had his hands full, but Prentiss took the time to excoriate him, still not believing that this was a general engagement. "I will hold you personally responsible for bringing on this engagement," Prentiss shouted at Colonel Peabody. Incredulous and disgusted that Prentiss had still not yet grasped the obvious, Peabody spat, "I am personally responsible for all my actions ... and if I brought it on I will lead the van[guard]."[23] The 16th Wisconsin regiment barely got the news and was angling from fronting south to southwest when they were hit by crossfire. Derickson never presented his request to General Prentiss. Prentiss impressed Lt. Richard Derickson as an immediate aide.

Derickson's own son John was acting as orderly sergeant to Company

K's Captain Williams and was wounded in the arm; then Captain Williams was wounded as well. The line command of Company K was taken over by Lt. David Vail near Corporal Valentine. In the crossfire, O.J. Valentine took two balls to the left arm and leg, allowing him only a short time to live, so the request for his services would never be received and signed by Brigadier General Benjamin M. Prentiss.[24] He was not the only early casualty of the 16th Wisconsin. Forty-one-year-old private William Tousley and his son, eighteen-year-old Private Stowell Tousley, were killed outright next to one another, yards in rear of the 16th Wisconsin Camp.

The order was given to withdraw to the front of the camp while the two batteries of Munch and Hickenlooper blasted. With this murderous advantage, the 16th Wisconsin made a stand in front of their camp. The Confederates attacking this sector were General Gladden's brigade. A shot from one of the cannons tore his arm off at the shoulder, ensuring his death. The brief lack of command bought some time for the 16th Wisconsin, but in a sector receiving the attention of Supreme Commander Albert Sidney Johnston, the weak spots were found, and the 16th was flanked on both sides. Colonel Daniel Adams took control in place of Gladden and the onslaught continued.[25]

The 15th Michigan could offer no resistance on the left and retreated in somewhat of good order. The 18th Wisconsin was torn to pieces. It lost all of its field officers, killed or wounded, and most of its line officers. The 61st Illinois resisted and then melted under the Confederate fire. Brigade commander Madison Miller was astonished, and as the rebel onslaught poured into his camp, he tried to find a place to rally. He did not rally until reaching the sector later famous as the Hornet's Nest.

On the far right of Peabody's Brigade, though holding the line for more than an hour, it finally collapsed as Shaver's Brigade unrelentingly blasted away. A rebel battery took great toll on the right of Peabody's Brigade. Peabody himself took four bullets before finally receiving one through the forehead that killed him. According to Lt. Oliver Newberry, this happened while he was trying to take the Confederate battery that was doing so much damage. Two Confederate batteries were part of Shaver's assault, Miller's and Swett's.

Next to Peabody's 25th Missouri was the 12th Michigan. It had a split command due to infighting. Colonel Quinn, according to one source, went into his tent and shot himself in the foot, but because the command was divided between Quinn and Lt. Colonel Graves, this incident is not certain. The regiment broke into two factions and retreated toward the long arc that comprised the sunken road, Hornet's Nest and Peach Orchard line. Colonel Moore of the 21st Missouri, to the right of the 16th Wisconsin, had already been borne from the field and was being carried to the *Iatan*, where he would soon have his leg amputated, and the 21st Missouri would have few representatives at the stand made in the middle of the Hornet's Nest line.[26]

The 16th Wisconsin held until, first, its Lt. Colonel Cassius Fairchild was felled by a ball near the hip. Then Colonel Allen had his horse shot from under him, ordered his second, and it was killed as he mounted it. Major Thomas Reynolds was under arrest back at the landing due to Grant's order, so he was of no value at this time. Company K was the last to leave front line and take a stand in the rear of its camp by Barnes Field. As it moved backward, Lt. David Vail tapped his young men on the behind with his sword, telling them they could not hold because they had been flanked on both sides. Quartermaster Derickson helped make a momentary rally as they emerged from the trees onto the field.[27] General Prentiss began to give the call to fall back and fight from tree to tree as best as each man could. Prentiss steadily retreated himself until he reached the camp on the edge of Sarah Bell's cotton field. There Hurlbut's Division had mobilized on its south edge, and Prentiss asked permission to pass through the lines. It was granted, and a new line began to form with fragmented bits of regiments of the 6th Division now combining with the 4th and 2nd Division.

Even as the Confederate press was being made on Colonel Peabody's Brigade, at the landing this matter did not have urgency, part of the general reluctance to move from the Cherry Mansion. The Grant headquarters was not just hours late; it was a whole week late. There can be no excuse for lives lost by the 15th Michigan and others of the 6th Division that morning. It was the fault of General U.S. Grant.

More terrible treatment was to come to the 15th Michigan and the battered 6th Division. Although they were able to retreat in good order for awhile, the 15th Michigan returned to the landing with others in a flash flood of men. The 15th Michigan had no camping ground and there was no place to go but back to the landing. Now all the camps of the 6th Division were lost. The other Michigan unit at Shiloh, the 12th Regiment, was dismembered by the first attacks on the 6th Division as well. Most of the stories of the men who fled to the landings are related with disdain, in such terms as, "They all had the Bull Run story," or "We are all cut to pieces," as if it were an exaggeration. These were the facts; they had been cut to pieces. If any demonstration of the "Sir Walter Scott" disease could be cited, it applied to just about every Union officer who criticized these men as cowards.

Now disorganized and growing by the thousands of all ranks and cowering for safety, they were berated by Grant's staff and Grant himself when he finally arrived after 9:00 A.M., along with men of other units who were struggling to control their panic. The 15th Michigan especially had been betrayed, yet the growing crowd was described as runners and cowards, and described by Grant himself as "so scared they would have been shot where they stood rather than go as ordered." These statements reveal an incredible lack of understanding as to the real state of affairs. The pitiable condition of the crowd of men of all ranks who huddled beneath bluffs has to be credited to the week-long tardiness of moving Grant's headquarters to Pittsburg Landing, and further, to his late morning arrival at Pittsburg Landing on April 6. The whole 6th Division was broken up by the time Grant arrived. General U.S. Grant was dilatory in arrival on the field.

This was the very charge that was leveled at Major General Lew Wallace after the Battle of Shiloh. The fact is, Wallace was only perceived late. He had done almost everything right. Some accounts have implied Wallace stupid. That title belongs elsewhere, to the ones who were really late to arrive on Sunday morning, April 6, 1862.

8

"I smell the blood," said an Englishman

The boy who became Henry Morton Stanley was a runaway from an English poorhouse. He boarded a ship bound for America and served in the brutal, unenviable position of a cabin boy. When he reached New Orleans, he jumped ship with another boy. On the road to a predictable lifestyle he was found, adopted and baptized as a Christian by a New Orleans business-man. His father trained him and later sent him up the Mississippi River to mind one of his mercantile stores in Arkansas. Then the Civil War closed the river and severed his communication with his adoptive parent. So young Stan-ley closed the store and joined one of a multitude of militia companies that became part of the 6th Arkansas regiment of Confederate colonel Shaver's Brigade. It was one of the first engaged at Shiloh.[1]

Confederate private Henry Morton Stanley started that April 6 Sabbath morning with flowers in his hair. He and another young fellow, also named Henry, picked some purple blooms from the forest floor, and the nervous, competitive, testosterone-filled adolescents began to show off goofily. Feigning as females in front of the other boys in butternut about to march forward, they chortled in high-pitched girly voices: "Perhaps the Yanks won't shoot us if we have these violets in our hats." The ranks broke into laughter. Nobody would be laughing in a few more minutes.

The order to march came soon enough, and these soldiers very soon crushed the opposition that Colonel Everett Peabody had sent out to produce an alarm for the rest of the Union Army. It was likely the following sound that was heard by the army in general about 7:30 A.M., the way Stanley described it: "Still advancing, firing as we moved, I, at last saw a row of little globes of pearly smoke streaked with crimson, breaking out with spurtive quickness from a long line of bluey figures in front; and, simultaneously, there

81

**The portrayal of Arkansas troops at the Hornet's Nest from the back cover of the
Manual of the Panorama of the Battle of Shiloh reflects the similar experience of Private Henry Morton Stanley of the 6th Arkansas and Shaver's Confederate Brigade
(author's collection).**

broke upon our ears an appalling crash of sound, the series of fusillades following one another with startling suddenness, which suggested to my somewhat moidered sense a mountain upheaved, with huge rocks rumbling and
thundering down a slope, and the echoes rumbling and receding through
space."[2]

Among the "bluey figures" in that long line was Lt. O.P. Newberry, making a line officer's stand with Company I of the 25th Missouri of the Union
Army.[3] Stanley's ball, fired through the pall of smoke, could have been one
of several that struck Colonel Peabody himself. When young Stanley ran
through and past the camps of Peabody's Brigade, his bullets could have
whizzed past the ears of Lt. Richard P. Derickson and Lt. David F. Vail as the
men of Company K, along with the rest of the 16th Wisconsin, retreated tree
by tree.[4] The shots fired in the battle were less often sharpshooting and much
more a conglomerate effect. Few could really say they recognized that it was
their own ball that hit a particular mark. Henry Morton Stanley's path through
the fields of Shiloh that day and the killing marks they may have found are
less remarkable than the keen insight he possessed and the conscience he con-
fessed he violated.

In his autobiography after a lifetime of reflection, his participation at
Shiloh is seen to be imprinted in his memory more vividly than his later

adventure in Africa, where he located the missing and mysterious missionary David Livingstone. That meeting gave rise to very popular mimicry. Stanley's supposed glib English statement, "Dr. Livingston, I presume," continued as a trite party greeting for more than a hundred years.

Shiloh was no party, and repartee about Shiloh was not uttered cleverly until the waning days and memories of the Grand Army of the Republic and the United Confederate Veterans. The memories of Shiloh were too painful for many. Some more of the words of Henry Morton Stanley, the Shiloh veteran, journalist and friend of Mark Twain, bear serious consideration:

> An object ... indelibly fixed in my memory ... I cannot forget that half-mile square of woodland, lighted brightly by the sun, and littered by the forms of about a thousand dead and wounded men, and horses and military equipments. It is formed a picture that may always be reproduced with an almost absolute fidelity. For it was the first Field of Glory I had seen in my life, and the first time that Glory sickened me with its repulsive aspect, and made me suspect it was all a glittering lie.

Laying the responsibility at the feet of failed religion, Stanley went on:

> My thoughts reverted to the time when those festering bodies were idolized objects of their mothers' passionate love, their fathers standing by, half-fearing to touch the fragile little things, and the wings of civil law out-spread to protect parents and children in their family loves, their coming and going followed with pride and praise, and the blessing of the Almighty overshadowing all. Then, as they were nearing manhood, through some strange warp of Society, men in authority summoned them from school and shop, field and farm, to meet in the woods on a Sunday morning for mutual butchery with the deadliest instruments ever invented, Civil Law, Religion, and Morality complaisantly standing aside while 90,000 young men, who had been preached and moralized to, for years, were let loose to engage in the carnival of slaughter.... Only yesterday, they professed to shudder at the word "Murder." Today by a strange twist in human nature, they lusted to kill, and were hounded on by their pastors, mothers and sisters. Oh, for once, I was beginning to know the real truth! Man was born for slaughter! All the pains to soothe his savage heart were unavailing! Holy words and heavenly hopes had no lasting effect on his bestial nature, for, when once provoked, how, how swiftly he flung aside the sweet hope of Heaven, and the dread of Hell, with which he amused himself in time of ease! ... As I moved, horror-stricken, through the fearful shambles where the dead lay as thick as the sleepers in a London park on a Bank Holiday, I was unable to resist the belief that my education had been in abstract things, which had no relation to our animal existence. For, if human life is so disparaged, what has it to do with such high subjects as God, Heaven, and Immortality? And to think how devotional men and women pretended to be on Sunday! Oh cunning and cruel man! He knew that the sum of all knowledge and effort was to know how to kill and mangle his brothers, as we were doing today! Reflecting on my own emotions, I wondered if other youths would feel they had been deluded like myself with

man's fine polemics and names of things, which vanished with reality.... A multitude of angry thoughts surged through me, which I cannot describe in detail, but they amounted to this, that a cruel deception had been practiced on my blank ignorance, that my atom of imagination and feeling had been darkened, and that man was a portentous creature from which I recoiled with terror and pity. He was certainly terrible and hard, but he was no more to me now than a two legged beast: he was cunning beyond all finding out, but his morality was only a mask of his wolfish heart![5]

Henry Morton Stanley gives some of the most vividly horrible descriptions of what was seen at Shiloh. Many veterans were not able to express their experiences the way he did. His object was to portray the reality of killing other humans: "A little further were some twenty bodies lying in various postures, each by its own pool of viscous blood, which emitted a peculiar scent, which was new to me, but which I have since learned is inseparable from a battlefield"—the smell of blood by an Englishman.[6]

Private Stanley of Confederate Shaver's Brigade was not alone in these sentiments. A *New York Tribune* reporter present at Shiloh, right in Peabody's camp, not limiting it to either Union or Confederate faces, described this frightening transformation that belied claims of Christianity: "Men lost their semblance of humanity ... and the spirit of the demon shone in their faces. There was but one desire, and that was to destroy." In the full context of the article he could not think of them as Christian soldiers, or even of beings that were fully human.[7]

In the years following the Civil War, groups of like-minded individuals gravitated toward one another, trying to make sense of it. Like other thinking men of other wars, certain minds found one another. If Hemingway, Fitzgerald, Gertrude Stein and other writers exemplified the "lost generation" after World War I, Henry Morton Stanley, Ambrose Bierce, Robert Ingersoll and Mark Twain exemplified a kind of "lost generation" after the Civil War. All had experienced the Civil War, and it had changed them. Yes, even Mark Twain had participated in a military action that resulted in the grisly death of an innocent man, as he recounted in his short nonfiction account, "The Private History of a Campaign That Failed."[8] These men became the great cynics and skeptics of the 19th century. They produced some of the best literature, with thought-provoking content and parody of man's nature, that has ever been written. All but Twain were at Shiloh, but all were acquainted with one another and influenced one another.

Ambrose Bierce, who had been an artillery sergeant in the 36th Indiana, seized the guidon of Church and Clergy and trampled it as best he could under the definition he wrote for "Religion" in his *Devil's Dictionary*. He defined it this way: "A daughter of Hope and Fear, explaining to Ignorance the nature of the Unknowable."[9] In memoir form, his mélange of impressions, he wrote *What I Saw of Shiloh*. He descended into burnt-out ravines and wrote this about what he saw there:

> I obtained leave to go down into the valley of death and gratify a reprehensible curiosity. Forbidding it was in every way. The fire had swept every superficial foot of it, and at every step I stepped into ashes to the ankle. It contained a thin undergrowth of saplings, every one of which had been severed by a bullet, the foliage of the prostrate tops being afterwards burnt and stumps charred. Death had put his sickle into this thicket and fire had gleaned the field. Along a line that was not that of an extreme depression, but at every point significantly equidistant from the heights on either hand, lay the bodies, half buried in ashes; some in the unlovely looseness of attitude denoting sudden death by the bullet; but by far the greater number in postures of agony that told of the tormenting flame. Their clothing was half burnt away, the hair and beard entirely, the rain had come too late to save their nails. Some were swollen to double girth; others shriveled to manikins. According to degree of exposure, their faces were bloated and black or yellow and shrunken. The contraction of the muscles had given them claws for hands and had cursed each countenance with a hideous grin. Faugh! I cannot catalogue the charms of these gallant gentlemen who had got what they enlisted for.[10]

A writer as popular as his friend Mark Twain during that time, Ambrose Bierce spoke more bitterly than Twain with an entitlement of ironic cynicism that only a veteran receives as a legacy. He was like Cain, the murderer of his brother, who was allowed to stay alive but condemned and banished to a dreaded existence east of Eden.

Twain did not suffer as much this way, but he had participated in a militia encounter, killing an innocent civilian. Twain cloaked his revulsion of religion's hypocrisy in artful humorist stories. In unpublished writings after the death of his wife who had helped keep him somewhat tactful in certain situations, he revealed his true disgust with all that was hypocritically religious and political. Perhaps there was a mutual envy between Bierce and Twain which forged a similar outlook between the two. Twain had avoided major participation in the slaughter at Shiloh, but held a kind of envy for the man, Bierce, who had been perverted, having seen the (battle) elephant. Bierce was literally a wounded man who used his experience to throw down the ivory towers of religious hypocrisy, while treasuring the remains of humanity that he knew existed somewhere in the scarred souls of veterans. On the other hand, at the same time he may have envied the wisdom of Twain, the "man who was better at retreating than the man who invented retreating."

Twain wrote scathingly like Bierce soon after the war, but created a parody in short story form called "burlesque." It was called "Extract from Captain Stormfield's Visit to Heaven," but it was not published until after the turn of the 20th century. In it he ridiculed the content of Elizabeth Stuart Phelps's *The Gates Ajar*, a novel of supposed Heaven, where family reunions took place amid paradise conditions. It was certainly a chord that struck millions of families who had lost loved ones in the war, but Twain was disgusted with the glossing over of religion's culpability for the bloodshed. *The Gates Ajar* perpetuated the sentiment of the "good death" and Christian-soldier mentality as justification for war. Twain countered Phelps's descriptions in his short story by portraying an "imagined little ten-cent heaven about the size of Rhode Island — a heaven large enough to accommodate about a tenth of one percent of the Christian billions who had died the last nineteen centuries." In Twain's burlesque, he mocked Phelps's Captain Stormfield. Twain's version portrayed Stormfield as a man who had trouble managing his angel wings and flew so badly he had regular collisions with other angels. Upon collision, he was surprised that these American angels were in fact Indians and not Christian white men at all. They had been accumulating in the American section of heaven because of the depredations of said Christian white men during the centuries after the arrival of the Europeans. A reversal had taken place in heaven. Captain Stormfield was a poor flyer and in a small minority of a few white Christians who actually deserved to be in heaven. In this story, Mark Twain made the "good death" with its pie-in-the-sky promises an absurdity. He was hiding much more. He specified that his autobiography not be published until one hundred years after his death. It now has been published and contains blistering indictments of church and state that he could not publish while alive.[11]

Robert Green Ingersoll, the cavalry colonel who reported first to Lew Wallace and then to General Prentiss at Shiloh, has hardly any historical information about his specific experience at Shiloh, but it can be assumed the experience shaped his agnostic cynicism. Twain called him the greatest orator of the age. His words echo Ambrose Bierce in his disdain for religion. The fiery hell-like conditions that Bierce saw in the Hornet's Nest no doubt were seen also by Colonel Ingersoll. His camp was only a few hundred yards from it. In Ingersoll's treatise *Crumbling Creeds* he states: "The doctrine of eternal punishment is in perfect harmony with the savagery of the men who made the orthodox creeds. It is in harmony with torture, with flaying alive, and with burnings. The men, who burned their fellow-men for a moment, believed that God would burn his enemies forever."[12]

In still a more acrid condemnation of doctrine that manipulated men in 1877, he spat in "The Liberty of All":

> If there is a God who will damn his children forever, I would rather go to hell than to go to heaven than keep the society of such an infamous tyrant. I make

my choice now. I despise that doctrine. It has covered the cheeks of this world with tears. It has polluted the hearts of children, and poisoned the imaginations of men.... What right have you, sir, Mr. Clergyman, you, minister of the gospel to stand at the portals of the tomb, at the vestibule of eternity, and fill the future with horror and with fear? I do not believe this doctrine, neither do you. If you did, you could not sleep one moment. Any man who believes it, and has within his breast a decent, throbbing heart, will go insane. A man who believes that doctrine and does not go insane has the heart of a snake and the conscience of a hyena.[13]

War affects men in different ways. Some could never reconcile themselves with what they had done. Lew Wallace found his own literary way of dealing with the harm wrought at Shiloh in the novel *Ben-Hur: A Tale of the Christ*. The haunting description of what Henry Morton Stanley and Ambrose Bierce described of Shiloh can be felt at the National Military Park today. It is difficult to walk across the beautiful preserve that it is today and not think of what really took place there and the failure of religionists who did not remember these words: "And the Lord said unto Cain. Where is Abel thy brother? And he said I know not. Am I my brother's keeper? And HE said: What hast thou done? The voice of thy brother's blood crieth unto me from the ground" (Genesis 4:10, 11).[14]

9

Setting the Stage
for a Scapegoating

He was a veteran soldier dedicated to the cause of the country. He even contributed to the great victory at Ft. Donelson that saved and catapulted the reputation of his commander, General U.S. Grant. Then that commander turned on him and blamed him for the casualties of thousands of fellow soldiers. Yet he had done everything his commander had asked. The accusations continued to snowball for decades, to the extent that at one of the most spectacular venues in the country, it featured Gen. Lew Wallace as a bungler and a manslaughterer. That venue was the great Panorama of the Battle of Shiloh in Chicago. People came from all over the world to see this attraction. In the manual guide for that remarkable 400-foot circular painting of Shiloh's universe of battle, millions of vistors accepted verbatim the following, written expressly for this work by Lucien B.Crooker, late Captain of the 55th Illinois Infantry:

> Certain it is that Wallace had received early notice to be ready, and through the day repeated orders to march to the field. All his marches and counter-marches, however, did not bring him upon the scene the first day. All the published comments, his own included, fail to afford a satisfactory solution. The bald fact remains, that although so ordered he did not during the day get into the battle, only six miles away. His men, if left to their own instincts would have reached the battle-field sooner on their hands and knees.

As he stared out over the bow of steamboat *Tigress*, air resistance blew tobacco smoke back in General U.S. Grant's face. He chomped his cigar while going up the Tennessee River toward Crump's Landing on the morning of April 6, releasing nicotine juices that had a calming effect. He needed it for the unfolding events. Cigars were his nationally famous trademark since victories at Ft. Henry and Ft. Donelson. Patriots sent boxes to him in appreciation. His voice was deeper than what it would have been had he not smoked.

The Manual of the Panorama of the Battle of Shiloh slammed General Lew Wallace as late, inept and blood-guilty on a circular stage that was viewed by millions of national and international visitors in Chicago (author's collection).

The affect it had on his larynx gave him a more mellifluous tone and a more authoritative voice. That was an asset for a commander, but he was unaware of the effect his long-term contact with tobacco was having on the cells in his throat.

He was also on crutches from a horse mishap two nights before. Sloppy road conditions on the way to visit General Sherman near Shiloh Meeting House had caused his horse to fall on him in the dark. His ankle was so badly sprained that his boot had to be cut off. Small things like that could have big consequences. An example was back at the Cherry Mansion headquarters in Savannah, his West Point mentor and 2nd Division commander, General C.F. Smith, was bedridden from the simple mishap of jumping from steamboat to rowboat. It had peeled the flesh from his shin and an infection set in. It was killing Smith, but he did not know it. With his severely sprained ankle, Grant could have drunk some whiskey to dull the pain. It would be reasonable if he did, but nobody would ever admit that. Today, a plaque still outside the Cherry Mansion one hundred and fifty years later makes an effort to dispel the idea that a military man of his stature could possibly have been under the influence at Shiloh.

The *Tigress* rounded Wolf Island and the headquarters boat of Grant's 3rd Division commander, Major General Lewis Wallace, came into view. Wallace was eagerly waiting orders to move, having been wakened early by his adjutant, Captain Frederick Kneffler, because of the clear sounds of battle to the south. The *Tigress* pulled in close and the two steamers were lashed together for a short conference, the logistics of it consuming time. It was between 8:00 and 8:30 A.M. Neither of the generals realized in those moments the sounds of battle meant that Prentiss's Division was breaking apart, Sherman's Division was in deep trouble, too, and thousands of men were falling dead or wounded. Contrary to later mythologies of those moments, Grant was perplexed, not a man in complete grasp of the situation. One account says when he heard artillery fire from the Cherry Mansion, holding an untasted cup of coffee in mid-air, he said with aplomb: "Gentlemen the ball is in motion."[1] That was an artfully embellished description, as if an orchestra conductor were conducting a symphony. Here at Crump's it probably eased Grant's mind to have Wallace clear up the situation as to the real point of attack through this consultation. He had suspected Wallace's Division and a huge amount of supplies at Crump's Landing might be the location of the attack that was underway now. Getting that information, he addressed an already eager-to-go General Lew Wallace in terms that enabled Wallace's professional downfall later. Grant ordered him to "wait in readiness" until he received orders to move.

Wallace was extremely disappointed to be instructed to "wait in readiness." Now he had to languish the same way he had at Ft. Donelson, waiting for Grant's orders to move while the rebels savaged the Union Army. Ironies ruled April 6, 1862. This day Wallace was six miles away from the scene of battle at Pittsburgh Landing along a river. At Ft. Donelson, Grant had been six miles away on a river when Wallace needed a similar order from Grant to come to the aid of General McClernand, but he was told to wait in readiness for Grant there, too.[2] Likely, Wallace brushed off the disappointment at Crump's and reasoned this situation would turn out well for the both of them, as it had with the Confederate surrender of Ft. Donelson and the capture of almost 15,000 Confederates.

Wallace had technically disobeyed orders at Donelson by rushing to help General McClernand, but only after a second request by that general. He had masterfully reinforced the right wing of the army before it could be pulverized by the enemy, and he had prevented a rebel escape from the garrison. His action had saved the right wing of the army, but ruffled Grant and his aides; Captain William Hillyer may have reflected Grant's mixture of embarrassment and gratitude for being away from the field at the nadir of the battle in a dispatch to Wallace after Ft. Donelson had been taken: "You are not going to be left behind.— I know General Grant's views. He intends to give you the chance to be shot in every important move.... I speak advisedly — God bless you. You did save the army on the right."[3] It sounds an attempt at humor communicated from Grant, but also could be construed as a veiled warning. Reading between the lines one could interpret the message, "Even if the result was good, General Grant did not like being shown up by you, or having his orders sidestepped by a subordinate." Grant had chastised Wallace for not noting the three-day rations in the sacks of the enemy, saying that he should have known the enemy was desperate to escape. Grant minimized what Wallace had done by saying he should have gone ahead and charged the works of Ft. Donelson after his coming to the aid of the attack on General McClernand. This was easy for Grant to say; Grant had been six miles away at the time.

In the above case, Grant privately realized that if Wallace had not done what he had done, the victory might not have happened; "Unconditional Surrender" Grant would not have become his moniker. Wallace helped Grant to come out smelling like a rose, but Wallace's aggressiveness set Grant's staff on edge that he might prove to be a rival. Captain Hillyer attempted to be good natured and grateful in framing the communiqué to Wallace, but this commendation had been channeled through Grant's adjutant general Captain John Rawlins. Rawlins was fiercely protective of Grant. That was to be expected of the right-hand man on any general's staff, but Rawlins was in a different category. He was psychologically attached and viewed Grant as a father figure.[4]

Under Rawlins's Watchful Eyes

In 1862 Grant at Shiloh was surrounded by a posse of young men picked from his own town of Galena, Illinois, and haunts in St. Louis. Grant and other West Pointers complained of politically appointed generals, which is how they viewed Lew Wallace. Colonels with little military acumen were considered a plague by West Pointers, but Grant saw no problem in drawing from the same pool of inexperienced civilians for his staff.

John A. Rawlins was the same age as Lew Wallace. Wallace was a major general already. Rawlins was a captain, and likely the green-eyed monster of jealousy welled up in Rawlins with regard to Wallace. Yet Rawlins was in the enviable position of being prime advisor to the rising star of U.S. Grant. Rawlins hitched his wagon to that star and was not just there for the ride but to act as the sometimes coy, sometimes virulent supporter of the man he loved. So much was this the case that he wrote in a lengthy defense of General Grant to Congressman Elihu Washburne: "I regard his interest as my interest ... all that concerns his reputation concerns me; I love him as a father; I respect him because I have studied him well, and the more I know him the more I respect and love him. But I pledge you my word, that should General Grant at any time become an intemperate man or a habitual drunkard, I will ask to be removed from duty on his staff or resign my commission."[5]

Rawlins was at his general's side during the conference at Crump's Landing. He witnessed Grant binding Wallace with a hurry-up-and-wait conundrum. Wallace had been promoted to major general for his command at Ft. Donelson, the youngest of that rank early in the War. It was a heady experience to be in the rarefied atmosphere of major general meeting major general under battle conditions, yet for Wallace, that mixed message to "wait in readiness," with Rawlins watching, reminded him of the message through Hillyer back at the Donelson victory. It may have given him pause.

After the *Tigress* pulled away from the short conference, everybody in the Union Army would have been better off if Wallace had obeyed the instincts he showed at Ft. Donelson, not waiting for orders from Grant to move. This order to wait at Crump's Landing proved to be a no-win situation that damned Wallace for the rest of his life. In a galling self-protective lie a year later, Grant impaled Wallace in an official report: "Had General Wallace been relieved from duty in the morning, and the same orders communicated to Brig. Gen. Morgan L. Smith (who would have been his successor), I do not doubt but the division would have been on the field of battle and in the engagement before 10 o'clock of that eventful 6th of April. There is no estimating the difference this might have made in our casualties."[6]

It is a fact that Grant himself did not get the complete picture before 10 o'clock. It was only then that he sent the first messenger to General Lew Wallace to come up. Grant's statement that Major General Wallace's subordinate, Colonel Smith, could have made it to Pittsburg Landing by 10 o'clock is preposterous. It is like saying Morgan L. Smith could have ridden a telepathic brain beam emanating from Grant's head, arriving upon on it with a whole division of over 5,000 men and several sections of heavy artillery at the exact moment Grant had the thought.

It is probable that Grant was advised in a lawyerly way by John Rawlins what words to use in that later report about General Lew Wallace to the Chief of all Armies, General H.W. Halleck in Washington. When that report was made a year later, before Vicksburg, a fly on a headquarters wall tent might have witnessed congratulatory back-slapping among Grant's staff members, which kept Major General Lewis Wallace off the military stage. A reorganization had taken place while Major General Wallace was on leave, since there was little place for another major general. Grant had dissolved Wallace's whole division in his absence. Mischief was clearly afoot to keep Wallace away from the intimate organization Grant was building around himself.

But at the time of this steamboat conference at Crump's Landing, there was no diabolical agenda or glaring animosity between General Grant and General Wallace. Ten years older than Wallace, Grant, the middle-aged man, had tempered life experience, compared to the younger, more impetuous Wallace. However, the order Grant gave to Wallace to "wait in readiness" proved to be a serendipitous situation that set the stage for Wallace to be used as a scapegoat. He would be blamed later for the slaughter taking place on the fields of Shiloh in those very moments while Grant was with him. Here at Crump's Landing, no one was a prophet about what was happening at Shiloh. Though Wallace felt chafed at the wait order, he was the tutored son of a West Point graduate and understood the importance of chain of command. He had been through this before with Grant, and it had turned out wonderfully for both of them.

Wallace now did what was cohesive, more cohesive than Grant, on his way to the Confederate surprise party. Wallace readied his troops that were stretched out in three brigades across five miles, already moving to centralize toward Adamsville at a place called Stoney Lonesome. The name was a harbinger for Wallace. It could have been his pen name in his later search for vindication after Shiloh. He would become "Stoney Lonesome" as he bore the slanders of Shiloh.[7]

The name of the road to the scene of battle also had a peculiarly haunting sound. It was the Shunpike. If he had shunned it that day, maybe it would have turned out differently for Lew Wallace. Shunpike: it could have been a name out of the great literature Wallace liked to read. It could have been out of Shakespeare play with a ghostly sentinel standing before it warning: Do not pass! The literary tones of that day would resurface in Lew Wallace's mind some fifteen years later. Characters in his novel *Ben-Hur* have correlations to Lew Wallace and U.S. Grant. The accident that changed everything for Ben-Hur in the novel parallels what happened with Grant's orders to Wallace on the Shunpike road starting at Stoney Lonesome.

What-Ifs

Despite his romantic bent, Wallace was not a man of premonitions. He was prepared before the hour of need. He had corduroyed the road he took, previous to the meeting with Grant at Crump's Landing. He and the other division general, also named Wallace (W.H.L. Wallace) who was acting as division commander in place of the dying General C.F. Smith, had coordinated for just this sort of contingency. W.H.L. Wallace preserved the record of the road's preparations, perhaps in his valise. It disappeared with his death. What if, what if ... so many what-ifs. If Lew Wallace had access to that communication, his scapegoating would not have been as easy.

What if a Minié ball had not found its mark in W.H.L. Wallace's brain? By the time Lew Wallace got to the battlefield, W.H.L. Wallace was lying with a mortal wound in his head behind enemy lines. His wife, who just happened to be down at the landing on the steamer *Miniehaha,* hoping to surprise her husband, would leave with his personal effects after her heartrending deathbed vigil at the Cherry Mansion. Among them was the record of preparations that had been planned for in the event of attack. What if she had not shown up? Those particular papers of General W.H.L. Wallace's battlefield records disappeared for twenty years. It is strange that Mrs. W.H.L. Wallace carried away vital records pertaining to military actions on the Shunpike road. How did she get that record about the road preparations? At the very least it shows the pandemonium of bloody Shiloh. The turning over of military papers to the civilian wife may have been intended as benign, but the Cherry Mansion had been Grant's headquarters, and Captain John Rawlins had not closed up shop there. Two Union generals lay dying in the bedrooms of the mansion. Captain John Rawlins was the paperwork man. It cannot be ruled out that John A. Rawlins purposefully hid the record of the road preparations. By the time of W.H.L. Wallace's death, U.S. Grant was under extreme duress, having been relieved of his command by General Halleck. The national news was looking for someone to hang the blame on about the massive casualties. Foremost for blame would have to be the general who commanded at the time of the battle. Even President Lincoln had read reports of ineptitude by Grant and had demanded an accounting. The disposal of the records of General Lew Wallace and General W.H.L. Wallace would facilitate a turning of attention to Lew Wallace and away from Grant. The focus did in fact become planted on Lew Wallace and his march.

Finally, when the record of the road preparations did surface, Rawlins was long dead, and Grant was dying of throat cancer. In his shawl, writing on his front porch, he finally ameliorated the lie that had been perpetrated by assenting that preparations had been made by the two Wallaces, yet he never totally recanted his impression that the so-called River Road was the road Lew Wallace should have taken. He only states in a footnote of his memoirs that if he had known of the arrangements between the two Wallaces he would have a different opinion of the route General Wallace chose to take. The fact was he did know of preparations along that route, but the curious way that Grant expresses himself in later life lends credence to the idea that no specific road had been optioned by him when the event actually happened. He simply states: "I never could see and do not see now why any order was necessary further than to direct him to come to Pittsburg Landing, without specifying by what route."[8] The River Road issue smacks strongly of an introduced controversy by adjutant general John A. Rawlins. The focus on the road taken diverts attention away from an issue in plain sight. Grant had ordered "someone" to take the message to General Lew Wallace to come up. It is not clear that Grant made the selection of the messenger. In any case, it was Captain John A. Rawlins who instructed Captain A.S. Baxter to take the message to General Lew Wallace. Baxter was the head of supply and transportation corps. Sending him as a mere errand carrier deprived the army of seasoned logistical support. This was an astonishing decision. Whoever made the selection, whether it was specified by Grant or left to the discretion of Captain John A. Rawlins, it was a mistake. Grant and Rawlins were inextricably linked in the decision. Now, it had to be covered up.

The contentions that Wallace took the wrong road look suspicious in their intent. Grant and engineer Colonel James McPherson should have been aware of the Shunpike road preparations towards Owl Creek Bridge. The closest road to the river was well-nigh impassable due to the very rainy days before April 6, the same conditions that had caused Grant's horse accident. McPherson did rebuild a bridge at Snake Creek, which was the last watercourse on the river road before the main Pittsburg Landing Road, but Macpherson's preparations went no further than that. McPherson was a colonel at the time, actually directly accountable to Halleck. One of his surveys on the fields of the Union encampments at Shiloh involved the platting of a place that would satisfy General H.W. Halleck's wishes for breastworks. Some historians report McPherson had recommended to Grant that no breastworks be constructed. If true, it was another curiosity. Why would a West Point–trained engineer controvert supreme commander Halleck's explicit instructions? It is well known that McPherson got along famously with Grant. What was the explanation for that lack of follow-through about breastworks? The reason given was it would pose problems for easy access to springs of water in the case of attack. The flimsiness of this reason floats over the graves in the National Cemetery. If this abrogation of orders originated with McPherson, the astonishing consequences of the disastrous Confederate attack make any deficiencies of Lew Wallace pale to insignificance. The worst Wallace did was to arrive later than expected. Macpherson's survey for breastworks, had it been implemented, was the true place a difference could have been made, the right place for Grant to place blame in an official report. "There is no estimating the difference this might have made in casualties." The lack of knowledge about the communication between the two Wallaces falls on Grant, with McPherson sharing culpability. McPherson was the engineer.[9]

In fact there is a communication about this very subject that makes a cover-up to scapegoat Wallace more than an implication. On April 4, Grant wrote to General Sherman:

> Gen W.T. Sherman
> Commanding 5th Division
> Gen:
>
> Information just received would indicate the enemies are sending a force to Purdy, and it may be with view to attack Gen. L.Wallace Division at Crump's Landing. I have directed Gen. W.H.L Wallace, Comndg 2nd Division, temporarily to reinforce Gen. L. Wallace in case of an attack with his entire Division, although I look for nothing of the kind, but it is best to be prepared.
>
> I would direct, therefore, that you advise your advance guards to keep a sharp lookout in that direction, and should such a thing be attempted, give all the support of your Division and Gen. Hurlbut's if necessary. I will return to Pittsburg at an early hour tomorrow and will ride out to your camp.
>
> I am Gen, Very Respectfully,
> Your Obt. Servant
> U.S. Grant
> Major Genl. Commanding.[10]

This communication between Grant and Sherman shows Grant himself had attentions placed along the very road that the two Wallaces prepared. The emphasis was enough that Grant had directed the bulk of his army to be ready to travel that way, the Purdy Road crossing over Owl Creek. It was in accord with these ideas from Grant that Lew Wallace proceeded to the battlefield on April 6 on the Shunpike road with intentions of joining Sherman on the his right wing.

Subsequent to this message, the two Wallaces corresponded, in obedience to Grant's directives involving the road to be taken in emergency:

Headquarters 3rd Division
Adamsville, April 5th 1862

Gen. W.H.L Wallace
Comdg 2nd Division
    .Sir:

Yours recd. Glad to hear from you. My cavalry from that point have been to and from your post frequently. As my 3rd Brigade is here, five miles from Crumps Landing, my 3rd two and a half miles from it, I thought it would be better to open communications with you from Adamsville. I will tomorrow order Major Haynes of the 5th Ohio Cavalry to report to you at your Quarters; and if you are so disposed probably, you had better send a company to return with him that they may familiarize themselves with the road, to act in case of emergency as guides to and from our camps.

Very Respectfully
Your Obdt. Servant
Lewis Wallace
Comdg 3rd Div.[11]

General Grant himself set the stage for these preparations. None of Grant's staff ever makes mention of this in the correspondences against Lew Wallace a year later. General Lew Wallace did things correctly, but the chance circumstances of the first day of battle had certain intricacies that later enabled Grant to use Lew Wallace as a scapegoat to cover the huge mistake of decapitating his supply and transportation corps.

10

The Need for a Cover-up

Getting at the truth can be like stutter-stepping. U.S. Grant was stutter-stepping as he came downstairs Sunday morning, April 6, 1862, still hurting from the fall he had taken with his horse on Thursday, April 4. What happened between the time he sat down to breakfast in the Cherry Mansion and arrived at Pittsburg Landing is open to question. Official reports of many commanders at the Battle of Shiloh are recorded in great detail, but U.S. Grant gives little actual detail of his own activity. The most reliable information would be written closest to the actual events.

Reports of Grant Closest to the Battle

The first of Grant's transmissions, the second day of the battle, was to General Henry W. Halleck, his superior then residing in St. Louis, Missouri:

> PITTSBURG, April 7, 1862.
>
> Yesterday the rebels attacked us here with an overwhelming force, driving our troops in from their advanced position to near the Landing. General Wallace was immediately ordered up from Crump's Landing, and in the evening one division of General Buell's army and General Buell in person arrived. During the night one other division arrived, and still another to-day. This morning, at the break of the day, I ordered an attack, which resulted in a fight which continued until late this afternoon, with severe loss on both sides, but a complete repulse of the enemy. I shall follow tomorrow far enough to see that no immediate renewal of an attack is contemplated.
>
> **U.S. GRANT,**
> Major-General.
> Maj. Gen. H. W. HALLECK,
> Saint Louis, Mo.[1]

The next transmission from U.S. Grant came on Monday while some hostilities were still taking place between General W.T. Sherman and Nathan Bedford Forrest's and other groups of cavalry in a place of fallen timbers.

PITTSBURG, *TENN. (via SAVANNAH), April* 8, 1862.

Enemy badly routed and fleeing towards Corinth. Our cavalry, supported by infantry, are now pursuing him, with instructions to pursue to the swampy grounds near Pea Ridge. I want transports sent here for our wounded.

U.S. GRANT.[2]

The fullest report closest to the time line of battle was written Tuesday.

HEADQUARTERS DISTRICT OF WEST TENNESSEE,
Pittsburg, April 9, 1862.

CAPTAIN [McLean, Halleck's adjutant]: It becomes my duty again to report another battle fought between two great armies, one contending for the maintenance of the best government ever devised, the other for its destruction. It is pleasant to record the success of the army contending for the former principle.

On Sunday morning our pickets were attacked and driven in by the enemy. Immediately the five divisions stationed at this place were drawn up in line of battle, ready to meet them. The battle soon waxed warm on the left and center, varying at times to all parts of the line. The most continuous firing of musketry and artillery ever heard on this continent was kept up until nightfall, the enemy having forced the entire line to fall back nearly half way from their camps to the Landing.

At a late hour in the afternoon a desperate effort was made by the enemy to turn our left and get possession of the Landing, transports, &c. This point was guarded by the gunboats Tyler and Lexington, Captains Gwin and Shirk, U.S. Navy, commanding, four 20-pounder Parrott guns and a battery of rifled guns. As there is a deep and impassable ravine for artillery or cavalry, and very difficult for infantry, at this point, no troops were stationed here, except the necessary artillerists and a small infantry force for their support. Just at this moment the advance of Major-General Buell's column (a part of the division under General Nelson) arrived, the two generals named both being present. An advance was immediately made upon the point of attack and the enemy soon driven back. In this repulse much is due to the presence of the gunboats Tyler and Lexington, and their able commanders, Captains Gwin and Shirk.

During the night the divisions under Generals Crittenden and McCook arrived. General Lewis Wallace, at Crump's Landing, 6 miles below, was ordered at an early hour in the morning to hold his division in readiness to be moved in any direction to which it might be ordered. At about 11 o'clock the order was delivered to move it up to Pittsburg, but owing to its being led by a circuitous route did not arrive in time to take part in Sunday's action.

During the night all was quiet, and feeling that a great moral advantage would be gained by becoming the attacking party, an advance was ordered as soon as day dawned. The result was a gradual repulse of the enemy at all

This later photograph of General U.S. Grant (seated) and his adjutant general John A. Rawlins in the Wilderness Campaign is suggestive of the close cooperation between the two. (An unknown aide is standing.) Evidence shows they worked together at Shiloh to divert attention away from Grant's mistakes by focusing attention on General Lew Wallace and his supposed dilatory march (Library of Congress).

parts of the line from morning until probably 5 o'clock in the afternoon, when it became evident the enemy was retreating. Before the close of the action the advance of General T.J. Wood's division arrived in time to take part in the action.

My force was too much fatigued from two days' hard fighting and exposure in the open air to a drenching rain during the intervening night to pursue immediately.

Night closed in cloudy and with heavy rain, making the roads impracticable for artillery by the next morning. General Sherman, however, followed the enemy, finding that the main part of the army had retreated in good order.

Hospitals of the enemy's wounded were found all along the road as far as pursuit was made. Dead bodies of the enemy and many graves were also found.

I enclose herewith report of General Sherman, which will explain more fully the result of this pursuit.

Of the part taken by each separate command I cannot take special notice in this report, but will do so more fully when reports of division commanders are handed in.

General Buell, coming on the field with a distinct army long under his command, and which did such efficient service, commanded by himself in person on the field, will be much better able to notice those of his command who particularly distinguished themselves than I possibly can.

I feel it a duty, however, to a gallant and able officer, Brig. Gen. W.T. Sherman, to make a special mention. He not only was with his command during the entire two days' action, but displayed great judgment and skill in the management of his men. Although severely wounded in the hand the first day his place was never vacant. He was again wounded, and had three horses killed under him.

In making mention of a gallant officer no disparagement is intended to the other division commanders, Maj. Gens. John McClernand, and Lewis Wallace, and Brig. Gens. S.A. Hurlbut, B.M. Prentisss and W.H.L. Wallace, all of whom maintained their places with credit to themselves and the cause.

General Prentiss was taken prisoner in the first day's action, and General W.H.L. Wallace severely, probably mortally, wounded. His assistant adjutant-general, Capt. William McMichael, is missing; probably taken prisoner.

My personal staff are all deserving of particular mention, they having been engaged during the entire two days in conveying orders to every part of the field. It consists of Col. J.D. Webster, chief of staff; Lieut. Col. J.B. McPherson, chief engineer, assisted by Lieuts. W.L.B. Jenney and William Kossak; Capt. J.A. Rawlins, assistant adjutant-general; Capts. W.S. Hillyer, W.R. Rowley, and C.B. Lagow, aides-de-camp; Col G.G. Pride, volunteer aide, and Capt. J.P. Hawkins, chief commissary, who accompanied me upon the field.

The medical department, under the direction of Surgeon Hewitt, medical director, showed great energy in providing for the wounded and in getting them from the field regardless of danger.

Colonel Webster was placed in special charge of all the artillery and was constantly upon the field. He displayed, as always heretofore, both skill and bravery. At least in one instance he was the means of placing an entire regiment in a position of doing most valuable service, and where it would not have been but for his exertions.

Lieutenant-Colonel McPherson, attached to my staff as chief engineer, deserves more than a passing notice for his activity and courage. All the grounds beyond our camps for miles have been reconnoitered by him, and plats carefully prepared under his supervision give accurate information of the nature of approaches to our lines. During the two days' battle he was constantly in the saddle, leading troops as they arrived to points where their services were required. During the engagement he had one horse shot under him.

The country will have to mourn the loss of many brave men who fell at the battle of Pittsburg, or Shiloh, more properly. The exact loss in killed and wounded will be known in a day or two. At present I can only give it approximately at 1,500 killed and 3,500 wounded.

The loss of artillery was great, many pieces being disabled by the enemy's shots and some losing all their horses and many men. There were probably not less than 2000 horses killed.

The loss of the enemy in killed and left upon the field was greater than ours. In wounded the estimate cannot be made, as many of them must have been sent back to Corinth and other points.

The enemy suffered terribly from demoralization and desertion.

A flag of truce was sent in to-day from General Beauregard. I enclose herewith a copy of the correspondence.

I am, very respectfully, your obedient servant,

U.S. GRANT,
Major-General, Commanding.[3]

The Mysterious Missing Man: Captain A.S. Baxter, District Quartermaster

The foregoing is the closest thing there is to an official report of the Battle of Shiloh by General U.S. Grant. He actually never wrote a comprehensive one. He needed all the reports of all the officers in command to do that, but when General Halleck arrived on April 11, he took over everything. The abbreviated report of General Grant is more remarkable for the things it does not contain than for the things it does.

In particular his report has little of his own activity, but especially omitted is his late arrival to the scene of battle or anything connected that might bring attention to that fact. The next primary omission that should be glaring, but shrewdly covered, is the absence of mention of arguably the most important member of his staff to the army in general, Chief Quartermaster A.S. Baxter. It is useful to repeat the wording as to how Grant deflected attention away from the loss of his district quartermaster's important function. He said: "My personal staff are all deserving of particular mention, they having been engaged during the entire two days in conveying orders to every part of the field. It consists of Col. J.D. Webster, chief of staff; Lieut. Col. J.B. McPherson, chief engineer, assisted by Lieuts. W.L.B. Jenney and William Kossak; Capt. J.A. Rawlins, assistant adjutant-general; Capts. W.S. Hillyer, W.R. Rowley, and C.B. Lagow, aides-de-camp; Col G.G. Pride, volunteer aide, and Capt. J.P. Hawkins, chief commissary, who accompanied me upon the field."

There is *no mention* of Captain Algernon Sydney Baxter, Grant's staff and district quartermaster, head of supply and transportation. This points to Grant's recognition that a great mistake had been made in selecting and sending Baxter away to order up General Lew Wallace. His name is omitted purposefully in the "all" part of "All of my personal staff are all deserving of mention."

Back at the Cherry Mansion headquarters early that morning of April 6, normal procedure for a close staff member would have been to join staff meetings at breakfast. Captain A.S. Baxter was a personal staff member. It seems logical that he would have been there at breakfast, but there is no mention of his presence in any recorded accounts. This is more than curious.

This soon after the battle, General Grant's real-time outlook toward his 3rd Division Commander General Lew Wallace, as it related to Wallace's performance, reflects no animosity toward Wallace. He only states: "General Lewis Wallace, at Crump's Landing, 6 miles below, was ordered at an early hour in the morning to hold his division in readiness to be moved in any direction to which it might be ordered. At about 11 o'clock the order was delivered to move it up to Pittsburg, but owing to its being led by a circuitous route did not arrive in time to take part in Sunday's action." Then, showing no indications of lack of performance toward Wallace, he actually gives commendation when he says: "In making mention of a gallant officer no disparagement is intended to the other division commanders, Maj. Gens. John McClernand and Lewis Wallace, and Brig. Gens. S.A. Hurlbut, B.M. Prentiss and W.H.L. Wallace, all of whom maintained their places with credit to themselves and the cause."[4] Juxtaposing these points, there is an indication of a cover-up in the selection of Captain Baxter to deliver the message to Major General Lew Wallace to come up from Pittsburg Landing. Grant held no malice toward Wallace; on the other hand, he was concerned with drawing attention to the fact that his major logistics officer, the main supply and transportation man, District Quartermaster Captain A.S. Baxter, was not present when he was needed the most. With all the problems that had existed in the Quartermaster Department prior to the appointment of Captain Baxter and with Grant's boss General H.W. Halleck being a stickler about procedures, General U.S. Grant stood to lose a great deal if attention became focused on Captain A.S. Baxter.

Conflicting Reports a Year After the Battle

The primary official information about the specific activities of General Grant on the morning of April 6, 1862, are stated a year after the fact. The information from these reports have a hostile slant because they were issued at the request of General Lew Wallace, who had felt wronged for the loss of his command and was seeking a board of inquiry in regard to derogatory remarks made against him by General U.S. Grant and his staff. It is interesting that suddenly the role of Captain A.S. Baxter has been emphasized, but again with the obfuscation that Baxter was greatly needed during the events of the first day of battle. As these next reports about Grant's movements that fateful morning are considered, it is important to notice that the specifics provided were controlled by a now promoted Lt. Col. John A. Rawlins as Grant's adjutant general. The first correspondence of the package is a short report attributed to U.S. Grant himself to the War Department:

Grant's Report
HEADQUARTERS DEPARTMENT OF THE TENNESSEE,
Before Vicksburg, April 13, 1863

Col. J.C. KELTON,
Assistant Adjutant-General, Washington, D. C.:

COLONEL: I have the honor to acknowledge the receipt of a copy of a communication of

Maj. Gen. Lewis Wallace to Major-General Halleck, of date March 14, 1863, relative to his failure to participate in the first day's fight at Pittsburg Landing, and submitted to me for my remarks.

Instead of making a detailed report myself in answer to said communication I called upon Maj. Gen. J.B. McPherson, Lieut. Col. John A. Rawlins, and Maj. W.R. Rowley, all of whom were members of my staff at that time and were cognizant of the facts, for their statements in reference to the same, and these I herewith respectfully transmit.

All these reports are substantially as I remember the facts. I vouch for their almost entire accuracy; and from these several statements, separate and independent of each other, too, a more correct judgment can be derived than from a single report.

Had General Wallace been relieved from duty in the morning, and the same orders communicated to Brig. Gen. Morgan L. Smith (who would have been his successor), I do not doubt but the division would have been on the field of battle and in the engagement before 10 o'clock of that eventful 6th of April. There is no estimating the difference this might have made in our casualties.

I am, colonel, very respectfully, your obedient servant,

U.S. GRANT,
Major-General Commanding[5]

Rowley's Report

The next enclosure to Washington is that of Captain promoted to Lt. Colonel Rowley. Addressing the pertinent information to the time between the Cherry Mansion and Pittsburg Landing, it is directed through Colonel John A. Rawlins:

COLONEL [Rawlins]:

Yours, requesting a statement as to my knowledge of the part taken by General Lewis Wallace in the first day's fight at the battle of Shiloh, on the 6th of April, 1862, is just received. In reply, I would state that at that time I was an aide-de-camp on the staff of General U.S. Grant, with the rank of captain, and on the morning of the 6th of April I accompanied the general together with the other members of his staff [including Captain A.S. Baxter], from Savannah to Pittsburg Landing. When the steamer upon which we were embarked arrived near to Crump's Landing General Grant directed that it should be run close in to the shore, as he wished to communicate with General Wallace, who was standing upon the commissary boat lying at that place. General Grant called to General Wallace, saying, "General, you will get your troops under arms immediately, and have them ready to move at a moment's notice." General Wallace replied that it should be done, adding (I think) that the necessary orders had already been given. This was between the hours of 7 and 8 o'clock A.M. We passed on up the river, meeting the steamer *Warner*, which had been sent by General W.H.L. Wallace (as I understood) with a messenger to inform General Grant that a battle had been commenced. The *Warner* rounded to and followed us back to Pittsburg Landing.

Upon reaching the Landing General Grant immediately mounted his horse and rode upon the bank, and after conversing a moment with some officers turned to Captain Baxter, assistant quartermaster, and ordered him to proceed immediately to Crump's Landing, and direct General Wallace to march with his division up the river and into the field on the right of our line as rapidly as possible.

    This order was given to Captain Baxter about the hour of 8 o'clock. I think not later than that....[6]

The inconsistency in this report is apparent almost immediately when compared with the other accounts called for by General Grant through his adjutant John A. Rawlins. The Rowley report makes it appear that Grant gave the transmission to Captain Baxter personally, saying he "turned to Captain Baxter." Even John A. Rawlins does not say that. Furthermore Rowley's report, coming a year later as do the other reports, conglomerates impressions of what happened. He makes it sound as if the transmission occurred immediately from Grant to Baxter saying Grant "mounted his horse and rode upon the bank, and after conversing a moment with some officers turned to Captain Baxter, assistant quartermaster, and ordered him to proceed immediately to Crump's Landing." This does not agree with the account of Major General McPherson.

McPherson's Report

    The next portion of the report against General Lew Wallace is by former Lt. Colonel McPherson at Shiloh, but now Major General McPherson. He was not at the Cherry Mansion that morning, but had apparently spent the night in the tent of General W.H.L. Wallace. He was at Pittsburg Landing and can only testify by hearsay what transpired for Grant between the Cherry Mansion and Pittsburg Landing. At the time of Shiloh he was actually officially a member of General Halleck's staff rather than Grant's. Notice that this correspondence had to be funneled through Rawlins.

> Lieut. Col. JOHN A. RAWLINS,
> *Assistant Adjutant-General:*
>
> COLONEL: I have the honor to submit the following in relation to the position of the troops and the battle of Shiloh:
>
> When the troops first disembarked at Pittsburg Landing the Tennessee River was very high, the water backing up in all the streams, covering the bottoms in the vicinity of river from 2 to 6 feet, rendering Lick and Snake Creeks impassable.
>
> Four divisions of the army were encamped on the field of Shiloh in the relative positions indicated in the sketch, and one division (Maj. Gen. Lewis Wallace's) at Crump's Landing, about 6 miles below.
>
> My attention was frequently called to the crossing of Snake Creek, on the direct road from Pittsburg Landing to Crump's, as it was considered very important that a line of land communication between the two portions of the army should be kept open.
>
> As soon as the water subsided sufficiently the bridge across the creek was reconstructed, and a company of cavalry sent through to communicate with General Wallace's command. This was on Thursday, previous to the battle.

At this point in McPherson's report it must be said that the records that exist of communications between General Wallace's command on the Thursday previous to the battle do not deal with the bridge over Snake Creek, but rather directions given to General Sherman to keep his eye out in the direction of the road to Purdy, with the bridge over Owl Creek being the obvious ford.[7] There is also a communication that was lost. Missing for more than twenty years, it turned up in possession of General W.H.L. Wallace's widow, and it shows preparations and communications over the Purdy Road/Owl Creek route were the way communications were being carried out.[8] McPherson continues:

> Sunday morning, the first day of the battle, I was with Brig. Gen. W.H.L. Wallace, who, in consequence of the severe illness of General C.F. Smith, commanded this division. It was well known the enemy was approaching our lines, and there had been more or less skirmishing for three days preceding the battle.
>
> The consequence was our breakfasts were ordered at an early hour and our horses saddled, to be ready in case of an attack. Sunday morning, shortly before 7 o'clock, word came to the Landing [where General W.H.L. Wallace's Headquarters sat] that the battle had commenced. I immediately started, in company with General W.H.L. Wallace and staff; found his division In line

ready to move out. At this time, not later than 7.30 A.M., General McClernand had moved a portion of his division up to support General Sherman's left. General Hurlbut had moved to the support of General Prentiss, and General W.H.L. Wallace's division was moved up to support the center and right. I was actively engaged on the field, and did not see General Grant until some time after his arrival, when I met him on the field, with Brig. Gen. W.H.L. Wallace. He informed me that when he came up from Savannah, at 7.30, he had notified Maj. Gen. Lewis Wallace, at Crump's Landing, to hold his command in readiness to march at a moment's notice, and that immediately on his arrival at Pittsburg Landing, finding that the attack was in earnest and not a feint, he had sent Captain Baxter, assistant quartermaster, with orders to him to move up immediately by the River road and take a position on our right. Shortly after this Captain Baxter returned, certainly not later than 10.30, and said that he had delivered the order....[9]

While this report was requested in order to cast aspersions on Lew Wallace, handled through Adjutant General John A. Rawlins, we also glean other information from former Lt. Colonel McPherson that does not reflect well on U.S. Grant when looked at closely. The time of Grant's arrival is important to the question of when Baxter was sent to take the message to General Wallace. The enclosure of McPherson states he "did not see General Grant until some time after his arrival." Here McPherson inadvertently exposes Grant's lateness, saying about the first contact he had with General Grant: "I was actively engaged on the field, and did not see General Grant until some time after his arrival, when I met him on the field, with Brig. Gen. W.H.L. Wallace." Gen. W.H.L. Wallace's headquarters was at the top of the hill at Pittsburg Landing. That was not the place that Grant consulted with W.H.L Wallace. Grant met him "on the field." John A. Rawlins stated that it was "about half a mile from the river you met Brig. Gen. W.H.L. Wallace...." The field of battle would be the area now known as the "sunken road" and "Hornet's Next" sector, for that is the area that General W.H.L. Wallace brought the majority of his division to when it was first engaged about 9:00 A.M., having come to the aide of Prentiss. Most park markers dealing with the division show this to be the case.[10] McPherson can account for his own activities but he was really in no position to comment on matters pertaining to the delivery of the message by Baxter to Wallace. He states: "He informed me that when he came up from Savannah," etc.; this shows anything that McPherson had to say other than his own activity about the transmission of the message by Baxter to Wallace was not firsthand. The report was malleable in the hands of John Rawlins. Rawlins used it to try to make appearances of validity. It was only hearsay with respect to the delivery of the now infamous message. Certainly the idea that Baxter returned by 10:30 is preposterous.

Rawlins's Report

Finally is the carefully prepared report of John A. Rawlins, which contradicts what the other two aides at Shiloh had stated, especially with regard to the times things happened. Rawlins addresses his report directly to U.S. Grant:

Maj. Gen. U.S. GRANT,
Commanding Department of the Tennessee:

GENERAL: I have the honor to submit the following statement of your orders to Maj. Gen. Lewis Wallace, who commanded the Third Division of the Army of the Tennessee on the 6th day of April, A.D. 1862, and the manner in which he obeyed them, together with facts and circumstances transpiring that day and the one immediately preceding, deemed necessary to a clear understanding of them:

In pursuance of the following order —
GENERAL ORDERS No. 30.
HEADQUARTERS DISTRICT OF WEST TENNESSE
Savannah, March 31, 1862.

Headquarters of the District of West Tennessee is hereby changed to Pittsburg Landing. An office will be continued at Savannah, where all official communications may be sent by troops having easier access with that point than Pittsburg Landing.

By command of Major-General Grant:
JNo. A. RAWLINS,
Assistant Adjutant-General. —

I was in charge of the office at Savannah, Tenn., with instructions to make out the necessary orders, and send forward to Pittsburg Landing all troops arriving from below. Up to the 5th day of April, 1862, from the date of said order, you had run up every morning to Pittsburg Landing and returned at night on the steamer Tigress, used for your headquarters boat, and on which boat steam was continually kept up.

April 5, 1862, a dispatch was received from Maj. Gen. D.C. Buell, commanding the Army of the Ohio, dated Camp 3 miles west of Waynesborough, April 4, 1862, stating that he would be in Savannah, Tenn., with one and perhaps two divisions of his army the next day, and requesting to meet you there; to which you replied you would be there to meet him.

General Nelson's division of the Army of the Ohio reached Savannah on the afternoon of the 5th of April, but General Buell himself did not arrive; and supposing the he must be near, you determined to ride out the next morning and meet him. That there might be no delay in getting off (and consequent detention in moving the office) to Pittsburg Landing, directions were given for breakfast and horses to be in readiness at an earlier hour than usual.

I was awakened by Capt. W.S. Hillyer, a member of your staff, who had arrived from Cairo on the boat that brought the mail from that place, about 3 o'clock A.M., and did not fall soundly to sleep again that morning. I got up at daylight, and in your private office was examining the mail, when you came down-stairs from your sleeping room. Your mail was handed you, and before you were through reading it Brig. Gen. John Cook, of Illinois, who had come in on a steamer during the night, reported to you in person his return from leave of absence for orders, and from that time until breakfast was announced, which was about 6 o'clock A.M., you were engaged in reading your mail and in conversation with General Cook.

While at breakfast, Edward N. Trembly, private Company C, First Regiment Illinois Artillery Volunteers, and on detached duty at headquarters, reported artillery firing in the direction of Pittsburg Landing. Breakfast was left unfinished, and, accompanied by your staff officers, you went immediately on board the steamer Tigress, then lying at the Landing. The horses being in readiness, as per orders of the night previous, were sent at once on the boat and orders given at once to start for Pittsburg Landing, delaying only long enough for you to write an order to General Nelson to move his division by the road from Savannah to the river opposite Pittsburg Landing, and a note to Maj. Gen. D.C. Buell, informing him of the supposed condition of affairs at or in the vicinity of Pittsburg Landing.

In passing, and where was stationed the division commanded by Maj. Gen. Lewis Wallace, the Tigress ran close alongside the boat on which Major-General Wallace had his headquarters, and addressing him in person, you directed him to hold his division in readiness to move on receipt of orders, which he might expect when you ascertained the condition of affairs above, but in the mean time to send out and ascertain if there was any enemy on the Purdy road, apprehending, as you did, that the real attack might be intended against his position. His reply was that he was then in readiness, and had already taken the precautionary steps you directed as to the Purdy road. This was not far from 7 or 7.30 o'clock A.M.

From thence you continued direct to Pittsburg Landing, which place you reached about 8 o'clock A.M., and, with your staff, started immediately to the front. About half a mile from the river you met Brig. Gen. W.H.L. Wallace, who commanded Maj. Gen. C.F. Smith's Second Division of the Army of the Tennessee. From him you ascertained the particulars of the attack and how matters stood up to that time. You then directed me to return to the river and send Capt. A.S. Baxter, assistant quartermaster, U.S. Volunteers, and chief of the quartermaster's department in your district, on the steamer *Tigress,* without delay, to Crump's Landing, with orders to Maj. Gen. Lewis Wallace to bring forward his division by the River road to Pittsburg Landing to a point immediately in rear of the camp of Maj. Gen. C.F. Smith's division, and there form his column at right angles with the river on the right of our lines and await further orders.

In obedience to your command I proceeded to the river, and found Captain Baxter at the landing near where the Tigress lay, and communicated to him your orders, who, fearing lest he might make some mistake in the delivery of the orders, requested me to give him a written memorandum of them, and I went on board the steamer Tigress, where a pen and ink could be procured, and at my dictation he wrote substantially as follows:

Major-General WALLACE:

You will move forward your division from Crump's Landing, leaving a sufficient force to protect the public property at that place, to Pittsburg Landing, on the road nearest to and parallel with the river, and form in line at right angles with the river, immediately in rear of the camp of Maj. Gen. C.F. Smith's division on our right, and there await further orders.

Captain Baxter took this memorandum and started on the steamer *Tigress* to convey your orders to Maj. Gen. Lewis Wallace. This was not later than 9 o'clock A.M. Captain Baxter returned and reported before 12 o'clock m. his delivery of your orders to General Wallace, bringing at the same time from General Wallace to you the report of Col. Morgan L. Smith, that there was no enemy in the direction of Purdy; the result of his reconnaissance that morning. About an hour after Captain Baxter had gone down on the steamer *Tigress* to General Wallace an officer of the Second Illinois Cavalry, who was well acquainted with the road leading to Crump's Landing, was sent by you with a verbal message to Major-General Wallace to hurry forward with all possible dispatch. This officer returned between 12 o'clock m. and 1 o'clock P.M., and reported that when he delivered your message to Major-General Wallace he inquired if he had not written orders. He replied in the negative, and General Wallace said he would only obey written orders. He further stated that it had been more than one hour since he left General Wallace, and that his division was then all ready to move. He should have been by this time on the field. His presence then would have turned the tide of battle, which was raging with great fury; saved the lives of many brave men, and ere the setting of that crimson spring day's sun secured to us certain victory....[11]

Determining Grant's Time to the Landing from the Later Accounts

The rest of Rawlins's report is not pertinent to the discussion at hand. At this point the movements of General Grant are of primary interest, those of Sunday morning, April 6, from the time at the Cherry Mansion to arrival at Pittsburg Landing. These later reports were composed for the possibility of a military board of inquiry that was requested by General Lew Wallace. Rawlins emphasizes superfluous details that divert attention away from Grant's mistakes. Had the board of inquiry actually taken place, each piece of information would have received a piercing examination. Without applying the rules of a military tribunal, it is still possible to extract certain information.

The above account by Rawlins is so exacting, ironically, as to make it unbelievable. The major astonishing point is that he has the audacity to state that the headquarters has been moved to Pittsburg Landing while at the same time narrating the timeline of events as they actually occurred from the true headquarters at the Cherry Mansion in Savannah. He proceeds to speak of the obvious events and command decisions that are still being made in Savannah, at Cherry Mansion. He scrambles to make it seem as if the very moment the battle was breaking out was the same moment when Savannah headquarters was to be closed and moved to Pittsburg Landing in the log house on the hill. It did not happen that way by Rawlins's own narration. Even after the battle, communications still issued out of the Cherry Mansion until General Halleck arrived, though reports are made to appear as if they were coming from the Landing.

The three accounts from one year later, considered together, contain contradictions of one another, especially the times when things happened. The chronology is massaged, making it appear that Grant was on the scene before he actually was. This pattern goes back as far as Ft. Donelson: Grant is not on the scene of important events when they break, and then his movements are spun into something more admirable by his aides. The events must be reconstructed with neutral testimony that is not loaded with acrimony toward General Lew Wallace.

Recall: "We are entirely out of coal here. Please send some at once." That is the urgent request General Grant made personally on April 3 to the post quartermaster in faraway Paducah, Kentucky.[12] Next note that Rawlins stated, "Up to the 5th day of April, 1862, from the date of said order, you had run up every morning to Pittsburg Landing and returned at night on the steamer *Tigress*, used for your headquarters boat, and on which boat steam was continually kept up." This information speaks for itself. "Entirely out of coal here," Grant stated. The likelihood that the filling of the requisition for coal extended to the morning of April 6 is great. The morning of April 6, 1862, it is highly questionable that, as Rawlins states, "the steamer Tigress, used for your headquarters boat, and on which boat steam was continually kept up," had steam continually kept up.

The clever wording, "Up to the 5th Day of April," also covers over the fact that because of his ankle injury he apparently did not go up to Pittsburg Landing on the 5th of April. He canceled reviews of troops, particularly that of the 6th Division commanded by General Benjamin Prentiss.

Next, Rawlins gives dissertation in great detail of the arrangements to meet General Buell, arrangements that appear to be urgent, but in the reality of how it worked gave Buell less consideration than Rawlins maintains. It must be kept in mind that Grant himself had telegrammed General Halleck, "I have not the faintest idea of an attack." So the specificity of preparations Rawlins relates a year later are quite disingenuous when he states: "General Nelson's division of the Army of the Ohio reached Savannah on the afternoon of the 5th of April, but General Buell himself did not arrive; and supposing he must be near, you determined to ride out the next morning and meet him. That there might be no delay in getting off (and consequent detention in moving the office) to Pittsburg Landing, directions were given for breakfast and horses to be in readiness at an earlier hour than usual." This business about the preparation of "breakfast and horses" is clearly a packing of the report with superfluous information in a kind of shell game to fool the reader as to where the headquarters actually resided.

Next Rawlins goes to great pains to mention timing. Recall that General Grant personally had no pocket watch, having sent it home to his wife, and was waiting for another, so Grant himself could not testify personally as to the times things happened. Only in the waning days of his life did he make any personal reckoning of the time, and it was based on the then deceased John Rawlins's reports. In a matter that is purely superfluous, Rawlins relates:

A lawyer in civilian life and the youngest major general in the Union Army at the time of Shiloh and not without his own arrogance, Lew Wallace was outwitted by a shrewder lawyer with Machiavellian skills, John Rawlins (Library of Congress).

"I was awakened by Capt. W.S. Hillyer, a member of your staff, who had arrived from Cairo on the boat that brought the mail from that place, about 3 o'clock A.M., and did not fall soundly to sleep again that morning." Interestingly, it is possible that the boat that brought mail from Cairo may also have been towing the load of coal Grant had requested from Paducah. Was it the racket of coal being transferred from the barge to the *Tigress*, located just below the mansion, that kept Rawlins from sleeping soundly?

The details become tedious in Rawlins's account, so it is necessary to focus on the times he claimed things happened. "I got up at daylight, and in your private office was examining the mail, when you came downstairs from your sleeping room. Your mail was handed you, and before you were through reading it Brig. Gen. John Cook, of Illinois, who had come in on a steamer during the night, reported to you in person his return from leave of absence for orders, and from that time until breakfast was announced, which was about 6 o'clock A.M., you were engaged in reading your mail and in conversation with General Cook."

Focusing on the object of the actual times that things happened concerning Grant's movements, Rawlins says he "got up at daylight." It could not have been at 6:00. Daylight at Savannah, Tennessee, can be quantifiably determined based on data from the National Oceanic and Aeronautic Administration (NOAA). NOAA gives the time of dawning for April 6, 1862, as occurring at 6:17 A.M. at Oak Ridge, Tennessee.[13] Oak Ridge is about two hundred miles east of Savannah. Dawn does not mean daylight. That means daylight at Savannah was later than 6:30. More time was consumed while Rawlins examined mail in Grant's private office while he waited for the limping Grant to come down to receive his mail. More time passed in its perusal, and then General John Cook entered from his leave of absence and engaged in conversation with Grant until breakfast was announced. The time had to be later than Rawlins states. It is at this point Rawlins has begun a subtle massaging of the time in his year-later report. If Rawlins arose at daylight, which was after 6:30 A.M., and all the minor theater of events he describes happened, obviously breakfast was not at 6:00 A.M. It is reasonable to deduce that it was, at the earliest, after 7:00 A.M.; Rawlins moved things back in time by at least an hour.

Grant Realizes a Battle Is On

The surest way to determine the time events occurred, based on the report of Rawlins, comes when he says: "While at breakfast, Edward N. Trembly, private Company C, First Regiment Illinois Artillery Volunteers, and on detached duty at headquarters, reported artillery firing in the direction of Pittsburg Landing." Here a suggestively named artilleryman reported the sound of artillery fire. He was not the only expert as to the nature of the sound of the firing. Grant himself, trained in artillery, had heard it many times from a distance in many battles going all the way back to the Mexican War. Others experienced in the sound of artillery were present, foremost being Colonel Webster, who acted as Grant's chief of artillery, but who was also his chief of staff. The West Point–trained officers, with vast battle experience between them, agreed it was artillery they heard. That enables identification of the time Grant was alerted to the Battle of Shiloh. One source, accepting the Rawlins account, states that it was "Presumably only musket fire, which the wind carried the nine miles to Savannah, and their imagination or memories changed into cannon fire."[14] This supposition that it was not artillery is unreasonable, although if musket fire was being heard it indeed rivaled the cannon fire. As Henry Morton Stanley described the first substantial clash about 7:30 A.M., "There broke upon our ears an appalling crash of sound, the series of fusillades following one another with startling suddenness, which suggested to my somewhat moidered sense a mountain upheaved, with huge rocks rumbling and thundering down a slope, and the echoes rumbling and receding through space.... Twenty thousand muskets were being fired at this stage...." Either way, the sound was heard at Savannah after 7:00 A.M.[15]

The most neutral source of the time Grant could have heard artillery comes from the reports of the Confederate Army. Confederate colonel William Preston on Albert Sidney Johnston's staff reported heavy firing on General Hardee's left at 7:10 A.M. and cannon fire at 7:15 A.M. Captain W. Irvin Hodgson, 5th Company Washington artillery, reported his battery firing at 7:10 A.M. Lieutenant Colonel S.W. Ferguson, aide-de-camp to General Beauregard, caught in the huge significance of the moment, gives a precise time: he recorded he heard the first cannon shot at exactly 7:09 A.M. With these witnesses it can be reliably considered that artillery fire was heard at this time at the Cherry Mansion. Shock waves from artillery disturb the atmosphere. The concussion is unmistakable. It is the reason the guns of Shiloh could be heard by some residing near Corinth, more than twenty miles away.[16]

Rawlins's explanations as to when Grant got away from Savannah are given nowhere near the consideration and exact detailing Rawlins designed into the report intended for Washington against Lew Wallace.

> Breakfast was left unfinished, and, accompanied by your staff officers, you went immediately on board the steamer Tigress, then lying at the Landing. The horses being in readiness, as per orders of the night previous, were sent at once on the boat and orders given at once to start for Pittsburg Landing, delaying only long enough for you to write an order to General Nelson to move his division by the road from Savannah to the river opposite Pittsburg Landing, and a note to Maj. Gen. D.C. Buell, informing him of the supposed condition of affairs at or in the vicinity of Pittsburg Landing.

It is interesting that in his care to give clock times to other mundane details and the times they happened, Rawlins does not give a time when the *Tigress* embarked. Simply stating that they all went immediately on board the *Tigress* does not account for the time it took to get off. A steamboat does not get underway with rapidity. Getting the horses on board took some minutes. Another factor is that steam could not have been at its peak; even if the *Tigress* had been fired up, a boiler has certain requirements, and a river pilot has certain procedures for disembarking. Lt. Colonel McPherson, by hearsay from

Grant, states, "I was actively engaged on the field, and did not see General Grant until some time after his arrival, when I met him on the field, with Brig. Gen. W.H.L. Wallace. He informed me that when he came up from Savannah, at 7.30, he had notified Maj. Gen. Lewis Wallace, at Crump's Landing, to hold his command in readiness to march at a moment's notice." This detail, which McPherson says Grant told him about the time he came up from Savannah, may be close to the actual time of debarking from the wharf at Savannah, but Grant did not have a watch, and it is not likely that it took only 15 minutes from the time of the first recorded cannon fire to get underway.

The man who acted most reasonably that day with General Lew Wallace, Captain W.R. Rowley, allows a full hour of leeway for Grant to accomplish getting away from Savannah to Pittsburg. He says:

> When the steamer upon which we were embarked arrived near to Crump's Landing General Grant directed that it should be run close in to the shore, as he wished to communicate with General Wallace, who was standing upon the commissary boat lying at that place. General Grant called to General Wallace, saying, "General, you will get your troops under arms immediately, and have them ready to move at a moment's notice." General Wallace replied that it should be done, adding (I think) that the necessary orders had already been given. This was between the hours of 7 and 8 o'clock A.M.[17]

Even allowing for this hour of leeway, Grant's debarkation could not have been 7:00, for they had not yet heard the sound of artillery in Savannah. It could not have been at 7:30, for that is when they could have left Savannah at the very earliest. That is what McPherson states Grant told him. Rawlins's words, "Crump's landing which is on the river between Savannah and Pittsburg Landing, and distant about 4½ miles from the former and 5½ miles from the latter place," help us to understand the time factor. A steamboat at full steam travels upstream safely at about 20 mph.[18] That would be on a good unimpeded stretch of river. An experienced pilot must read the eddies and vary his speed as the leadsman calls out the river's depth. That means it would take about fifteen minutes to get from Savannah to Crump's if those conditions existed. Crump's was located in a dogleg of the Tennessee River and the river was in flood, so care needed to be taken. The time Grant arrived at Crump's Landing would be at earliest after 8:00 A.M., already more than three hours after the Battle of Shiloh had begun.

The Missing Account of Captain Baxter

There is yet another witness on Grant's staff there on the *Tigress* who knew the timing of Grant's movements between Savannah and Pittsburg Landing. On March 30, 1863, U.S. Grant wrote to Captain Algernon S. Baxter, who was then resigned from the army and residing in Chicago. Baxter may have been tending to business interests of his wealthy brother Horace Baxter, adjutant general of the state of Vermont. Grant wrote: "You will please Send me a statement at your earliest possible convenience, of the time and circumstances at and under which you delivered my order to Maj. General Lewis Wallace at Crump's Landing, to move to the field of the battle of Pittsburg Landing on the 6th of April 1862 and the time as nearly as you can remember the time I passed Crump's Landing on my way to Pittsburg Landing. This is necessary to the answering of inquir[i]es made by Gen Wallace of Gen. Halleck."[19] There is no record of any reply. There is reason to believe Baxter did not want to be involved, or else the reply was not preserved. Again this reply would have been handled by adjutant general John A. Rawlins. The lack of record of Baxter's reply is consistent with a pattern of all things pertaining to Captain A.S. Baxter at Shiloh. The matters pertaining to Baxter are virtually expunged.

The time it took for the *Tigress* to pull away from Crump's Landing and get to Pittsburg Landing is educated guesswork. If the captain of the *Tigress* was being safe, normal steamboat operations would consume numerous minutes. That would have been most seriously advisable, since General C.F. Smith was disabled and dying from a simple accident involving a steamboat. Then as the *Tigress* headed upstream, another steamboat, the *John J. Warner*, came downriver, and the *Tigress* slowed for a midriver conference. That had to have been a delicate maneuver. The *John J. Warner* was coming down a flooding river, so to slow and rendevous with the *Tigress*, the captain would have had to reverse engines in order to back-paddle, while the *Tigress* would have had to slow. A courier from W.H.L. Wallace was aboard and informed Grant that indeed it was a general attack. The *John J. Warner* then turned around and followed Grant's boat back to Pittsburg Landing.[20]

Neutral Accounts That Might Help Determine the Time of Grant's Arrival

In official correspondence and official reports closest in time to the Battle of Shiloh, the commanders were required to turn in their accounts of what happened. They often go into great detail about the times they arose, details of their activities, their first mustering on their color lines, their first line of battle. In Grant's reports in his own hand, there are no details and there is a glaring absence of the time things happened. Other sources must be sought as to what time Grant got to Pittsburg Landing with his staff.

One way to detemine what time Grant arrived at Pittsburg Landing is through an order Grant issued through his aide-de-camp Captain Clark B. Lagow about releasing the officers who were under arrest. If the arrested officers make any statement in their reports as to what time they went into action, they might give clues as to the time of Grant's arrival, without being filtered through Grant's protector Captain John Rawlins. What had to have been an immediate concern when Grant arrived was that certain regiments, even brigades, were without their commanders. Aide-de-camp Captain Clark Lagow transmitted an order upon Grant's arrival at Pittsburg Landing that read simply this way: "Brig Gen McArthur Lt Col A.S, Chetlain 12th Ills. Lt. Col. Morgan 25th Ind Col Reed (of Cruffs Brigade) & Col Gaddis 8th Iowa are hereby released from arrest & will resume their Swords and returnt to duty with their respective commands."[21] What times do the officers who were arrested state they came into action? What do all the arrested officers say as to the time they brought their men into line? Time must be allowed for them to get back to their units and take command.

General McArthur has nothing to say at all about time in his after-battle report.[22] He only refers to Colonel Tuttle for information. Colonel Tuttle's report is similarly silent as to the time things occurred. General McArthur's is the most incredibly short report of all the one hundred thirty-three turned in by Union officers. The shortness of his report could be because he was wounded, but in the Derickson documents he was active enough to have conducted an inquiry into the disappearance of thousands of pounds of corn from the *Iatan*. (See Appendix A.) He should have been able to turn in a full report with the stated time or approximate time he began operations after his release from arrest. Why this report is so abbreviated is one of the curiosities of the battle. It makes it impossible to determine the time when Grant arrived according to General John MacArthur's report. The effort grows increasingly frustrating to find specific witnesses as to the time of Grant's arrival. Since McArthur was the highest ranking officer under arrest, it might be understandable that he would not mention that he was released from arrest to go into battle, but when in action with his troops he certainly would have given more detailed information. While McArthur turned his report in on April 16, it is interesting that U.S. Grant — that is, through John A. Rawlins — forwarded McArthur's short report the day after Grant came under scrutiny by President Lincoln. The report that exists gives some plausibility to the idea that there may have been more pages to McArthur's report before it was filtered through Captain John Rawlins. McArthur's report reads as follows:

HEADQUARTERS SECOND DIVISION
April 16, 1862.

SIR: Herewith I transmit to you the report of Col. J.M. Tuttle [No. 18], who commanded the Second Division during the greater part of the engagement. The list of casualties, as far as I have yet had reports, is as follows:

	Killed.	Wounded.	Missing.	Aggregate.
1st Brigade	36	171	666	873
2d Brigade	100	458	16	574
3d Brigade	86	349	482	917
Batteries (four)	4	55	....	59
Total	226	1,033	1,164	2,423

Two regiments, the Fifty-second and Fifty-eighth Illinois, have not yet reported.

All of which is respectfully submitted.

J. McARTHUR,
Brigadier-General—

HEADQUARTERS ARMY OF THE TENNESSEE,
Pittsburg, April 25, 1862.

Respectfully referred to headquarters of the department. From the casualties occurring in the Second Division it is not probable that any further reports than those now sent will be received.

U.S. GRANT,
Major-General.[23]

A colonel, who was not under arrest, is more specific as to the time McArthur showed up. In report No. 22, Colonel August Mersy states: "At 9:00 the regiment in the company with the 12th Illinois infantry was ordered by Brigadier General McArthur to a part of the lines about one-fourth of a mile in advance of General Hurlbut's Headquarters, Stuart's sector."[24] General McArthur, who was a brigade commander of W.H.L. Wallace, was released close to 9:00 A.M., the time Grant most likely arrived. A further search for corroboration, based on the arrested officers, conflicts with the attested time of Grant's arrival.

The report of Grant's under-arrest friend Lt. Augustus Chetlain contains an obfuscation. In his report No. 23, he states, "I arose from a sick bed and took command of my regiment.... By order of General McArthur commanding the brigade." Since he was under arrest with McArthur at the provost marshall's camp, that would have been also about 9:00 A.M. He makes no mention that the sickbed he arose from was while he was under arrest with General McArthur.[25]

The report of Colonel James L. Geddis is less definitive because he makes out his report on November 13, 1862, after six months as a prisoner of war. Already the nation was moving on to more mournful disasters of battle. Like

McArthur and Chetlain, he makes no mention of his release from arrest in order to begin performing. He says it was "about 8:00" that he ordered the regiment under arms in front of his camp.[26] He could have derived this time from other reports already in public record by the time of his parole by the Confederates. If the time is close to correct as to when he gave directions, he could have given orders to his second in command to put them under arms even while under arrest, as he was part of the 2nd Division encamped at the top of the landing, this being the same general area the provost marshals were located.

Lt. Colonel Morgan was in charge of the 25th Indiana. He did not make a report. In addition to being under arrest, his regiment was pulled out of normal command of General Hurlbut's 4th Division and placed under supporting General McClernand of the 1st Division. He had trouble finding it. His second, Major John W. Foster, makes the report for the 25th Indiana, but Foster gives no time in which the regiment went into line. The park marker for the 25th Indiana says it was 9:00 A.M.[27]

Arrested Colonel Reed of the 44th Indiana says he marched his troops to the front at 8:00 specifically. It was probably later, but it cannot be ruled out that these qualified officers, who would suffer arrest willingly for minor violations, would be willing to violate arrest and leave the provost marshal tents to help their men, consequences be damned.[28]

The Surest Way to Determine Grant's Arrival Time

Why is it so difficult to find a sure mention of Grant's arrival time? He was the chief of the whole army. Trying to find the time should not be that hard, yet in the records it is elusive. It has the same feel of misdirection that was accomplished with the District Quartermaster Captain A.S. Baxter. It cannot be ruled out that because Captain John A. Rawlins controlled all the record keeping, the exact times become unavailable except where Rawlins dictates; therefore, the most reliable source for determining the time of Grant's arrival must be examined.

Veteran of the Battle of Shiloh and park historian on the Battlefield Park Commission, D.W. Reed was most interactive with the numerous veterans of the Battle of Shiloh when they revisited the battlefield. He showed 9:00 as the time that is most often cited. D.W. Reed is probably conservative in deference to veterans who had suffered much. Major Reed had himself been captured at the Hornet's Nest, so the book *The Battle of Shiloh and the Organizations Engaged* is a very fair presentation to all veterans both North and South. He tries as best as possible to give everyone his due. His most credible statement about when Grant arrived at Pittsburg Landing says: "Arriving on the field about the time Prentiss was driven from his camp, he immediately dispatched orders to Gen. Lew Wallace to bring his division to the battlefield." Almost all Shiloh National Military Park markers of Prentiss's Division show that the breakup occurred about 9:00 A.M. Therefore, allowing for the incidents that occurred between the time of Grant's arrival and the sending of Captain Baxter away from the field of action, Baxter probably got off to go to General Wallace closer to 10:00 A.M. District Quartermaster Baxter had been away from his most important duties since the beginning of the battle. Now he would be of no value to the army for several hours more. It was a major blunder.

11

Critical Decisions

There is a blessing and a curse to being in reserve and behind battle lines. The obvious blessing is that one may live longer; the curse is the suspense of not being involved in the action, knowing that friends and relatives are out there in the thick of it. Awaiting orders to move and feeling conflicted at Lick Creek were the Confederate 1st Tennessee under Colonel Maney, the 19th Tennessee and Forrest's and Adams's cavalry.[1]

Sunday morning opened for them as a clear, beautiful and still day. The cavalry had a stretch of some miles to cover between Hamburg and Greer's Ford. The eyes and ears of the army included Samuel Garrett among the squads of riders who were continually being sent out to observe various sectors of the approach to Shiloh.[2] On Saturday evening this contingent of cavalry and infantry had been the advance, but early Sunday, Gladden's Brigade had passed just to the left. The regiments were positioned some distance in front of them, making this sector a small reserve with little to do but wait. They could hear the rolling of caissons up on higher ground where the Shake-a-Rag slave church was and could conclude that artillery was setting up there. Some handled the anxiety by joking around with ironic humor, like Sam Watkins of Company H. Watkins, who liked to play with words and manipulate the sound of them, turned his company letter H into "Aytch." When Gladden's Brigade passed, Watkins was close enough to hear part of a report between one of the mounted couriers and the general. He did not get what the courier said, but heard General Gladden say, "Tell General Bragg that I have as keen a scent for Yankees as General Chalmers has."[3] It was a telling statement, revealing that the same kinds of personal rivalries existed among Confederate officers that existed in the Union camps. Portly Brigadier General Adley Gladden got to demonstrate his keen scent for the Yankees about the same moment that acting Union Brigadier General Everett Peabody's scent led him to the Rebels. Their brigades were facing one another. On both sides there had been personality conflicts within the respective military organizations. Both Peabody and Gladden saw their personal conflicts with fellow officers end when they experienced their own violent deaths.

Sam Watkins listened with the rest of the reserve troops he was with to what was probably the engagement of the left of Peabody's Brigade, the 16th Wisconsin, facing off against Gladden's Brigade at Spain's field. In his book, *Company Aytch: The Sideshow to the Big Show,* Sam described the onset of battle: "The fire opened — bang, bang, bang, a rattle de bang, bang, bang, a boom, de bang, bang, bang, boom, bang, boom, bang, boom, bang, boom, bang, boom, whirr-siz-siz-siz — a ripping, roaring boom, bang! The air was full of balls and deadly missiles. The litter corps was carrying off the dying and wounded. We could hear the shout of the charge and the incessant roar of the guns, the rattle of the musketry, and knew that the contending forces were engaged in a breast to breast struggle."[4]

Colonel Forrest took his orders seriously to continue guarding the approach from Hamburg Landing. He believed there was good reason to assume that more Union troops might suddenly appear across the Tennessee River at Hamburg. Squads of Forrest's and Wirt Adams's scouts spread out across Tennessee had brought back reports that Buell's Army of the Ohio had moved out of Nashville and was headed south to Alabama. Nobody knew that what they had observed was a feint of some "troops in force" to take away attention from the main of Buell's Army of the Ohio marching towards Savanah. The feint worked with the Confederate high command, but the Alabama state line was only fifteen miles away across the Tennessee, so to have ignored a possible threat from that direction would have been unwise.[5]

For several hours all that Maney's and Cummings's troops, along with Forrest's and Wirt Adams's cavalry, could do was anguish. Waiting was one thing; seeing the gore of wounded men being carried to the rear was another. At one point things became too much for a man named Smith; he stepped out of the ranks and shot off his finger to keep out of the fight.[6]

Some relief from the tension came with news. Over in the Union front the 16th Wisconsin, along with the rest of General Prentiss's Division, was giving way. Union colonel Peabody went down, and Confederate general Gladden, also, as one by one the Union camps were overrun. Defensive stands in the Union camps were turning to a crumbling front, then a panicked rout. The stalwarts of the 16th Wisconsin and other clusters of soldiers resorted to a retreating fight from tree to tree.[7]

Forrest would bolt off and return, trying to get a sense of things; he sent out scouts and demanded news of what was happening to the north and west of his position. He was all but forgotten at Greer's Ford. The reports trickled back from his cavalry and others returning from the line of battle. Each report was greeted with cheers that rolled through the forest as the news was passed along. When a man would call out, "Well, what news from the front?" the reply came back, "Well, boys, we are driving 'em! We have captured all their encampments, everything that they had, and all their provisions and army stores, and everything."[8]

The Confederate battle lines had been deployed in three corps, one behind the other. The Rebels had the momentum, but an indiscriminate grim-reaping scythe was mowing down both gray and blue grass a mile away. In the reserve, Maney's Brigade, Cummings's battalion, and Forrest's and Adams' cavalry waited their part of the second and third cuttings in this human hayfield.

Nathan Bedford Forrest and Wirt Adams were now chafing over their assignment. They had not signed on for this. The waiting was making Forrest's blood boil. The fact that Forrest was the most successful element of the Ft. Donelson defense seemed lost on the generals, most of them West Pointers. He had saved his own command from the surrender at Ft. Donelson. Back there it was insufferable to him when Generals Floyd Pillow, Simon Buckner, and Bushrod Johnson had voted to surrender.[9] Now Johnson had a command here at Shiloh in the Confederate Army of the Mississippi. Forrest had been trying to play the way of the Southern aristocrats since the beginning of the war. He was near the end of his apprenticeship among these types. Of course, this self-made man who had built his fortune as a slaver was distasteful to the more elite social movers and shakers of antebellum society.

Ironically, Forrest's outlook toward Pillow and Buckner was something he shared with U.S. Grant. At Ft. Donelson, Grant had sized up the psychology of the Confederate leadership there, knowing some of them from West Point. General Simon Bolivar Buckner had been his roommate at West Point and had once helped Grant by going security for his unpaid hotel bills in 1854.[10] Buckner was a believer in the "art of war" and was lost in imaginary pictures of Revolutionary heroes graciously bowing and discussing humanitarian options. All of Grant's brooding years in California, and now his successes, had created something of extreme military value. It was a head-down, bulldog, skip the frills and get it done, whip the rebels, nothing but victory attitude. When Buckner seemingly attempted to play on their previous friendship, it was then that Grant countered, "No terms except an unconditional and immediate surrender can be accepted. I propose to move immediately on your works." Buckner replied to this like a parlor dog with his tail between his legs, "I am forced to comply with your ungenerous and ungracious terms."[11]

Forrest had no illusions about war. He viewed it realistically. "War *is* killin'," he retorted to those who questioned his aggressiveness. At Greer's Ford, Forrest was still withering on the vine of hypocrisy among the aristocracy. He was not well-spoken and lettered like most of these genteel generals. His grammar was not always correct. His letters written in his own hand were filled with misspellings. His reputation as a slave-trader always went before him in contact with the upper social strata. The view held was that slave owning was acceptable, even a Christian duty to save Africans from themselves; but to actually run a foul auction house where the stench of "nigger" livestock caused Southern ladies to hold kerchiefs to their noses, well now, that was different. Forrest had tried to enter the upper class. He was a member of the Odd Fellows Lodge in Memphis. He involved himself in city management of the town where his slave mart was successful and prominent. His realistic and forceful attitude in attacking civic problems did not set well with mannerly sorts steeped in the romantic etiquette of the day. Somehow he had attracted Tennessee governor Isham Harris's attention; probably it was because Forrest's slave-sale money was needed in Confederate coffers. Originally Forrest was told by Harris he could outfit his own regiment, with a promise of repayment by the embryonic new secessionist government. To make a comparison, General G.T. Beauregard had enlisted as a private in the Orleans guard in a posturing move for higher rank, but it is doubtful Forrest enlisted as a private in the "Tennessee Mounted Rifles" with the same deliberate ulterior motive as Beauregard. Forrest was more spur-of-the-moment. He would have fought as a true private. Forrest was now a colonel, but his talents lay impotent back in the far forest, away from the sound of the heaviest firing. All he could do was send out couriers and make brief personal forays to find out what was going on and be of service wherever the need arose. His cavalry was unattached to any specific corps, division, or brigade.[12]

More than all of his men, Forrest was a master horseman. He was so at ease in the saddle, he might as well have been part of the horse. As word of the increasing number of falling bodies came back to him, his face took on a warp-spasm. As for Colonel William Wirt Adams and his men, it was also discomfiting to merely sit in their saddles with occasional sorties off to Hamburg to look for a nonexistent enemy force.

When the war broke out, Jefferson Davis offered Wirt Adams the position of postmaster general of the Confederacy. Although he was a lawyer, he could not see himself as a paper pusher. After turning the Confederate president down, he asked permission to raise a regiment for constant movement and reconnaissance of the enemy and was granted that commission.[13] It was almost noon and there was sporadic movement here at Greer's Ford. They had the time to notice the natural sulfurous salt licks that deer and livestock used, giving the creek its name.

It was surely true that at this point in time the Confederate High Command could not see Forrest from the trees at Shiloh. The disuse of these companies was like the proverbial loss of a "horseshoe nail" and most certainly a loss of the Confederacy's best rider. But a critical change was near for this rear-guard contingent of Confederate troops. Countermanding the orders from Confederate High Command, Colonel Maney could take it no longer and put his troops in motion under his own authority. It was about 11:00 A.M. Forrest made one last foray personally, down the road, all the way to Hamburg. Assured there was no Union threat for a final time, he galloped back with his personal bodyguard. He assembled all of his and Adams's subordinate troopers in battle line and rode up and down the line like the Scottish legend William Wallace. This is something of what the men, who were as down to earth and low talking as he, heard:

> "Boys, do you hear that rattle of musketry and the roar of artillery?"
> A yell from Private Samuel Garrett and the rest came back "Yes, Yes!"
> "Do you know what it means? It means that our friends and relatives are falling by the hundreds at the hands of the enemy and we are here guarding a d_ _ n creek! We did not enter the service for such work, and the reputation of this regiment does not justify our commanding officer in leaving us here while we are needed elsewhere! Let's go and help them!"
> Yells all along the line, "Yes! Yes!" and with this reply he moved his command at a gallop into the fight.[14]

It was past midday. Over in a far western sector from Forrest, English rebel Henry Morton Stanley was finally catching up with Shaver's Brigade after a bullet-enforced nap-time. It had hit him in the belt buckle and knocked the wind out of him.[15]

Backing away from Private Stanley's unit, Shaver's Brigade, was the Union 17th Illinois regiment commanded by Lt. Colonel Enos P. Wood. Brigade command had devolved on him in the smoke, and chaos reigned while the adjutant general Abram Ryan tried to find Wood to tell him Colonel Raith was probably dead. Here the mistake of using Captain A.S. Baxter, the chief of the quartermasters, becomes accentuated in records never seen before. The whole right of the Union Army was suffering a supply breakdown. This was because Baxter was gone, and nobody had figured that out. The fog of battle covered a major error by General U.S. Grant. Lt. Col. Wood, not knowing about Raith's fate, was out of ammunition and horseless. The quartermaster corps was breaking down, so Wood consulted with his officers and moved away toward the river about noon himself for the needed supplies. He had a choice of a few rutted, muddy roads used formerly as meandering paths to the farms of the area. They were all sloppy and jammed with traffic, but he found his way to the main landing road, looking for an ordnance train. The breakdown of the Union supply line was more than evident. Where was the head of Grant's quartermaster corps? He was near his return on the *Tigress* at Pittsburg Landing from a virtual errand boy's duty. Union regiments were scavenging for cartridges of the right caliber for their bewildering array of weaponry on the Union right; Hurlbut's Division on the Union left had no real arrangements for supply cartridges. A critical but expedient change regarding the chain of command was about to take place for gaining ammunition for the Union right. The quartermaster of the 6th Division, Lt. Richard P. Derickson, would be called on by the finally returned Captain A.S. Baxter to supply the 1st and 5th Divisions with ammunition.

Lt. Richard P. Derickson had been riding back and forth across the Hornet's Nest as Colonel Prentiss's aide, delivering messages to other officers and bringing forward supplies with the wagons assigned to him as the 6th Division quartermaster on the Eastern Corinth Road.[16] That road was a lifeline as it came directly to the Hornet's Nest sector. At the same time, Derickson was keeping track of what was happening with his own 16th Wisconsin, who were now positioned in reserve behind the pond in Wicker Field.[17] There were only pockets of each regiment of the 6th Division left, most fighting with or in support of other regiments.

Among the remnants of Prentiss's 6th Division was Peabody's 25th Missouri Regiment. Lt. O.P. Newberry of Company I had distinguished himself as a brave man in the midst of battle, but the little Major Powell who had led the reconnoitering party that opened the Battle of Shiloh had been killed. His young son, "the idol of the 25th Missouri Regiment," present on the field, was left an orphan.[18] This remnant of the 25th Missouri of Prentiss's 6th Division, along with other remnants commanded by General Prentiss, was acting at the angle of the "sunken road" sector, in its most defensible position amidst thickets and trees, the reason that the Confederates called it the Hornet's Nest. Colonel Madison Miller, the only remaining brigade commander of the 6th Division, was with Prentiss. Gone was Miller's free black body servant James Milton Turner, in a saving maneuver to protect him. Turner was now rendering some curious liquid supply assistance to U.S. Grant himself.[19]

This "Hornet's Nest" salient seemed providential to men who had lost almost everything but their pride. In the morning after he finally arrived, Grant told Prentiss and W.H.L. Wallace to hold that line at all costs. They had done so admirably. The apex of the battle was fast approaching; the Hornet's Nest was not far away from being overrun.

It was well after noon when Lt. Richard P. Derickson received a message coming from John Ryan at the *Iatan*. There was pandemonium at the landing. On official quartermaster paper, the message read to the exact hour John Ryan had written earlier:

12M

Str "Iatan" April 6th 1862

Lt. Derickson

Sir,

Your presence

is required <u>immediately</u> here
Many requisitions are made
which we cannot fill. & the Corn is being
taken & no one will give vouchers

(In Haste)

John Ryan[20]

This message shows that District Quartermaster A.S. Baxter had not returned to the landing by 12:00 noon, for surely he would have taken charge to handle this raid on his quartermaster stores. For Lt. Richard P. Derickson out on the field at the Hornet's Nest, the middle defense section of the Union Army, the raid on the *Iatan* quartermaster stores was ominous. If the corn was being taken, what else was being taken and who was taking it?[21] Derickson is likely to have presented this message to General Prentiss since the *Iatan* was the 6th Division quartermaster and commissary boat.[22] With the general's assent, he took off to the *Iatan* landing. Almost to his destination, he encountered Captain A.S. Baxter, Grant's quartermaster of the whole army, and line officer "EPW." This likely occurred about 1:00 P.M. Captain Baxter, the district quartermaster, chief of the whole army's supply and transportation corps, was now in the place he should have been all day. But who was this line officer EPW? A search of the *Civil War Soldiers and Sailors System* reveals the only man with those initials, EPW, and rank of line or field officer on the field of Shiloh is Enos P. Wood. He was lieutenant colonel of the 17th Illinois and now, at this juncture by attrition, commander of McClernand's 3rd Brigade. His official report dovetails with the long-hidden document of Lt. Richard P. Derickson, the 6th Division quartermaster.[23] This critical document, preserved by Lt. Derickson, may now be seen after one hundred and fifty years and reveals stunning information. Lt. Colonel Wood needed ammunition badly for his sector of the battlefield, which was on the Union right. Captain Baxter was breathless and exasperated, just returning from a long horse and boat ride to and from General Lew Wallace. He was faced with reconstructing his supply corps. What was about to happen was a substantial shift of supply from the

Hornet's Nest to the Union right. Lt. Derickson had a total of 26 wagons at his disposal, 16 six-horse teams, and 10 four-horse teams. Baxter ordered him to take all teams he had available to serve the interests of the field from whence "EPW" came. It looks as if the 6th Division supply line to the Hornet's Nest under the control of Lt. Richard P. Derickson was sacrificed to go to the aide of Sherman and McClernand's Divisions. Indeed, what backs this up is an incident involving Colonel Reed of the 44th Indiana and General Buell. Reed was scrambling to find ammunition about 3:00 P.M. He had an altercation with General Don Carlos Buell while looking for ammunition. The desperate Colonel Reed, not finding the Union left readily supplied, had to resort to finding supplies himself. Lt. Derickson was using critical supply wagons to supply the Union right at this time.[24] Two hours later the Hornet's Nest would be surrounded and almost all Federals in it would be dead, wounded or captured. It is not unfair to say the General U.S. Grant allowed the Hornet's Nest ammunition trains to be sacrificed in order to advantage or even save the Union right.

12

For Want of a Horse

Lt. Colonel Enos P. Wood of the 17th Illinois had been riding against rebels since early in the war. He was with U.S. Grant at the Ft. Donelson victory and was glad to be serving with him as an infantry officer rather than a surgeon. Back in Missouri he had written to U.S. Grant requesting permission to either seize or burn rebel granaries. He had rounded up a slave who had been running ahead of the 17th's patrols, warning secessionists that the Federals were coming. This is a study in itself of the captivity culture of slaves. They often identified with their owners, knowing no other way of life. To many untraveled slaves, a person out of county was an alien, a foreigner. All the black man probably knew was that these white men were coming to burn down things he had helped grow and that were feeding everybody he knew.[1] Enos P. Wood's willingness to destroy was a harbinger of things to come. He joined his 17th Illinois regiment to General William Tecumseh Sherman's left wing at Shiloh Church April 6, 1862. It was Sherman who would later take the scorched-earth strategy to an art form on his march to the sea.

Lt. Colonel Enos P. Wood, commander of the 17th Illinois regiment, awoke shivering Sunday morning and could not be sure if the popping noises he was hearing in the distance were musket fire or the shooting pains his muscles sent his brain. Even the neigh of horses and braying of mules had a startling effect. Of course he knew what he had, being the town doctor of the tiny upper Mississippi river town of New Boston, Illinois. He had ague.[2]

It came and went, this ague. He hoped the form of ague he was experiencing, with its uncontrollable shaking and fever, was not a deadly variety like typhoid or malaria, rampant in army camps. In medical articles there was use of the new word "germs," after discoveries with microscopes by the Frenchman Louis Pasteur. "Germs," invisible bugs that could spoil milk, were now suspected to cause a host of other forms of havoc. Yet few got the connection on the battlefield in 1862. Doctors did not even routinely wash

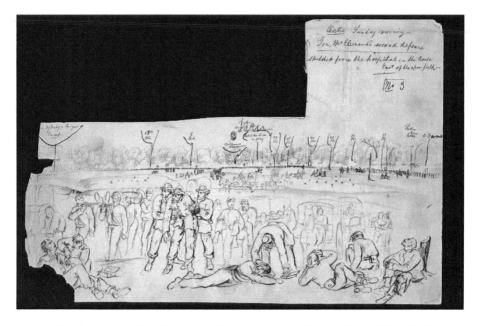

In this sketch artist Henri Lovie caught the moments when Lt. Colonel Enos P. Wood ("EPW") of the 17th Illinois regiment was forced by lack of ammunition supply to personally move off toward the river at about noon (Becker Collection, Boston College; thanks to Prof. Judith Bookbinder).

their hands going from patient to patient at the time. By the end of the day at Shiloh, transmission of deadly germs would figure in thousands of medical procedures, and death would result in many cases from wounds that should not have been fatal. The death count at Shiloh was much higher than recorded because many victims expired far away from Shiloh as a result of infection. Just common sense told a layman rain and ground water drunk from streams and wells that ran through privies and polluted fields on this plateau would make a man sick. Details weren't necessary; the plague of the ague was common enough in towns along a river where thick clouds of mosquitoes and flies that people thought were only pesky actually carried diseases like malaria.

Here at this military city along one of the biggest rivers in the country, Camp Shiloh was full of sickness. The sick list was 15 percent of the army at Pittsburg Landing, in addition to the sutlers, black servants, women and other visitors. There were at least 6,250 men reporting sick plus 203 officers in the Federal forces. Enos P. Wood was in the 3rd Brigade of McClernand's 1st Division, out of which 273 soldiers and eight officers reported sick. Wood was sick, but doctors will work sick. Enos P. Wood had chosen not to enter the army as a surgeon, but he was sticking with that role with field officer rank of lieutenant colonel. He would work and fight sick until he dropped.[3]

Lt. Colonel Enos P. Wood was second in command of the 17th regiment to Colonel L.F. Ross, who was also 3rd Brigade commander of General McClernand's 1st Division, but Ross was away because of the death of his wife.[4] When the battle reached McClernand's sector, Colonel Rearden of the 29th Illinois was temporarily commanding the brigade, but he was among the very sick and could hardly rise. Lt. Colonel Enos P. Wood, who may have preferred to go by his initials E.P.W. rather than be called Enos, rose in his wall tent and began to dress despite his weakness. Getting a little more clear-headed, Wood realized the shots he had heard were not fevered imagination in his head, for the sound of the long roll beat, announcing impending battle, was reverberating across camps nearby. Adrenaline surged, overcoming his weakness, and he purposefully readied his accoutrements and sword to order his men into battle as field officer. Just then, brigade adjutant general Lt. Abram Ryan galloped into the camp of the 17th Illinois and informed Wood that Colonel Rearden was down and Colonel Raith of the 43rd Illinois was now brigade commander by seniority and would command the brigade of three regiments in the impending clash.[5] The communication may have been accompanied by a scribbled authorization on a piece of lined foolscap, such as most officers typically carried in their valises. It would have contained an authorized signing of the officers involved. Lt. Colonel Enos P. Wood preferred to use his initials EPW as his authorization in such cases. He was the only one with those exact initials at the Battle of Shiloh.[6]

German-born Colonel Raith, through Lt. Ryan, instructed Wood to move the 17th regiment as right wing of McClernand's 3rd Brigade into line of battle onto the left wing of Sherman's Division at Shiloh Church. McClernand's whole 3rd Brigade had to move south in an extended line west to east through a deep ravine that disrupted continuity. Colonel Raith directed from the left of the brigade. For the 17th Illinois the movement was logical because the 17th Illinois camps were yards behind General Sherman's headquarters tent on a knoll behind Shiloh Church.[7] Next to Shiloh Church, the 17th regiment was partly on the ridge of Shiloh Church and partly in a big broken ravine with several branches; really it was many smaller ravines within the larger one. This meant disaster for the 3rd Brigade as the oncoming rush of Confederates hit their front in pockets of men disconnected from their fellows. Enos P. Wood's command had thus devolved to the third man in seniority, German-born Colonel Julius Raith. The attrition rate was accelerating, and Lt. Colonel Wood was next in line of succession.

Wood had his horse brought round by the orderly. His head was swim-

ming with fever as he brought his regiment in column and marched it to a
position only yards south and east of the log meeting house called Shiloh.
The left of his regiment, along with the rest of the brigade, had to form down
through a wide ravine. Already in play was a section of some Union battery
on a hill overlooking the far field. Wood became rigid in his saddle, looking
across Rhea field to the opposite hill. Skirmishers were popping away in the
field at something blurry gray and moving. It was heavy columns of men in
gray and butternut uniforms, their officers forming regiments in long lines
and deploying them. The gleam of bayonets flashed across the ranks, strangely
thrilling Wood and each man seeing the advancing columns of the enemy.
That excitement continued to overcome his fever flashes.[8] Many of the officers
on both sides were Freemasons in civilian life, like himself. This was certainly
an extraordinary situation, but from that distance, he could not ascertain any
fellow Mason. It made it easier, for he had not truly contemplated what it
would be like to kill a brother in the secret society.[9]

    Dr. Enos P. Wood had been of character strong enough to be elected
captain of the Mercer County (Illinois) Militia, and then had ascended to
lieutenant colonel of the 17th Illinois when it was mustered. He was not
given to putting on airs or a show of ambition for fame and glory that was
another epidemic plague of this army here at Camp Shiloh. Early on he
chose to heal men, and now this change ... to lead a sanguinary effort that
could be construed as contrary to the Hippocratic Oath of "First, do no
harm." Enos P. Wood was not the only physician willing to exchange scalpel
for sword. On both sides there were medical men who chose to play this
role. He had reasoned like so many others that the rebellion would be over
shortly anyway. Better to make this conflict short by quick amputation than
nurse the festering wound of traitorous Confederate gangrene. The session-
ists would cave in if shown a strong hand. They already had at Ft. Henry, Ft.
Donelson, Clarksville and Nashville. He would show his strong hand this
morning.[10]

    General Sherman was setting the example. The enemy approached and
scattered, firing peppered the ridgelines from sharpshooters on both sides,
and men were dropping like occasional acorns in autumn. Sherman appeared
and reappeared, galloping back and forth to discover what he could. They
faced the oncoming mass. The general of the 5th Division looked steady, griz-
zled and determined, though he had a bandage wrapped around one hand.
Sherman hastily rode over to check Taylor's battery that was blasting deadly
grape and canister to good effect right on the road in front of Shiloh Meeting
House. Then a ball hit Sherman's horse and both went down. The general
arose as if out of a haystack, brushing his already begrimed uniform and

calling to an aide for another mount, inspiring to every soldier who witnessed it. He would lose a few horses this way.[11]

The fire from the Union battery of Waterhouse was hot, about two hundred yards to the left of where E.P.W. sat in his saddle, observing. The 3rd Brigade was effective enough for a time; the enemy had been giving way some. The 3rd Brigade was facing south behind some Ohio regiment in front. Then rebels who had been masked by trees began appearing to the east. There was time to avoid being flanked, so Colonel Raith ordered a change obliquely to the right; the whole brigade was to exercise the maneuver they had drilled often. The extreme right was the pivot point, acting like the hinge of a gate. The regiment shuffled back diagonally to be clear of the ravine where most of the regiment was resting. About two thousand men along the long line of McClernands 3rd brigade were coordinated by its dozens of company captains.[12]

Wood felt a swoon of fever and with the loss of concentration dismounted his horse about this time to gain a better sense of himself. Whether it was the blasts of artillery unsettling his horse, or something as simple as a loose horseshoe, the lieutenant colonel lost control of the reins. He watched the animal dash away. He was now sick in a different way. He could not bolster his troops the way Sherman did by example when he lost his horse. There was no other horse available to remount. It was the kind of mishap that could misconstrue the true character of an officer. Lose a horse and find a remount in a fierce fight and it might make you famous; lose a horse and be forced to command on foot, and men don't perceive you as a field officer anymore, but instead a line officer of lesser authority. Field officers were supposed to command on horseback. He saw no other available. Now it might inhibit later promotion due to lack of visibility and someone to witness the valor. These were the vagaries of perceived merit in the midst of battle ... all for the want of a horse. There was no time to think of that now.

Hundreds of Confederates broke through the timber in large numbers. They charged the Waterhouse battery like wild creatures with the shriek of banshees. They took possession of the artillery pieces, killing and wounding cannoneers, some jumping up and down on the cannon pieces in delirious jubilation, appearing and disappearing amidst the smoke drifting through the trees. One planted a rebel flag. A private of the 17th was hit by a Minié ball and fell, and as he did, an officer near Wood grabbed the boy's weapon and aimed. The rifled projectile, engineered for just such accuracy, found its mark, though two hundred yards away. The flag disappeared along with the man under the pall of smoke. It rose again in the hands of another determined patriot of the South, but that marksmanship was so impressive Wood determined to mention it in his report.

Frozen in the grim grandeur of these events and with his body also struggling with illness, Enos P. Wood was not completely cognizant that the regiments on his left and right were breaking apart, and men were scattering to the rear. He was able to summon enough strength to concentrate on directing the tenacity of his own regiment. Soon they were left isolated in front with only the cannon of Taylor's battery to the right, sitting on the section of Corinth road. It was a stone's throw from the log church, with few men left to face the oncoming throngs.[13]

The exasperated artillery commander of Taylor's battery had been holding the ground and did not understand why the regiments close by had melted away behind him. He was forced to limber up and fly, caissons rattling north up and off the ridge on the Corinth-Pittsburgh Road back past the crossroads of the Hamburg-Purdy and Pittsburg Landing. About the same time Lt. Abram rode up, belatedly delivering to Wood the order General McClernand had communicated to the rest of the regiments in the brigade. The 17th was to retreat to the road that passed in front of the field used for reviewing, with what was remaining of 400 men of the regiment. Enos P. Wood's 17th regiment backed away about sixty to a hundred yards to the crossroads. There they made a stand. They inflicted some casualties on the rebels. Behind them Schwartz's battery was blasting away. Captain Schwartz felt the situation deteriorate despite Lt. Col. Wood's attempt to reverse the situation with a charge.[14]

It was about 10:00 A.M. and unbeknownst to the army in general, Captain A.S. Baxter, chief of supply, was headed away from the battlefield back down to Crump's Landing with a message for General Lew Wallace to "come up." His absence would seriously be felt in this sector. For now there was enough ammunition, but soon there would not be. The 17th Illinois camp was only a few yards away, but the Confederates were exploding through it. Sherman's headquarters tent was in their possession, too.

A stand was made at the crossroads located at this place. It was where the main Corinth road that ran past Shiloh Church and the Hamburg-Purdy road intersected. Along with a bold move by artillery Captain Swartz, who left his guns in play with others, Colonel Raith and Lt. Colonel Wood made an advance. It was enough to stay the Confederates for a time. Some attribute the stand here as so critical that it prevented the rebel advance from a stampeding takeover of the right sector of the Union Army, perhaps even preventing total defeat the first day of the battle. Shortly Colonel Raith was wounded severely. He refused to have his men taken out of service by helping him, demanding that they leave him behind. There in the smoke and confusion, Lt. Colonel Wood became the brigade commander, but did not know it yet. Until this became apparent, he was told to fall back again by McClernand.

Schwartz's battery limbered up and flew further back down the road along a field containing an oak tree-lined pond. No cannon were lost, but the man leading the 3rd Brigade was lost, Julius Raith. He lay wounded for two days on the field of battle only to die after an amputation.[15]

Shaver's Brigade was there, helping push Enos P. Wood and his men back; but Henry Morton Stanley had been hit in his belt buckle by a spent ball somewhere in all of this. With the wind knocked out of him, he dragged himself exhausted to the cover of a tree and rested. Awaking, he took nourishment from his own rations; others had consumed theirs on the march from Corinth. After a much needed rest, but with his momentum gone, he stumbled. As he went he examined the carnage, yard by yard, as he kept going north to find his regiment.[16]

The loss of the crossroads sealed the road of access that the two General Wallaces had prepared for reinforcement from Stoney Lonesome. While Wallace still awaited his orders to move, he readied his division to march that way. Wallace could not know how badly the Union was being beaten by 10 A.M., and he would be given information to the contrary, that the enemy was being beaten back. From General Lew Wallace's standpoint six miles away, the sound of the firing was all along the plateau in one continuous roar. Wallace could not pinpoint anything in the normal way an army officer would, to listen for the sound of the most firing.

Somewhere in the smoke, Colonel Julius Raith recognized the seriousness of his wound: no bone support in his thigh, which was shattered, guaranteeing amputation and making him useless to anyone on the field. His German constitution held up, hands gripping the earth as spent lead pattered around him, and bullets and shrapnel buried themselves into the tree above his head. Some trees on the battlefield were being transformed to metal. Rebels began to run past him, some hollering with accents of various sorts, even Germans as Confederate attackers from Louisiana and Alabama had German American immigrants and settlements.[17] Back, back away fell the Federal line. On came the Confederate juggernaut.

Sherman and McClernand formed several defensive lines that day, but a major problem is revealed in several official reports. Lt. Colonel Enos P. Wood, adjutant general Abram Ryan, Colonel Adolph Engleman of the 43rd Illinois, Colonel Marsh of the 20th Illinois, and others attest to the failure of the supply line. The whole 3rd brigade was nearly out of ammunition. E.P.W. was horseless and sick, but still kept fighting. McClernand's and Sherman's Divisions fell back steadily, sustaining massive casualties along the way. No comfort was drawn that masses on the Confederate side were also falling. As Confederate Henry Morton Stanley put it: "They stood obstinately ... and not all the honors of the day were to be with us."[18] The remains of regiments fought desperately, and the 17th Illinois finally found pause in a field owned by Mr. Jones. Here Lt. Col. Wood consulted with his officers and then moved off toward the river for ammunition. Having been horseless for much of the engagement, he may have taken a horse from the diminished Taylor's battery. However, in a remarkable sketch by Henri Lovie that caught the action in Jones Field about this time, teamsters are seen heading toward the Pittsburg Landing road. Henri Lovie may have actually sketched Lt. Colonel Wood moving off toward the river in one of these. It was about noon.

In his quest along the way, a man on horseback emerged from the confusion of troops choking the road. He was wearing quartermaster insignia on his uniform and looked bewildered and angry. Captain A.S. Baxter had just returned from delivering the message to General Lew Wallace. Lt. Colonel E.P.W. waved him down, and put in his request about his extreme need for ammunition.

A breathless Captain Baxter mistook the dismounted Enos P. Wood for a line officer, rather than a field officer. Even in the midst of the fog of war, Baxter possessed writing materials and a pen. He drew from his saddlebag a valise. Along this road the quartermaster of the 6th Division was coming. He had gone to check on the status of things aboard the *Iatan* after the frantic note from John Ryan that the corn was being taken. It was Lt. Richard P. Derickson of the 16th Wisconsin, Baxter's key transportation corps officer at the moment. Baxter dismounted. Placing the little desk on a wagon surface, Baxter withdrew a briefcase that contained a smooth portable mahogany laptop writing surface. He unsnapped the cover, reached in and pulled some writing materials from the built-in accordion file. He unscrewed the small inkwell that sat in a designed niche. Then he slid back the cover of a compartment in the clever little desk. He dipped pen into an ink reservoir and dashed off a hurried note authorizing Derickson to pick up ammunition. He was to immediately go to the ordnance vessel down at the landing to the steamer *Rocket*:

> Lt. Derickson
>
> Send all teams available to Steamer Rocket to haul ammunition to the field immediately.
>
> By order of
Capt. A.S Baxter — aqm
E P.W line officer
>
> Pittsburgh April 6[19]

To look at that order today is a time-traveling experience as to what was happening on the battlefield of Shiloh on April 6, 1862. As compelling as its brief message is about the need for ammunition, the casual observer would not realize more importantly it holds the only existing, visible, recorded key to understanding the character of the transmission of General U.S. Grant's order to General Lew Wallace. District Quartermaster A.S. Baxter illustrates his form of writing and protocol after one hundred and fifty years, right on the battlefield. This is most interesting, because Baxter did not participate in the later scapegoating of Lew Wallace that happened a year later. Reasonable if not definite conclusions can be drawn from it that may help General Lew Wallace stop rolling over in his grave about the slanders that affected him all his life.

13

No Arrangements for Supply

The Confederate Army had concentrated much of its force against the Union left until about 9:00 A.M. when it overran the camps of Prentiss's 6th Division. It was the impression of the Confederate High Command that the Union Army was lined up north to south, so they had attacked in strength with the idea of flanking what they had considered was the left wing of the Federals and accomplish the goal of turning them away from Pittsburg Landing. One geographical feature that affected their plan was Locust Creek ravine, which hindered them from easily spreading out all the way to the Savannah-Hamburg road. They also had not realized the utmost left of the Union was the brigade of Colonel David Stuart, which was separated from Sherman's 5th Division. The main body of Confederate troops was dense for a time in thick numbers over a narrower field of operations; however, initial rebel success brought change to the density of the Confederate corps on their right. Having enveloped the 6th Divison camps, the breadth of Confederate masses in this sector had the personal attention of General Albert Sidney Johnston. Thinking he had turned the Federal left completely, he diverted most of the Confederate brigades away to the northwest of Prentiss's camps. He unknowingly damaged his battle plan in doing so. Now there were fewer Confederate troops to push the Federals back along the river corridor, and that single brigade of Colonel Stuart's men put up a remarkable fight, inhibiting the original Confederate strategy intended to turn the Federals away from Pittsburg Landing and drive them into the swamps beyond Owl Creek, where they would be forced to surrender.[1]

Those Confederate brigades that went to the northwest spread out into more meadowed territory, and then into large areas of swampy morass. It disheveled most of the Confederate army and resulted in a mixing up of commands. Few units could recognize organizations they had marched with to Shiloh. Lining the Confederate corps up one behind the other revealed the

In the original on scene drawing "Woods on Fire" by Henri Lovie, the 44th Indiana was commanded by Colonel Hugh B. Reed. Not only were injured men dying in the flames, no arrangements had been made for supply of ammunition. Because Chief Quartermaster A.S. Baxter was sent to Lew Wallace, it broke down the efficiency of the supply corps. Reed, like Lt. Col. Enos P. Wood, had to seek ammunition personally (Becker Collection, Boston College; thanks to Prof. Judith Bookbinder).

plan's flaws. Organization disintegrated because of the terrain. The Waterloo strategy of line formation that had been implemented was beginning to take shape as déjà vu for the Confederates. Time was consumed closing gaps in their lines, and worse, disastrous friendly fire incidents were in the offing; yet the spirit of the Confederate press continued relentlessly.

As the 6th Division of General Benjamin Prentiss broke up and retreated in confusion, he and remnants of his division sought a place to make a stand. Fortunately for him, the reserve 4th Division of General Stephen Hurlbut was coming to his aide. They first formed an angle at the skirts of Sarah Bell's cotton field. As the Sixth Division men retreated pall mall, many broke through Hurbut's lines in an unsettling affect until General Prentiss came up and in battle protocol asked permission to pass by and through this angle.[2]

It was granted; then, with a relatively small number of men remaining of his division, he found a thicketed curve on a wagon road where they would make a stand. Demoralized and clamoring with the loss of his camps, he kept urging what men remained with him to rally and retake them. Thoughts of warnings by Colonel Peabody must have entered his mind in the pandemonium for survival; however, in Prentiss's official report, his pride did not allow him to state anything significant about his 1st Brigade commmander Everett Peabody's warnings, only that he commanded the 1st Brigade and that he, Prentiss, had ordered advance to the front. Conversely he heaped credit on Colonel David Moore, who had actually opposed Colonel Peabody's ideas of a Confederate attack in mass.[3]

General Prentiss's staff quartermaster Lt. Derickson facilitated supply as best he could, but there were only remnants of the division taking hold in this place, and they were spread out all along the little-used wagon road, mixed with regiments of Hurlbut and the 2nd Division commanded by General W.H.L. Wallace. This defensive line comprised what became known as the "Sunken Road," "Hornet's Nest" and "Peach Orchard" defense. Lt. Richard P. Derickson inexorably looked for scattered parties of his own 16th Regiment. Some began forming as a decimated reserve behind the 44th Indiana later in Wicker Field behind what would become known as the "Bloody Pond." By the next morning, Lt. Derickson stated, "We only found 30 of our own company."[4]

It is to the credit of the men of the 6th Division that they held out as long as they did. From about the time of the first firing at 4:55 A.M. in Woods and Fraley Field, until the final stands at their camps about 9:00 A.M., they resisted a larger force stubbornly, inflicting and receiving heavy losses. Prentiss himself gives an exact time in which he rallied a portion of his division at the angle as "9:05." This must have been a precise clock notation made by his adjutant general Henry Binmore, who escaped the later encirclement of the "Hornet's Nest" with his memos. All through this period of more than four hours, the Union high command of General U.S. Grant with all of its command staff officers, including District Quartermaster Captain Baxter, were absent and of no value to anyone on the field.[5]

Hurlbut's and W.H.L. Wallace's Divisions, which had been sitting in reserve camp positions at Pittsburg Landing, had moved forward to assist Prentiss just before 9:00 A.M. Williams's and Lauman's Brigades of Hurlbut's 4th Division first came to the assistance of the 6th Division, almost at a right angle on the west and south sides of Sarah Bell's field. It was behind Sarah Bell's property line that the remnants of Prentiss's troops found a place to muster and face the Confederates. The old trace of a road arced along a fence-line and then continued in a northwesterly path along field property owned by the Duncan family.[6]

Shortly after the time Hurlbut's Division lined up along the edges of the cotton field, there began a Confederate artillery barrage trying to "shell them out." Colonel Nelson G. Williams of Hurlbut's 1st Brigade was disabled by a cannon shot that killed his horse and threw him to the ground. He was replaced by Colonel Isaac Pugh. Here supply became a critical issue in the absence of Captain Baxter, the chief quartermaster. With growing concern of the general attack all along the Union lines, Colonel John Logan of the 32nd Illinois looked ahead to what they were facing. In his official report, he states a crisis existed. That crisis has never been examined in depth. Obvious apprehension happens when a commander becomes a casualty, but there was more to it than that. Logan went to Colonel Isaac Pugh, the wizened commander of the 41st Illinois with his long white beard, who had taken

Colonel Isaac C. Pugh definitively referred to the chief quartermaster's absence during Sarah Bell's cotton field defense. Col. John B. Logan of the 32nd Illinois asked him what arrangements had been made for supply of cartridges. He replied that he didn't know of any (author's collection).

Colonel Williams's place. Colonel Logan states the problem: "At this place I went to the colonel (Pugh) and inquired what arrangements there were to supply us with cartridges. His reply was ... none that he knew of."[7]

"None that he knew of." There were no arrangements for ammunition! The person who made arrangements for ammunition was District Quartermaster Captain A.S. Baxter. He was not on the field because he was with General Grant, who was not there yet. Hurlbut's Division could sustain with the ammuniton they had for a period of time, but for how long was nebulous with no arrangements for resupply of cartridges. This made standard practices gauged on firing drills in Hardee's *Light Infantry Tactics* fairly useless to the Union men. This handbook, authored by one of the Confederate corps commanders, was used on both sides. Standard practice did not work that well for infantry at Shiloh. Each man had a standard issue of 40 rounds in his cartridge box. Going by the book, an excellent infantry musketryman could fire three rounds per minute. That means his cartridge box would be empty in just over 13 minutes if an ideally efficient situation existed. At Shiloh in general, and at this place specifically where Colonel Logan asked Colonel Pugh about arrangements for cartridges, the firing was much more erratic. The lines of each column did not consistently act in the fire, fall back, reload/ next line fire, fall back, reload tactic. Lying on the ground or hiding behind trees, they were under orders to conserve ammuniton.[8] To gauge how ammunition might be consumed in a model situation, consider the following. If the ammunition wagons carried cartridge packets of 40 rounds per man to resupply a soldier's box, the weight of each bullet or ball was about an ounce or more; being conservative, that made 40 ounces per man (two and a half pounds). When multiplied by a conservatively numbered 400-man regiment, that meant 1000 pounds of lead per regiment. Based on the treatise by Harvey Riley, Superintendent of the Government Corral, Washington, D.C, a humanely, fully loaded ammunition wagon pulled by six mules might carry 6000 pounds of cartridges. Ideally, one wagon would be enough to replenish a 400-man regiment six times.[9] A single wagon thus might keep a regiment supplied for about an hour or more. Conservation of fire would help, but what then? The quartermaster would have to return to the quartermaster boats clustered at the landings and the steamer *Rocket* for more ammunition. Not factored into this were the many different calibers of weapons in use. The lack of uniform weaponry caused great problems at Shiloh and was exacerbated by the absence of Captain Algernon Sydney Baxter. He was responsible for the accounting of where certain calibers of cartridge could be found. It is obvious Baxter was at the core of the army's needs, but he was nowhere on the field because Grant was not on the field. When Grant finally arrived on transport *Tigress* with his staff including Baxter on board, incredibly Baxter was sent away again for hours more.

Shortly because of steady pressure from the rebels, the 4th Division of General Hurlbut determined a withdrawal should be made back across the cotton field to the peach orchard. Colonel John Logan of the 32nd Illinois, who had asked about provision for cartridges, brought his men into line on the north side. When he had asked about provision made for cartridges, Logan recalls, Colonel Pugh asked him in return "if I was not supplied. I told him yes, we had 40 rounds to the man, but I expected to use more if the battle continued. Colonel Pugh said that was enough." The unsatisfactory situation caused Logan to practice shrewd economy of firing, having his men lie flat on the ground and fire only when ordered.[10]

For Colonel Logan to have made such an inquiry of Brigade Commander Pugh about "what arrangements there were to supply us with cartridges," he must have previouly had the inquiry conveyed from his own regimental quartermaster, Lt. Charles Morton. The general question about what to do about supplies must have existed among all the quartermasters of all the regiments. The supply teams were likely corraling in Wicker Field behind the peach orchard defense screened by forest. That field had an excellent transportation line along the Hamburg-Savannah road back to the landings where the central ammo depot at the steamer *Rocket* lay. However, all these quartermasters had been instructed to follow exact procedures for procuring everything, especially ammunition. As a colonel in Sherman's Division commented, the quartermasters were under restrictions not to answer requisitions outside of immediate command, and "Baxter will only answer the requisitions of the Division Quartermasters."[11]

According to the statement of Col. Pugh, then, all of the following troops would have had no true arrangements for ammunition resupply. On the south side of the cotton field/peach orchard, the regiments of William's 1st Brigade lined up east to west: 41st Illinois, 28th Illinois, 32nd Illinois and 3rd Iowa. Likewise in the same situation with no arrangements for resupply of cartridges was Lauman's Brigade. They were along the western edge of the field, and lining up south to north comprised the 17th Kentucky, the 25th Kentucky, the 44th Indiana and the 31st Indiana. All these regiments suffered because of the absence of Chief Quartermaster A.S. Baxter. Had it not been for situational issues, the problem would have been more manifest in the reports of these regiments, as it was especially in the 32nd Illinois. For example, Col. Armory Johnson of the 28th Illinois states the ammunition issue was not incumbent along the edges of the peach orchard, an area he "maintained for some time with little loss or firing."[12] The supply arrangement crisis of Colonel Logan's 32nd Illinois and others of Hurlbut's 4th Division after having moved east of the peach orchard is stated pathetically as the battle progressed: "In a few minutes I was notified we were getting out of cartridges. I rode along the line and the report was, 'We are out of cartridges.' I then ordered my command to fix bayonets.... I therefore, as the only means left to prevent our falling into the enemy's hands, gave orders to fall back...." In a spirit of contrite humility over a supply situation he was not responsible for, Colonel Logan took the blame himself, saying: "I am aware that I subject myself to the criticism of military men by changing my position without an order from a superior officer, knowing it to be the duty of every officer to remain with his command where he is put until ordered from there by the proper officer — believing as I did, for good reasons, that our situation had been overlooked or our brigade commander had fallen having received no order during the whole contest."[13]

So confused as to the cause of being later forced to retire, a problem directly related to the ammunition supply, Captain Alfred C. Campbell of the 32nd Illinois, turning in his report to General Hurlbut, stated with bewilderment: "I fear a mistake has been made somewhere, and that you have not been fully informed."[14]

Colonel Isaac Pugh of the 41st Illinois, whose comments about the lack of arrangements for ammunition were recorded by subordinate Colonel John Logan, strangely does not mention the bad situation in his report. However, his major does: John Warner in the 41st Illinois states that near 11:30, after two and a half hours, that the ammuniton supply became critical: "Our men continued with almost superhuman effort to return fire until the last cartridge became exhausted." General Hurlbut then ordered their withdrawal, and they were not replenished until after they had retired all the way back to the landing and near dark were posted behind the siege guns.[15]

The conservation and efficiency that these regiments maintained under heavy fire are reflected in the report of Col. Charles Cruft of the 31st Indiana. He is specific as to the expediture of cartridges, saying: "After the expediture of some 30 rounds the enemy was repulsed ... a second attack was shortly made with increased fury. The line stood unbroken until the last cartridge again repulsed the enemy." There was enough supply close at hand for the regiment to be replenished two or three times more, but Col. Cruft states that the regiment fired "an average of 100 rounds to the man" during this action. Certainly this was enough to wreak havoc on the Confederates, but a relatively small amount of ammunition was expended. This was probably due to the favorable position of defense at the Hornest's Nest sector until about 2:30. The regiment then moved to the left and fought when ammunition became a concern again of a number of regiments including the 44th Indiana.[16]

Interestingly, there is battlefield sketch that captured the approximate time these supply problems first began to manifest themselves. Due to the artillery barrage at the edges of the cotton field defense, the woods had caught fire, trapping many wounded men, burning them to death. Artist Henri Lovie was on the scene and sketched the defense and horror screened by smoke. On the reverse side of his drawing, he significantly noted that the regiment he captured on the page was the 44th Indiana commanded by Colonel Hugh B. Reed. Reed's presence in this sketch gives some indication of when U.S. Grant and his staff finally arrived at the landing because an order was issued to release Colonel Reed from being under arrest when Grant arrived.[17] Since Reed is present in Henri Lovie's sketch at the location where his regiment had come to the assistance of General Prentiss along with other members of Hurlbut's Division, the artist's sketch was made after the time Grant arrived, which was after the breakup of Prentiss's 6th Division. This is the same sector where Colonel Pugh stated he knew of no arrangements for ammunition. The 44th did, in fact, run out of ammunition in course of time. So evident was the lack of a supply line arrangement, Colonel Reed later had to seek the supply himself.[18] Most regimental battlefield markers of the 6th Divison show the breakup as happening about 9:00 A.M. Colonel Reed's after-battle report does not speak of his being under arrest, but the wording of his report allows for that fact. Instead of stating that he as Commander of the 44th Indiana ordered his men into line, as many others begin their reports, Reed merely states, "We left our encampment about 8 o'clock Sunday morning." It is therefore likely Reed used the collective term "we" in his report shrewdly. He joined his men after they had gone into line of battle under the direction of Colonel Reed's second-in-command in the 44th Indiana, Colonel William C. Williams.[19] The battlefield sketch is suggestive of this.

This area at the Peach Orchard for the Union reveals the ball of confusion and uncertainty that was increased by Captain Baxter's absence. Thousands of Union lives were in the balance. Baxter was certainly badly needed to make arrangements for cartridges, but he would only be at Pittsburg Landing for a brief time. In what vies for one of the biggest blunders of Grant's command at Shiloh, though it may have been actuated by Grant's adjutant general John A. Rawlins, Captain A.S. Baxter was chosen almost immediately to return to Crump's Landing. The army had waited all morning for his arrival with Grant; now this supply head would be gone again for hours. Why was Captain A.S. Baxter, of all people, the one chosen for what amounted to a mere errand?

Captain A.S. Baxter was really a general, the quartermaster general for the whole Union army of the West Tennessee. It becomes increasingly amazing that Baxter was sent to General Lew Wallace. With the brigade and regimental quartermasters in confusion as to where to go and how to get their requisitions filled for cartridges, what were the corps members under their own oversight to do? Ammunition would not be granted in large quantity to just any sergeant, corporal or teamster in an ordnance train. Pandemonium could result. In fact, in one of Lt. Derickson's documents, this situation is illustrated. Hundreds of supply and transportation corpsmen were without leadership. The confusion of battle has been the typical explanation for the roads choked with wagons, but that was not the only explanation for the quartermaster corps. With the head of the quartermaster corps gone, there was no plan for resupply. Some regimental commanders ended up having to expedite quartermasters' responsibilites. This would not normally have been needed to get the supplies. One of these regimental commanders was Colonel Enos P. Wood of the 17th Illinois; another was Colonel Hugh B. Reed of the 44th Indiana.[20]

Colonel Hugh B. Reed had a remarkable encounter with General Don Carlos Buell in this regard. This regimental commander of the 44th Indiana had gone to seek the whereabouts of critical ammunition after several hours of valiant effort to stem the Confederate tide. Seeing General Buell directing a wagon train, he rode up to him and "inquired if he were able to direct me to where I could find ammunition." Buell gave Reed a reply that revealed the total lack of understanding as to how hard the fighting had been for Reed and the lack of supplies. "No sir," General Buell replied, "nor do I believe you want ammunition, sir." Reed was incredulous at the reply. He asked the General his name and got the reply: "It makes no difference, sir, but I am General Buell." Apparently he gave the general enough of a disgusted look as he whirled his horse around to continue his search that it angered the general further. Buell had been riding about, waiting for his command to arrive with nothing to do but exhort the men who had fled to the landing as "cowards." He apparently lumped Colonel Reed in with the stragglers. Buell rode after Reed with an apparent intention of placing him under arrest. Buell demanded his name, but was greeted with a barrage of insults by Reed, who was right-eously indignant after the hours he had spent with valiant fighters, dead and dying soldiers, some of whom he had heard scream in the flames as they lay wounded.[21]

This encounter occurred probably around 2:30 in the afternoon. The 44th ran out of ammunition on the far left Union flank near the pond about that time and were relieved temporarily by a reconstituted segment of the 16th Wisconsin regiment. The Derickson documents point to a logistical sup-ply shift that had occurred shortly before this hour. Colonel Enos P. Wood, on the far right of the Union defensive line, "moved off to near the river" about noon to obtain ammunition. He encountered the recently returned Captain A.S. Baxter probably near 1:00 P.M. and explained the crucial need for ammunition on the Union right. Captain Baxter, trying to regain control after his absence, then acted in an altered chain of command and ordered Lt. Richard P. Derickson, who was 6th Divison's General Prentiss staff quarter-master, to divert all teams available to go to the steamer *Rocket*, obtain ammu-nition, and deliver it to the field immediately.

The field Baxter was referring to was not the area that Derickson had just come from in the performance of his duty with General Prentiss and the Hornet's Nest sector. It was to take ammunition to line officer EPW's field of operation. Among all the regiments that served at Shiloh, there is only one officer who matches those initials, Lt. Colonel Enos P. Wood. As regimental commander of the 17th Illinois, he was not aware that as he asked for this ammunition he had just ascended to third brigade command of McClernand's Division. Reflecting on the dovetailing of these incidences, Colonel Reed's encounter with General Buell illustrates the Hornet's Nest was undersupplied with ammunition after this order was delivered. Hurlbut had no arrangements, so certainly Prentiss would have no arrangements, for his quartermaster had been redirected away for the Hornet's Nest.

General Grant had to have involvement in this order of District Quartermaster Baxter to Lt. Richard Derickson since it altered command structure, but it may have been at Grant's advisement in general terms. Since Baxter had finally returned, Grant now had his services again, though it was way late. There was indeed critical need on the Union right; official records of the Battle of Shiloh report shortages of ammunition and supply on the right especially between 11:30 and around 2:00. The chief of supply and transportation had been away for hours, and his absence had a telling adverse affect. After he returned to Pittsburg Landing from Lew Wallace, Baxter was playing catch-up with his dismembered corps. The best assessment of the supply situation is in the reply Colonel Tuttle gave to General Buell when he asked Tuttle what was the battle plan: "By God, sir, I don't know."[22]

An examination of the Shiloh Church sector is neccessary to understand what was happening with the ammunition supply throughout the other divisions to the right of the army.

14

Cutting Off the Head of the Supply and Transportation Corps

I AM TRANSPORTATION ... the Spearhead of Logistics ... I am movement by air, land, sea and rail. My humble beginnings hail from the Quartermaster Corps. I was there from the hills to the shores. Long before the Navy, my vessels sailed rivers and oceans; I supported a fledgling Continental Army as it moved across the Delaware. I moved forward, steadfast and true because I AM TRANSPORTATION! In the Civil War I moved against my brother, ever wondering who would live and who would die. I moved the first soldiers at Bull Run.... I carried men, munitions and equipment ... **to Shiloh**.... I remember, for the weight of battle I always bear—because I AM TRANSPORTATION!

—Excerpt from THE ARMY TRANSPORTATION CORPS CREED

The accounts of how masterful General U.S. Grant was when he debarked upon his arrival at Pittsburg Landing vary. Some agree that Grant needed assistance getting into the saddle because of his ankle injury. There is no question that there was a growing crowd of thousands beneath the bluff comprised of demoralized men and three undeployed regiments that were assigned to Prentiss's Division. Grant had to make his way through this assembly, which would go against the idea that Grant bounded up the hill. The observation involving the ankle injury and his needing help in mounting probably happened, but Grant would have been anxious to find out what the battle situation was, and once saddled, would have been off as quickly as the crowding at the landing allowed. Some men onshore, observing the late arrival and the help General Grant needed getting into the saddle because of the ankle injury, might have thought him to be drunk, such were the aspersions that plagued him. Aide-de-camp to Grant, Captain Rowley, says he "immediately mounted his horse and rode upon the bank." Rowley testifies that "after conversing a moment with some officers [Grant] turned to Captain Baxter, assistant quartermaster, and ordered him immediately to Crump's Landing, and direct General Wallace to march his division up the river and to the field to the right of our line as soon as possible."[1] This contradicts Grant's adjutant general John A. Rawlins, who states that Grant "started immediately to the front.... Then about a half mile from the river you met Brig. Gen. W.H.L. Wallace." After that Rawlins testifies he himself went back to the landing and ordered Captain Baxter to take the message to General Lew Wallace.[2] Another prime aide, Lt. Colonel James B. McPherson, testifies that he did "not see General Grant until some time after his arrival when I met him on the field with Brig. General W.H.L. Wallace." Reasonably, there was a fair amount of "some time" consumed before Grant reached Lt. Colonel McPherson and W.H.L Wallace. McPherson could personally say that "he was actively engaged on the field" and met Grant "on the field." This lends a sound assertion that Grant first met Wallace and McPherson on the field of battle before the mission to send General Lew Wallace was transmitted from Grant to Rawlins. The field of battle at the time was farther than "about a half a mile from the river" (the

Henri Lovie's engraving "Final Stand of General U.S. Grant at Pittsburg Landing" shows the chaos in the supply and transportation corps. The heroic spin given the event belies the mistake of sending Captain A.S. Baxter, chief of supply, on an errand to Lew Wallace that kept Baxter from commanding his corps of quartermasters (*Frank Leslie's Illustrations, American Soldier in the Civil War*).

way Rawlins described it). In fact, McPherson gives details about the deployment of troops of the division commanders Generals McClernand, Prentiss and Sherman, showing that Grant most likely moved close to the Hornet's Nest sector before he gave the order to bring Lew Wallace up. However, McPherson could not testify directly to what took place at the landing and testifies only by hearsay what he knew of Grant's first arrival, what went on at the landing, and the later transmission of the order going to General Lew Wallace.[3] One historian describes how on arrival Grant found Pittsburg Landing "a comparatively serene spot. Then Grant began exercising his command. He ordered the 23rd Missouri to proceed to Prentiss' headquarters and form up with the Sixth Division."[4] Another account surmises, "Grant attempted to bring some order to the landing sector," and "immediately organized an ammunition train," as well directing the 15th and 16th Iowa to form a reserve line to stop stragglers.[5] If the sources of this information are correct regarding the organization of an ammunition train, Captain A.S. Baxter would have been involved in this organization. He was head of supply and transportation. Grant would have directed his chief quartermaster in the same way he directed the commanders of the three regiments at the landing. What followed a short time later baffles comprehension. Baxter was instructed to leave this corps of quartermasters and teamsters he was coordinating just to deliver a message that any junior officer could have delivered. The importance of that decision and the time Baxter took in accomplishing this relatively simple task can be measured in lives lost, so this is an important issue.

The details of what General U.S. Grant's aides Rawlins, Rowley and McPherson said a year after the fact blurs the order's timing and the decision-making process to bring up Lew Wallace's Division. It is about who, what, why, when and where. The *who* chosen to take the message, of course, turned out to be the District Quartermaster, Chief of Supply and Transport of the whole Army of West Tennessee, Captain Algernon Sydney Baxter. *What* the thinking was in selecting him to be the one to deliver the message may be that no one was thinking straight in the excitement of the hour. *Why* he was chosen has never been explained, but rather attention has been diverted from it. *When* exactly the order was given takes some educated guesswork. As with the timing of most other things, the timing of when the order was transmitted is obfuscated by Grant's adjutant John A. Rawlins. Rawlins states it occurred an hour before it could possibly have taken place. *Where* this order was transmitted by Grant is uncertain, and suppositions of where the order was transmitted can shorten or lengthen the time factors involved in getting the message to General Lew Wallace.

The foregoing information determines that when Grant arrived, he sought to find General W.H.L. Wallace, for Wallace had sent an advisory with a courier on the steamer *John J. Warner*, which had intercepted Grant's transport vessel the *Tigress* on its way up to Pittsburg Landing. W.H.L. Wallace's headquarters was at the top of the hill, but Wallace was not at the top of the hill when General Grant found him. When he reached W.H.L. Wallace, Rawlins says he was at least "a half mile inland." The evidence points to Grant's accompanying W.H.L. Wallace from that point as far as the so-called sunken road to assess the seriousness of the situation before giving the order to bring up General Lew Wallace. That is where W.H.L. Wallace had deployed most of his division. Grant's decision-making process never seemed rushed, even in battle situations. Keep in mind that though General Lew Wallace had informed him earlier the attack was a general one, he told General Lew Wallace that he should wait in readiness for orders. General W.H.L. Wallace would not have stampeded him either by simply stating the attack was general. Grant was a man who had demonstrated that he had to see things for himself before acting, so a knee-jerk reaction was not his form. General Grant himself states in his memoirs: "On reaching the front ... I found the attack on Pittsburg was unmistakable." So it was at the battle front. It was after this that he states, "Captain Baxter, a quartermaster on my staff, was accordingly directed to go back and order General Wallace to march to Pittsburg, by the road nearest the river." The wording of this memoir brings into question whether he had personally stipulated Captain Baxter as the choice to take the message. It has not been clear whether Grant actually made the specific order to use Captain Baxter as the courier. The fact attested in official records is that Grant's adjutant general Captain John A. Rawlins gave the actual order to Captain Baxter. Rawlins admits this himself.[6] Grant did take the responsibility for the decision, but there are subterranean intricacies that make it more likely that he merely told John Rawlins to send *someone* to get Wallace. Adding strength to the supposition of where Grant was when he turned to Rawlins and ordered that General Lew Wallace's Division be brought up is an anecdote related by a young paymaster, Douglas Putnam, Jr. He accompanied Captain Rawlins back to the front after the order to Captain A.S. Baxter was carried out. Putnam states he asked Rawlins where they would find Grant. Rawlins replied, "We'll find him where the firing is the heaviest," so it is reasonable that the decision to send orders for Lew Wallace to bring his division was made from the battle front rather than the top of Pittsburg Landing where General W.H.L Wallace's headquarters stood, or a mere half mile inland as Rawlins stated.[7] Every minute that passed elongated the time that it took to get the message to Lew Wallace. Every minute preyed on the mind of General U.S. Grant, giving him a distorted view of how long it would take for General Wallace to make it to the field of battle. It appears that the earliest Captain Baxter would have gotten the message from Rawlins would have been about 9:30 A.M. The defensive front where the Divisions of General Hurlbut and General W.H.L. Wallace came to the aid of General Prentiss's fractured and retreating division lined up at about 9:00. That was the time Grant was just arriving: "Arriving upon the field at about the time that Prentiss was driven from his camp,"[8] etc. A half hour is a stingy amount of time to allow for the chain of events involved in the transmission of the order to Lew Wallace in view of the mobbed conditions of the landing, the choked and sloppy condition of the roads and the retreating soldiers, the deployment of three idle regiments, and sundry orders to release officers under arrest as Grant rode to the front to determine the particulars of the attack. General confusion is an understatement; it was definitely *not* a "comparatively serene spot" when Grant arrived.

Chagrin would be too inadequate a word for Captain Algernon Sydney Baxter to use when he was asked by Rawlins to take the message to General Lew Wallace. He must have been astonished, there at the landing while directing his corps. But the only eyewitness reports of the order transmission are the two participants. It took a year for Baxter to get even a mention in official comment. He gets no specific attention as to how the transmission occurred in the time-line battle reports of General U.S. Grant. He is excluded, as if nonexistent on General Grant's staff, while all others are mentioned.[9] Adjutant General John A. Rawlins makes mention of the transmission a year later in an accusatory report against General Wallace, but there is no input from Baxter himself until decades later, after Rawlins was long dead. The way Rawlins put it a year after the battle, he subtly impugned Baxter by stating that he was "afraid he might make some mistake" in writing the information down, so he, Rawlins, was forced to act, and they "went on board where a pen and writing materials could be procured."[10] It is a carefully stated manipulation. The statement averts what astute observation shows plainly. Baxter was being wrenched away from his essential duties at the landing. All that is known about Captain Baxter and stated in previous chapters reveal he was not a man who was afraid he might make some mistake. Rather he was considered so competent by General Grant that Grant had requested a promotion for Baxter, upgraded from captain. The reaction Rawlins attributes to Baxter of being afraid of making a mistake was more likely the strong disinclination to leave his transportation corps without leadership. He was recognized as the "Chief Quartermaster of the Expedition."[11] Helpfully, the now available instances of Baxter's orders made in his own hand at Shiloh and preserved by Lt. Richard P. Derickson make that evident. They show Baxter possessed writing materials. The idea that he had no writing materials borders on preposterous. He was the quartermaster of the whole army. It was his job to have writing materials. He was a paper pusher and the logistical commander of six divisions, consisting of tens of thousands of men, with horses and mules and wagons all in need of ammunition and provisions. He was an accomplished leader who knew how to get things done. The Army Transportation Corps Creed calls out Shiloh as a successful example of how the quartermaster corps functioned during the Civil War. Unfortunately, it did not function quite so well the first day of the Battle of Shiloh, but it was not the fault of the quartermasters.[12] That is the shame of Shiloh regarding the Lew Wallace controversy. That is the shame of Shiloh regarding Grant's never-admitted blunder in sending Captain A.S. Baxter. The scapegoating of General Lew Wallace has screened that logistical error. It has never received historical examination.

This is the fact: In order to bring up the 3rd Division quickly, Grant through Rawlins chopped off the head of his own supply and transportation corps. Once it happened, it required some doctoring of appearances. As stated previously, Grant in his memoirs speaks of picking "a quartermaster on my staff" to go to Wallace, reducing Baxter to a mere courier. By minimizing Baxter, the quartermaster of the whole Army at Shiloh, to terms of "a quartermaster on my staff," U.S. Grant shows a lack of transparency. Even in his most reliable report, dated April 9, 1862, after the horror of the battle, Grant did not personally mention this critical player. Then, a year later in a packet of reports sent to the War Department about Lew Wallace, he delegates all framing of the issue to members of his staff through his war-long adjutant general John A. Rawlins. Grant's expression "*a* quartermaster on my staff" belies the fact that Baxter was *the* district quartermaster of the whole Army of the Tennessee. An examination of this overlooked historical blunder follows.

The impact of sending the district quartermaster of the Army of West Tennessee is palpable in the official reports of the Battle of Shiloh. The problem can be traced in the words of various commanders on the field. The accounts in the Official Records are a massive study in themselves, so these excerpts address some of effect of Captain Baxter's absence, chargeable first to the fact that General U.S. Grant was four hours late from the first shots fired to his arrival around 9:00 A.M., and then again chargeable to Captain Baxter's being gone an additional three to four hours more because of command decision.

The following excerpt from General McClernand's report points to problems of supply after a series of horrendous engagements with the Confederates on the Union right. He states: "Continuing this sanguinary conflict until several regiments of my division had exhausted their ammunition and its right flank had been borne back, and it was in danger of being turned,"[13] etc.

Notice that General McClernand commanded the 1st Division and reports that "several regiments ... had exhausted their ammunition." This ammunition shortage of several regiments occurred near 11 A.M. This can be determined by what General McClernand states in the same paragraph of his report. He states as ammunition ran out his

> right flank had been borne back, and it was in danger of being turned, the remainder of my command with the exception hereafter noticed, also fell back to the camp of the First Brigade. Here the portion which had fallen back reformed in obedience to my order, parallel with the camp and fronting the approach of the enemy from the west, while the other portion formed at right angle with it, still fronting the approach of the enemy from the south. The Forty-fifth Illinois, being the last to fall back, only escaped being surrounded and captured by boldly cutting their way through the closing circle of the enemy's lines and joining the division, under the daring lead of Colonel and Major Smith of that regiment.[14]

The markers in Shiloh Military Park show that these actions occurred around 11:00 A.M. Specifically, the Forty-fifth Illinois marker No. 26, placed by original Shiloh Park Historian and Shiloh veteran D.W. Reed, corresponds to General McClernand's description: "This regiment was engaged here at 11 A.M. April

Henri Lovie's "Center, Sunday Morning" shows General McClernand's "Desperate Retreat." Official reports show that McClernand was woefully unsupplied with ammunition (Becker Collection, Boston College; thanks to Prof. Judith Bookbinder).

6, 1862. After a short engagement it fell back to the ravine where it rallied and rejoined its brigade here at 12 m."

How long problems with supply on the Union right continued is stated next: "It was 2 o'clock P.M. when my fifth line had been thus formed. By that time Lieutenant Jones, ordnance officer of my division, had come up at great peril with ammunition, which was rapidly distributed among some of the most convenient regiments."[15] Captain A.S. Baxter was finally back to do his critical administration. In the recently discovered documents of Lt. Richard P. Derickson it is revealed that Lieutenant Jones was likely enabled due to the efforts of Lt. Colonel Enos P. Wood. More ammunition became available, as shown in the Derickson documents, due to the diversion of wagons of the 6th Division. Lt. Derickson was the head quartermaster of the 6th Division.

It is instructive that several regiments were experiencing the same problems with ammunition, and that it was taking great effort to get ammunition. While it is understandable that "great peril" is involved in a combat situation, the breakdown of the transportation corps had as much to do with the peril as the enemy. It goes without saying that an army cannot fight its enemy without ammunition. The enemy will keep pushing men short of cartridges back and cause great casualties. Great casualties: that is the shame of Shiloh, and on the Union side, it was greatly contributed to by the lack of a seasoned chief quartermaster on the field. It was 2:00 when McClernand was supplied. This coincides with Captain A.S. Baxter's return to his duties. Note the restoration in supply at this time, "when my fifth line had been thus formed."[16]

Although the problems were still not fully resolved, fortunately Captain Baxter was in position to coordinate better supply. As the Confederates relentlessly came on, General McClernand states, "I ordered my command to fall back toward the landing, across a deep hollow, and to reform the east side of another field in the skirts of a wood. This was my sixth line. Here we rested a half hour, *continuing* to supply our men with ammunition, until the enemy's cavalry were seen rapidly crossing the field to the charge...."

It was not just ammunition that had been in shortage. The quartermaster corps also furnishes food from the commissary department to the men and livestock. "An army travels on its stomach," as the saying goes. McClernand describes his division as a "worn and famishing remnant ... along a north and south road," and it was when a last line was formed that the crisis of ammunition saw its resolution toward the close of the first day of the Battle of Shiloh. General McClernand states that the Union right had been engaged in a conflict of ten and half hours, "from 6:00 o'clock A.M. to 4:30 o'clock P.M."[17] The head of supply and transportation had been absent for two-thirds of that time.

General McClernand gives special commendation to two men who would not have been able to perform as well without the return of District Quartermaster A.S. Baxter: "Lieutenant Jones, ordnance officer and aide, won the applause of all by his characteristic diligence and fearlessness in bringing up and supplying ammunition to our men, often within range of the enemy's musketry, and still oftener in range of his artillery. A similar tribute is due to Lieutenant Tresilian, acting engineer and aide, for unsurpassed activity and daring throughout the battle."[18] The Quartermaster Corps acted in accord with the ordnance department.

A closer look reveals that the transport issues could not be cured uniformly; that is, with Baxter's return it was still difficult to get an equalized supply maintained across the board. Under McClernand's command Colonel Hare states his issue of supply existed "until 4:30 o'clock P.M., all the officers and men behaving with the greatest gallantry. At that hour, my regiments having exhausted their ammunition and great numbers of them having been killed and wounded and the forces on my right and left having retired,"[19] etc.

One of the most acute shortages is described by Lt. Col. William Hall of the 11th Iowa. Note the time of day, "in the morning," his crisis began occurring:

> When about 50 yards in the rear of my position, when supporting Dresser's battery, in the morning, I received report from the commanders of companies that the men were out of ammunition, which fact I immediately reported to Major-General McClernand in person, and held my position until I was re-enforced, when I received orders from General McClernand to retire and procure ammunition. Before I issued the order to retire the troops ordered to occupy my ground broke in confusion, throwing my men into temporary disorder, but they rallied and formed at my camp, where I learned that my ammunition had been taken to the river half an hour before, and I could not learn, after repeated inquiries, where I could procure any, and the fire becoming very hot, I retired until I received ammunition, and was joined by part of Companies D, F, and I. While issuing ammunition I received orders from Major-General Grant to advance immediately, and ordering Companies B and C, who were armed with rifles and were then unable to procure cartridges of a suitable caliber, to remain until they procured them and rejoin the regiment.[20]

Colonel Marsh of the 20th Illinois, and commanding the 2nd Brigade of McClernand, mentions shortages this way:

> The enemy being heavily re-enforced and my ammunition running short, [when] I was forced to fall back without bringing off the guns, but on regaining possession of our camp on Monday morning the guns were found in the same position, and are now in our possession. During this attack Lieutenant-Colonel Richards, commanding the Twentieth Illinois, was wounded.... Fresh troops of ours having passed to the front, I equalized the ammunition of my command, and again moved forward, joined by the Forty-fifth, of my brigade, and engaged

the enemy till I had exhausted all my cartridges. At this time, my command having been reduced to a merely nominal one.[21]

It was not until "daylight on Monday morning the men in line were supplied
with some provisions."[22]

In the commendations section of Colonel Marsh's report, there is one of
the few mentions of a quartermaster who was able to perform beyond his
capacity despite the belated arrival and inability of Captain Baxter to be on
the field. He was not able to perform like this until after the time Captain
Baxter was back in control of his corps:

> Capt. G.W. Kennard, assistant quartermaster of the brigade, was constant in
> attention to his duties. Through his assistance I was able to promptly supply the
> command with rations on Sunday night and Monday morning. Major Smith, of
> the Seventeenth Illinois, assisted greatly in forming the line on Sunday evening,
> and during the engagements of both Sunday and Monday he well sustained his
> former reputation and that of the gallant regiment which he commands. Adju-
> tant Ryan, of the same regiment, was of great service as acting aide. To Lieuten-
> ant Jones, of the division staff, I am under many obligations for the promptness
> with which he supplied me with ammunition. Had a less efficient officer had the
> matter in charge my record might have been far more unpleasant. Lieut. Harry
> King, commanding Company G, Twentieth Illinois, employed as skirmishers,
> proved himself a daring and brave officer. Doubtless many other cases of indi-
> vidual daring occurred which did not meet my eye.[23]

In fact, it was due to a man who did not meet his eye that Lt. Kennard and
Lt. Jones had been able to get supplies. That man was Lt. Colonel Enos P.
Wood. Throughout the reports of the 1st Division, he remained unnoted as
to his quest to bring ammunition to "move off nearer the river and get a new
supply of ammunition. This was about noon."[24] It would take a robbery from
the left hand of the army to save the right hand. This extraordinary transaction
was not uncovered until almost 150 years later in the documents of Lt. Richard
P. Derickson of the 6th Division.

Helping to identify the time when ammunition problems began in
earnest is the report of adjutant general Abram Ryan, 3rd Brigade of General
McClernand's Division. Recall that Colonel Raith was the third in line of
accession of the 3rd Brigade; he participated in the defense of the crossroads
north of Shiloh Church. It was in this valiant defense that Raith received the
blow that killed him. The crossroads defense had been identified as taking
place about 10:00 A.M. Adjutant Ryan states:

> A few minutes afterward Colonel Raith fell mortally wounded. He was immedi-
> ately carried to the rear by four of his own men. I accompanied him a short dis-
> tance to receive orders, &c. When I returned the Twenty-ninth and Forty-ninth
> Regiments had fallen to the rear, having expended their ammunition. The

remainder of the brigade continued the fight until their ammunition gave out likewise, when they were ordered to the rear for a new supply. On gaining the encampment of the First Brigade, First Division, Lieutenant of Taylor's battery, requested a detail of men to assist in working the battery, many of his own men having fallen. I immediately detailed 20 men from the Seventeenth Illinois Regiment and reported them to Captain Barrett, commanding battery. Searching through the encampment of the Eighth Illinois Regiment, I found ammunition and carried it to the brigade, but it proved to be of a wrong caliber. Learning that it could be used by the Eleventh Regiment Illinois Volunteer Infantry, I turned it over to Colonel Ransom, commanding. After waiting a while, and no ammunition coming up, I fell back to meet the train. As I could do no further good remaining with the train, I rode forward to hurry up ammunition.

Meeting with Lieut. C.C. Williams, brigade quartermaster he gallantly volunteered to bring forward a train, designating a field where to meet the regiments. When I returned I found that the regiments had been separated. Halting the advance, I eventually succeeded in getting the Seventeenth, Forty third, and Forty-ninth Regiments into line, when Quartermaster Williams returned with an ammunition train, under the direction of Lieutenant Jones, ordnance officer, First Division, who, supplying the men with whatever was necessary gallantly moved with his train to the front. After getting everything in readiness for action I reported to Lieutenant-Colonel Wood, Seventeenth Illinois Regiment, who commanded the brigade the remainder of the day. For its operations during that time I would refer you to Lieutenant-Colonel Wood and to the report of Colonel Marsh, who commanded the brigade on the 7th instant.[25]

Ryan is oblivious in his report to the fact that it was due to Lt. Col. Wood (EPW) that this train moved forward. It must also be noted that a significant number of wagons in the supply trains were provided at the expense of the 6th Division. It was Lt. Richard P. Derickson at Captain Baxter's direction who diverted all teams available to this sector of the field away from the 6th Division. It is also telling to see that this only occurred because Chief Quartermaster A.S. Baxter was back on the field and support began to operate more efficiently again. (See Lt. Colonel Enos P. Wood's report, which narrates the part he played in the issue of supply and the saving of the right, as related in Chapter Twelve, "For Want of a Horse.")

It also must be kept in mind that to keep a supply and transportation corps fulfilling its duty, a semblance of order has to be maintained. Demands filled without order deprives ability to supply where it is most needed. (See in the Derickson documents an example of an urgent request by John Ryan that demonstrates this problem.) This was the situation produced when still another colonel, named Engelmann of the 43rd Illinois, found his troops without ammunition.

Having fallen back through the timber in front of the encampment of the First Division, it again formed in line forward of and to the right of General

Oglesby's headquarters. The ammunition of the regiment being almost completely exhausted, I sent one of the officers, with several men, to procure a supply, but before that officer could rejoin us the regiment was ordered forward by Captain Hammond, of General Sherman's staff, and advanced in double-quick past the battery planted in front of General Oglesby's encampment. [It is of note that they were ordered to advance without ammunition.] Being placed in the center of the line of attack, it advanced steadily and fearlessly upon the enemy's batteries, and then planted near General McClernand's headquarters. Within a short distance of the enemy the regiments to our right and left came to a halt and opened their fire. The Forty-third still advanced closer upon the enemy, but reduced in numbers, and its supports having come to a halt, it too had to stop, it being impossible for it to advance alone on the dense masses in front. The ammunition now being entirely exhausted, the men gathered a scant supply from the killed and wounded of the enemy, who here covered the ground thickly. The troops of the enemy opposed to us having been armed with the Enfield rifle, their ammunition being of English make and excellent quality, it could be used in our muskets. The men being cheered on by General McClernand, who was present in the thickest of the fight, for a long period, maintained a fearful conflict that cost great numbers on both sides. Our lines again giving way, the regiment retired down the branch on which the conflict had raged, and in the open field below again formed on the right of the Twentieth Illinois Regiment.

Being altogether out of ammunition, I again sent for a supply, but none being found, and the supply which had been promised Colonel Marsh failing to arrive, we were again compelled to retire as the enemy advanced. We now fell back by degrees, and a new line being formed, we found ourselves posted between the Forty-sixth Illinois and Thirteenth Missouri, our position being midway between the encampments of the Forty-sixth and Ninth Illinois. We here succeeded in getting a fresh supply of ammunition. The men, totally exhausted, lay heedless to the shower of shot and shell that passed over their heads. In this position we passed the night."[26]

This regiment was forced to scavenge ammunition from the enemy dead and wounded, and did not receive relief in the way of ammunition until the end of the harrowing day.

It was not just infantry that experienced ammunition shortage. Artillery had the firepower equivalency of multitudes of muskets, so its fire has a grim economy in the savings of musket and rifle fire, but even artillery units suffered the problem late in the day. The report of Lt. G.L. Nispel of Company E. Illinois Artillery demonstrates that being closer to the landing did not necessarily mean it was easier to get ammunition. That is another report that reveals a collapse of the quartermaster organization in the absence of the head of the corps. It would have taken a miracle worker to recover from ordering Captain Baxter away.

We next took position on the parade ground, by Major Taylor's order, and fired on the enemy's artillery and infantry for about three-quarters of an hour, when I ordered the howitzer back, because the ammunition was exhausted. The enemy advancing nearer, Major Taylor ordered me to take my battery toward the Landing, which I did, and rested my exhausted men and teams a short time, when I received an order from you to take a position on the right of the siege guns and support them. So soon as I had taken the position assigned me I ordered Lieutenant Carter back to the Landing for ammunition, which order was promptly executed, being ready for action on the receipt of the ammunition. The enemy advancing, a heavy fire was opened on him, the most terrific I ever heard. Every one seemed to be imbued with the idea that as this was our last stand, so should it be the most desperate. Being of that opinion myself, I used the most strenuous exertions to hold it, in which I was heartily seconded by my lieutenants encouraging our infantry to stand firm but a short time longer and we would drive them back. We kept our word, in conjunction with the other batteries. In this position we had 1 man and 2 horses wounded, with other slight casualties.

Thinking the enemy during the darkness of the night might make an attempt to charge and capture our guns, I threw up a little breastwork and self and men laid there all night exposed to the rain without any covering, and what was worse, anxiety. Firmly resolved to hold the position till the last man, I remained there until I was ordered back to my old camp.

The battery had six positions, fired 591 rounds of ammunition; 1 man killed and 4 wounded, 11 horses killed and wounded.... The battery is not fit for present use. I have taken the riding and spare horses to place on the guns and caissons. My caissons I have filled from the enemy's. I have not men enough to man my guns. I need ordnance stores very much, but am not able to procure them, because the ordnance officer has not a supply.[27]

Being a quartermaster was an enviable office from the standpoint of advancement. However, it was an arduous job, and not all could handle being quartermaster. The report of Lieutenant Colonel Thomas E.G. Ransom emphasizes the risk taken by quartermasters. Ransom in his commendations sadly relates, concerning his field supply officer: "Acting Quartermaster Goodrich, ever faithful to his trust, a brave soldier, was shot by my side through the head."[28] One individual who did master this was Lt. Richard P. Derickson on behalf of General Prentiss. Another is described in the report of the 2nd Division report of Colonel J.J. Wood of the 12th Iowa: "Quartermaster Dorr, though his position did not require him to go into action, volunteered to do so, and throughout the day behaved in a brave and gallant manner, daringly, if not recklessly, exposing his person to the enemy. He made himself very useful in carrying messages and spying out the positions and movements of the enemy and firing on them as occasion offered. Energetic and efficient in his own department, he would fill a higher one with credit to himself and honor to the service."[29]

While displays of bravery at the front have that glorious appeal, it's worth wondering whether Quartermaster Dorr would not have been of better service at Shiloh by staying with his department, but on the other hand, with shortages being difficult to satisfy, he may just have tried to do anything possible to help. The regiment that Lt. Dorr served was part of the Hornet's Nest–sunken road position. It appears that the Hornet's Nest was well supplied with ammunition until late in the afternoon, and this cannot help but credit the service of the quartermaster of the 6th Division, Lt. Richard P. Derickson. The fact that the salient positions there had three good roads to serve as supply routes contributed. The normal route that Derickson took to get to Prentiss was the Eastern Corinth Road, and it ran right to the center of the Hornet's Nest. So well was the Hornet's Nest served that it apparently allowed for a siphoning of its resources to save the Union right. Another way to look at it would be that General Grant, having told Generals W.H.L. Wallace and Prentiss to hold that position at all hazards, was willing to sacrifice that position to save the Union right. Still, with the Hornet's Nest sector, there is almost no mention of ammunition problems until the end of the day when it surrendered. Col. William T. Shaw of the 14th Iowa says: "The regiment still kept its ranks unbroken and held its position facing the enemy, but the men were almost completely exhausted with a whole day of brave and steady fighting and many of them had spent their whole stock of ammunition."[30]

On the far Union left, the ammunition problem was nearly similar to what was happening on the Union right. Some might argue that there will always come ammunition problems, but the reason there are such repetitive reports of them in the Union Army at Shiloh is that there were few individuals who knew how to get their men efficiently supplied. In concert with General Prentiss and his quartermaster Lt. Richard P. Derickson, W.H.L. Wallace also addressed the shortages with at least some success. Colonel August Mersy of the 9th Illinois describes:

At 9 o'clock the regiment, in company with the Twelfth Illinois Infantry, were ordered by Brigadier-General McArthur to a part of the lines about one-fourth of a mile in advance of General Hurlbut's headquarters. We there formed, and afterward marched about half a mile by the left flank, when we encountered a heavy force of the enemy, strongly posted in a deserted camp and skirt of timber.

While taking up a position in a ravine to the left of the Twelfth Illinois we received a severe fire of musketry and shell, which killed and wounded a number of men. After taking up this position we maintained a steady and destructive fire upon the enemy for an hour and thirty minutes, when our ammunition began to fail, and at the same time a most murderous cross-fire poured into our ranks from the left, which we were unable to silence by a partial change of front of the two left companies. We were then compelled to fall back some five hundred yards to the rear. The enemy were constantly re-enforced during this period, and fresh regiments were seen deploying to relieve those which had been some time under fire. Our loss up to this time was about 50 killed and over 200 wounded. We were ordered at this time by *General W.H.L. Wallace*, commanding our division, to retire to our camp, replenish the cartridge-boxes, clean the guns, and be in readiness for action as speedily as possible.[31]

The foregoing accounts are a portion of the places in the official reports that speak of the breakdown in the supply and transportation corps. Listed above as they are, they do not give the most comprehensive understanding of every situation that prompted the ammunition and rations problems, which deserve a fuller study. Even now hundreds, maybe thousands of unopened quartermaster documents sit in archives awaiting examination. With the emergence of just one set of quartermaster records, that of Lt. Richard P. Derickson, insights have been opened about the logistical progression of the Battle of Shiloh on its first day. Lt. Derickson preserved these in his own papers, but there may well be duplicates of them somewhere in government storage. The quartermaster corps under regulations from Washington were required to keep duplicates of everything that was done, even in the midst of battle. That being said, some doctoral thesis based on the quartermaster corps at the Battle of Shiloh is awaiting its author.

15

A Tangled Web

One of the focuses of this book has been to look at the Lew Wallace controversy differently. For one hundred and fifty years the finger has been pointed at Wallace for supposedly taking the wrong road. With the help of the found documents of Lt. Richard P. Derickson, a different and important component to the Wallace matter deserves more review. It has to do with the wrong messenger being chosen to take the message to Lew Wallace, a messenger who was indispensable to the army's performance. In the morning on April 6, 1862, at Pittsburg Landing, Captain John A. Rawlins approached Captain Algernon Sydney Baxter, district quartermaster of the whole army of West Tennessee, and ordered him to take the message to General Lew Wallace. Therein lies a tangled web.

The original circumstances of the transmission of the Lew Wallace order were benign in respect to General Wallace. The attitude toward the transmission of the order at the actual time of the battle is revealed by U.S. Grant in his first dispatch about the battle on April 7. He merely says: "General Wallace was immediately ordered up from Crump's Landing, and in the evening one division of General Buell's army and General Buell in person arrived."[1] By April 9 there was still no animosity shown toward the commander of the 3rd Division through the first official report General U.S. Grant sent to General Halleck about the Battle of Shiloh. Grant narrates in that report: "General Lewis Wallace, at Crump's Landing, 6 miles below, was ordered at an early hour in the morning to hold his division in readiness to be moved in any direction to which it might be ordered. At about 11 o'clock the order was delivered to move it up to Pittsburg, but owing to its being led by a circuitous route did not arrive in time to take part in Sunday's action."[2]

What Grant's report does not include is General Lew Wallace's actions on the second day. Wallace's Division was the first to fire on Monday, April 7, 1862. His troops fought efficiently and suffered fewer casualties because of

The scapegoating of General Lew Wallace is reflected in the May 3, 1862, *Harper's Weekly.* Though he performed admirably he is not shown among "The Heroes of the Battle of Pittsburg Landing."

Wallace's tactical decisions. General McClernand describes Wallace's division as aggressively advancing. General Sherman describes his "well-conducted Division." Especially of note is that General U.S. Grant gave Wallace the vanguard and told him, concerning special formation of attack, "I leave that to your discretion."[3]

Ironically, at the end of the day on Monday, General Lew Wallace's Division rested exactly where he would have come in the previous day if he had come in along the Shunpike route he had chosen, but had been turned away from by Grant's aides.

The only other accounts of the parties involved in sending the order to General Lew Wallace were written long after the battle. They are those of Adjutant General John A. Rawlins, who directly told Captain A.S. Baxter to go to Wallace, and the account of A.S. Baxter himself. Neither the account of Captain Baxter or (promoted to) Lt. Colonel Rawlins is related close to the time of the Battle of Shiloh. Baxter gives his account twenty-four years after the fact, and Rawlins gives his account a year after the fact with the specific intent to discredit General Lew Wallace. Two and a half decades after the Battle of Shiloh, Captain A.S. Baxter wrote: "On Sunday, between the hours of 8 and 9:00 A.M., April 6, 1862, Adjutant General Rawlins, of General Grant's staff, requested me to go to Crump's Landing (five miles below) and order General Lew Wallace to march his command at once by the River Road to Pittsburg Landing, and join the army on the right. At the same time General Rawlins dictated the order to General Wallace, which was written by myself and signed by General Rawlins."[4]

Captain John A. Rawlins tells his account this way:

> [Grant] then directed me to return to the river and send Capt. A.S. Baxter, assistant quartermaster, U.S. Volunteers, and chief of the quartermaster's department in your district, on the steamer Tigress, without delay, to Crump's Landing, with orders to Maj. Gen. Lewis Wallace to bring forward his division by the River road to Pittsburg Landing to a point immediately in rear of the camp of Maj. Gen. C.F. Smith's division, and there form his column at right angles with the river on the right of our lines and await further orders.
>
> In obedience to your [Grant's] command I proceeded to the river, and found Captain Baxter at the landing near where the Tigress lay, and communicated to him your orders, who, fearing lest he might make some mistake in the delivery of the orders, requested me to give him a written memorandum of them, and I went on board the steamer Tigress, where a pen and ink could be procured, and at my dictation he wrote substantially as follows:

Major-General WALLACE:

> You will move forward your division from Crump's Landing, leaving a sufficient force to protect the public property at that place, to Pittsburg Land-

ing, on the road nearest to and parallel with the river, and form in line at right angles with the river, immediately in rear of the camp of Maj. Gen. C.F. Smith's division on our right, and there await further orders.

    Captain Baxter took this memorandum and started on the steamer Tigress to convey your orders to Maj. Gen. Lewis Wallace. This was not later than 9 o'clock A.M."[5]

Determining the Circumstances and Character of the Order

    Unlike any other accounts of the transmission of the order to General Lew Wallace, the documents of Lt. Richard P. Derickson, the 6th Division quartermaster, preserve an order written on that very day in Captain Baxter's words. It is perhaps written on the same pad of ruled foolscap paper, maybe even the next order written by him after the order to General Lew Wallace, a time capsule written within minutes of Captain A.S. Baxter's return to Pittsburg Landing. It, along with other neutral information, gives a fuller picture of how the transmission of Wallace's order happened.

    One of the pieces of neutral information was brought out earlier in the accounts leading up to the Battle of Shiloh. Remember that on April 5 there was a huge reorganization of the quartermaster/commissary boats taking place. Captain Baxter as chief quartermaster had been supervising this from the steamer *John J. Roe*, and there was so much work to do for Captain A.S. Baxter that on the mother quartermaster boat it required a detail of 50 men from General Hurlbut's Division for fatigue duty for five days. They were not just standing idle; there were many provisions that needed to be distributed to each division assigned a boat at the landing and there would be transportation of goods and equipment to other depots on the field. As Rawlins had stated about the reorganization, the boats "now doing the issuing are sufficient for the entire army."[6] This makes it all the more interesting that Captain Rawlins picked Captain Baxter to take the message to General Lew Wallace. It is likely that Captain A.S. Baxter was astonished when John Rawlins asked him to be the one to take the message, considering the massive responsibilities he was charged with for "the entire army." But Baxter would not have questioned obedience. His understanding was that the order was coming from General U.S. Grant to him. The sticking point is that Grant may not have specified who should take the order, but left it to the discretion of Captain John A. Rawlins. It may be likely that Grant just told Rawlins to find someone responsible at the landing and send that person on the *Tigress* to take the order to General Lew Wallace. Nonetheless, since Captain A.S. Baxter was the one who took the order, Grant would have to assume all responsibility for the order sent, regardless of who sent it. Once again, therein lies intrigue.

It is possible now to get an actual visual look at the normal way Captain A.S. Baxter wrote things down when instructed to pass on an order. In the famous order that Captain Rawlins dictated to Captain Baxter it is possible with some reasonable degree of certainty to determine character by the way Baxter transmitted an order to Lt. Richard P. Derickson of the 6th Division on April 6. Below is a transcription of the order:

Lt. Derickson,
      Send all teams available
to Steamer Rocket to haul ammunition
to the field immediately
          By order of
              Capt A.S. Baxter a.q.m
                E P. W line officer

Pittsburgh April 6–

This order written on behalf of Lt. Col. Enos P. Wood for bringing ammunition to the field was written during the chaos of the battle on foolscap, ordinary lined blank paper called legal sheet today. These circumstances were also true of the order written to General Lew Wallace. Notice Baxter's instructions are brief and to the point. It was hurried, but not so much as to ignore normal correspondence protocol. It was written in ink in cursive, difficult to read. It is signed by Baxter, co-authorized assigned initials of EPW, line officer (Lt. Col. Enos P. Wood), and dated, with the place written simply "Pittsburg." All of these would have been true of the order written to General Lew Wallace. Among the Derickson documents are two other orders that demonstrate the character of instructions to be carried out, though they are not written during the press of battle. Taken together we see the character of the way Baxter wrote. (Appendix A.)

In the two accounts given by Baxter and Rawlins long after the battle, it is the germ of truth in them rather than the verbatim accounts that should be considered in regard to the Lew Wallace order. It can be confidently believed, based on the discovered orders signed by A.S. Baxter in the Derickson papers, that the order going to Lew Wallace was a signed order in some form, dated, brief to accomplish the task of simply bringing forward to a general location, and it was hard to read. The military rule of correspondence was to be succinct so as to minimize confusion. The lengthy description that Rawlins emphasizes twice in his antagonistic report a year later about Lew Wallace does not take the same character as the way Baxter wrote. The military maxim for any order, oral or written, is "Any order that can be misunderstood will be misunderstood." All who testified as to reading the order before it was lost say it was brief. That is, when Baxter arrived to deliver the order the immediate General Lew Wallace's staff members each read it and passed it around, essentially understanding that it was time to simply join the main body of the army.[7]

The several documents in the Derickson papers give character in Baxter's own hand that can be compared with the year-later claims of Grant's aides. (Appendix A contains actual Baxter orders. See the two-part order written April 4 by Captain Baxter and the captain of the steamer *Iatan*. Then one during the battle on the 6th and another April 10, 1862.) It would not be a hazard to say the character of the order he carried to General Lew Wallace followed the same pattern in a difficult-to-read cursive script. Whereas Rawlins states with great specificity what he claims the order said, Rawlins did not actually write the order. He dictated it while he was in a hurry, then rushed back to be at General Grant's side. Based on Baxter's style in the Derickson documents, in transmission of the order to General Lew Wallace, Baxter would have simply taken what Captain Rawlins said and recorded that General Wallace "leave enough force to protect the stores at Crump's Landing, bring his Division up on the best road near the river and form on the right of the Federal army, immediately." Another historian surmises it would have read, "You will leave a sufficient force at Crump's Landing to guard the public property there, and come up and take position on the right of the army. Form a line of battle at a right angle with the river and be governed by circumstances."[8] As to the nature of the signing, when Wallace received and read the order he could not make out who it was from. He asked who it was from and Baxter told him it was General Grant.[9] It is likely, based on the looseness of Rawlins's written transmissions in the days before the battle, he simply signed the order "Rawlins." He had shown inconsistency of form in the tense correspondence about the medical matters. He also did this three days before the battle when instructing Captain Baxter to move his quartermaster office out of the Cherry Mansion blacksmith shop. To sign simply as "Rawlins" or simply use his title "adjutant general" was not technically improper, as Captain Rawlins was U.S. Grant's adjutant general with power of military attorney to sign for General Grant. However, to sign merely as "Rawlins" or only use his title in difficult-to-read cursive script added visual difficulty to the order.[10]

The great detail that Captain Rawlins included in his later report was intended to build up the credibility of his account. It actually works against that. To say that the man whose job involved the most ink and paperwork in the army did not possess pen and paper and that he, Rawlins, had to go to the point of "board[ing] the steamer Tigress, where a pen and ink could be procured," stretches the point to unlikelihood. Most officers possessed writing materials in their equipment and saddlebags. Captain W.R. Rowley in his year-later report states he had writing materials in his haversack, when he quotes Grant in his anti–Wallace testimony, "'It has just been reported to me that that he has refused to come up unless he receives a written order. If he should require a written order of you, you will give him one,' at the same time asking me if I had writing materials in my haversack."[11]

The more details Rawlins gives of the transmission in his year-later report against General Lew Wallace, the more it does not comport with what was a simple instruction. That brings up the point of determining the length of time that was involved in Captain Baxter's fulfillment of carrying the order to General Wallace. Both Baxter and Rawlins approximate 9:00 A.M. as the time the order was sent, Rawlins says a year later: "Captain Baxter took this memorandum and started on the steamer Tigress to convey your orders to Maj. Gen. Lewis Wallace. This was not later than 9 o'clock A.M." Baxter says twenty-four years later: "On Sunday, between the hours of 8 and 9:00 A.M. the transmission occurred...." The evidence shows Grant and his staff were only just arriving at Pittsburg Landing at that time, 9:00 A.M.[12] The thousands of veteran interviews that Major D.W. Reed of the Park Commission made in the years after the battle convinced Reed that Grant's arrival was at the time of the breakup of Prentiss's Division. The park markers almost all state this occurred at 9:00 A.M. Therefore, giving allowance of perception for the hour of leeway that Baxter allowed, it was probably closer to 10:00 A.M. when Baxter got away from the landing.

The testimony that Baxter gave in his waning years bears weight in its succinct quality, and it can be inferred that he transmitted the order to General Lew Wallace in just as succinct a manner after having it dictated by Rawlins. This is true of his surviving orders among the Derickson documents. However, the mystery of the order to General Lew Wallace deepens considering that by army protocol, orders, even down to the smallest requisitions, required duplicates, and there were also extrapolations of orders given. For example: Grant gives a written order to an aide, then that aide gives his own written order to the party intended, then that party makes a record of orders received. There was redundancy built into the matter of recording orders given. This can be evidenced in the quartermaster papers kept by Lt. Richard P. Derickson that Baxter transmitted and signed originating with General Grant.[13]

There is a peculiarity that though the order hand-carried to General Lew Wallace was later lost by General Lew Wallace's adjutant general Captain Frederick Kneffler, Baxter had more than enough time to make out a duplicate on board the *Tigress*. He had office quarters on the *Tigress* in addition to the known office in the Cherry Mansion blacksmith shop.[14] It was Grant's transport for him and his staff; and Baxter was part of his personal staff. If Rawlins's year-later account is to be accepted verbatim, where he states that he, Rawlins, went personally on board the *Tigress* to procure writing materials, then even by Rawlins's account there would have been time and writing materials available to make a copy of the order being carried to General Lew Wallace. Since 6th Division Quartermaster Derickson's personal records have surfaced, the exact order duplicate of the Grant-Rawlins-Baxter-Wallace transmission may exist somewhere. In fact, there is a curious wording in the article U.S. Grant wrote for *Century Magazine* that suggests the possibility of a duplicate or recording of the order in another place. He says: "Captain Baxter, a quartermaster on my staff, was accordingly directed to go back and order General Wallace to march immediately to Pittsburg, by the road nearest the river. Captain Baxter made a memorandum of this order."[15]

"*Captain Baxter made a memorandum of this order.*" That statement could be construed more than one way. A definition in *Webster's Encyclopedic Unabridged Dictionary of the English Language* classifies a memorandum as "a short note, designating something to be remembered, esp. something to be done or acted upon in the future, reminder." This being the case, there is the suggestion in Grant's own words, in later life, that there was both an order and a memorandum of the order. It is well known that in army records, orders issued, whether oral or written, were recorded by the party responsible in a journal. This was true especially of chief quartermasters and adjutant generals.

The evidence of Rawlins's whole career as adjutant general to General Grant shows that Rawlins did everything in his power to suppress anything that would have detracted from General Grant's reputation. Curiosities pile up when events and correspondence are examined closely. A prime example at Shiloh is the record of preparations in the direction of Purdy Road, the road that Wallace took first to get close to the battlefield. The record of those preparations disappeared in the belated General W.H.L. Wallace's effects while Rawlins presided over things at the Cherry Mansion. It was Rawlins's job to keep track of Army business and keep detailed records. Rawlins would have gone through any army records the acting Division General W.H.L. Wallace possessed. It is a curiosity that written time-line records still exist for the orders sent to General Buell and General Nelson that same morning of April 6, 1862, but no time-line document has been discovered in regard to the General Lew Wallace order. The words *conspiracy to scapegoat* grow stronger in the Lew Wallace matter.

As Sir Walter Scott observed, "Oh, what a tangled web we weave/When first we practice to deceive." Close examination helps in getting at the truth of time factors. The search for neutral information is key. Interestingly, in Captain's Rawlins's testimony against General Lew Wallace, such neutral information is available in his contradictions. He says:

> Captain Baxter returned and reported before 12 o'clock m. his delivery of your orders to General Wallace, bringing at the same time from General Wallace to you the report of Col. Morgan L. Smith, that there was no enemy in the direction of Purdy; the result of his reconnaissance that morning. About an hour after Captain Baxter had gone down on the steamer Tigress to General Wallace an officer of the Second Illinois Cavalry, who was well acquainted with the road leading to Crump's Landing, was sent by you with a verbal message to Major-General Wallace to hurry forward with all possible dispatch. This officer returned between 12 o'clock m. and 1 o'clock P.M....[16]

Rawlins previously testified that Baxter got away no later than 9:00 A.M. Here he says, an hour after that, an officer of the Second Illinois Cavalry was sent to Wallace, returning as late as 1:00 P.M. This raises the question, if it took as long as three hours for a lone man, who knew the road well, to get from where General Grant was to General Lew Wallace and back, what took him so long? What it shows is that the rider was traveling through some of the most difficult country to traverse —*a poor choice of road to take*— the river road or Savannah-Hamburg road. It had, in fact, been completely submerged days previously. This was one of the reasons that there were alternate roads for the locals to get to communities on the west bank of the Tennessee River; the terrain included massive flood plains. It was six miles by riverboat to Crump's Landing and more or less the same along the swampy road the cavalry officer took. The officer then had about a two-and-a-half-mile ride to Stoney Lonesome, where General Wallace was concentrating his troops, a 14-mile round trip.[17] In Rawlins's own testimony, then, the cavalry officer made only five miles an hour or less on horseback in the urgent delivery of the order to General Lew Wallace and reporting back. The testimony about the two messages, Baxter's and the cavalry officer's, separate messages delivered, begins to trip upon itself in Rawlins's account. In Rawlins's testimony it took as long for the rider to get to Wallace and back as he says it took for Baxter to get to Wallace and back. These things just do not add up. Rawlins wants to make it look as if Baxter was gone only briefly from the field, when it was at least three hours by his own testimony. It was longer. He says that Baxter got back before the cavalry rider got back, and that is a clear fabrication. In the anti–Wallace report package a year later, Lt. Colonel McPherson even says that Wallace returned by 10:30 A.M.[18] According to the Rawlins time frame as given: "Captain Baxter returned and reported before 12 o'clock m, his delivery of your orders to General Wallace," and yet: "This [2nd Illinois Cavalry] officer returned between 12 o'clock m. and 1 o'clock P.M...." General U.S. Grant did not have a watch personally for the time-flow of events, so a year later, Captain John A. Rawlins was evidently massaging the times to make it look as if things happened at times they did not, in respect to the movements of Captain A.S. Baxter. There is clear attempt to minimize the time of absence by chief supply officer from the field.

It gets tedious to examine the belabored points of detail Rawlins makes, but in them is a costly reality, costly in human lives. The chief of supply was gone several hours. If it required the sending of a cavalry officer to hurry up Wallace, then he could have been sent in the first place, and the entire army would have still been serviced by its commanding corps supply officer.

The truth that it was ultimately General U.S. Grant's fault for sending Captain Baxter was something that had to be covered up. In the commendation portion of his report on April 9, 1862, U.S. Grant commends all members of his personal staff, with the curious exception of his staff quartermaster. By comparison, when Rawlins wanted a year later to put the onus on General Lew Wallace, he suddenly emphasizes the rank of Baxter: "Capt. A.S. Baxter, assistant quartermaster, U.S. Volunteers, and chief of the quartermaster's department in your district," but in the original report on April 9, 1862, Grant does not even include Baxter.[19] It is because Grant knew a mistake had been made sending Baxter away and did not want to draw attention to it, a kind of hidden-in-plain-sight maneuver.

This is not a far-fetched outlook, for consider another aspect of timing. On April 12, 1862, General Lew Wallace turned in his lengthy report of two days of his division's actions. This occurred one day after the Commander of all Western Departments, General Henry Wager Halleck, appeared on the scene. Halleck was flabbergasted that the battle had occurred before he expected it to occur. He had wanted the army not to engage until Corinth was brought under siege. He had instructed that breastworks be implemented at Pittsburg, and no breastworks had been installed, so just about everything in Halleck's plan to take Corinth had gone awry.[20] He was anxious to take command of the army in the field and did so. That left U.S. Grant in a subordinate position with little to do. He has been described as riding about trying to find something of importance in the way of command decision, worried that his career was over.[21] Next came something worse for U.S. Grant. Halleck received this correspondence:

Hon. E. M. STANTON,
Secretary of War.

WAR DEPARTMENT, *April* 23, 1862.

———

The President desires to know why you have made no official report to this Department respecting the late battle at Pittsburg Landing, and whether any neglect or misconduct of General Grant or any other officer contributed to the sad casualties that befell our forces on Sunday.

EDWIN M. STANTON,

Secretary of War.[22]

This query directed by the president of the United States, Abraham Lincoln, was dated April 23, 1862. General U.S. Grant and his adjutant general Captain John A. Rawlins would go into scrambling mode when they read it. Grant had had more than two weeks to review reports that had been turned in to General Halleck and nothing untoward had been asserted against General Lew Wallace. There had even been praise in Grant's report about General Lew Wallace and the other division commanders. He said there was "no disparagement intended ... all whom maintained their places with credit themselves and the cause."[23] So what happened to start turning the screw on General Lew Wallace? Halleck must have faced Grant with the letter from Lincoln questioning "whether any neglect or misconduct of General Grant or any other officer contributed to the sad casualties that befell our forces on Sunday."

The reply Halleck gave the Secretary of War the very next day said this:

Major-General HALLECK,
Pittsburg Landing.——

PITTSBURG LANDING, *April* 24, 1862.

The sad casualties of Sunday, the 6th, were due in part to the bad conduct of officers who were utterly unfit for their places, and in part to the numbers and bravery of the enemy. I prefer to express no opinion in regard to the misconduct of individuals till I receive the reports of commanders of divisions. A great battle cannot be fought or a victory gained without many casualties. In this instance the enemy suffered more than we did.

H.W. Halleck
Major-General.

Hon. E. M. STANTON.[24]

After two weeks and plenty of time for General Grant to have reviewed the report from General Lew Wallace and not finding fault with it, there is a sudden surfacing of disapproval of General Lew Wallace from General Grant. His tune changed. The scapegoating had begun. It began the day after the questioning from President Abraham Lincoln.

HEADQUARTERS ARMY OF THE TENNESSEE
Pittsburg, April 25, 1862.

Respectfully forwarded to headquarters of the department.

I directed this division [Wallace's] at about 8 o'clock A.M. to be held in readiness to move at a moment's warning in any direction it might be ordered. Certainly not later than 11 A.M. the order reached General Wallace to march by a flank movement to Pittsburg Landing. Waiting until I thought he should be here, I sent one of my staff to hurry him, and afterwards sent Colonel McPherson and my assistant adjutant-general.

This report in some other particulars I do not fully indorse.

U.S. GRANT,
Major-General[25]

This report was turned in behind the scenes and behind the back of General Lew Wallace. By the time *Harpers Weekly* came out two weeks later, May 5, 1862, with pictures of all the "hero" generals of the Battle of Shiloh, General Lew Wallace was totally excluded from among them.

Masking the Deliveryman of the Order to General Lew Wallace

Captain Baxter had come up the river with General Grant as part of his staff in a tension-filled atmosphere aboard the headquarters' transport. Now he was to go back down the Tennessee on the *Tigress*. With his departure went the opportunities of a repulse of the Confederate Army the first day of the Battle of Shiloh. Ringing in Baxter's ears was "the most continuous firing of musketry and artillery ever heard on this continent."[26]

At the time, the battle, according to Grant's incomplete evaluation, "waxed warm on the left and center." He had not yet visited General Sherman and General McClernand, who were waxing more than warm on the right. In fact, as the *Tigress* backed out of moorage and rounded to follow the flow of the river, Sherman was retreating back from the Shiloh Church area, and McClernand was making his second stand along the Purdy Road at the crossroads. At this place the ammunition supply was already becoming an issue, but there was now nobody familiar enough with the transportation corps officers to adequately organize ammunition distribution or to provide provisions to men who were burning calories at such a rapid rate that they were in as much danger from exhaustion, loss of water, lack of sustenance and famishing, as from stray bullets.

Apparently, Grant did make some effort to remedy the mistake that had been made in sending the chief of his supply and transportation corps, but it would not be enough. There is no specific mention at all given as to their duties, but in his April 9, 1862, report, Grant mentions a "Col. G.G. Pride, volunteer aide, and Capt. J.P. Hawkins, chief commissary, who accompanied me upon the field."[27] Captain J.P. Hawkins was actually General Halleck's department commissary officer from St. Louis.[28] If he made attempts to supply provisions, he was just arrived and would not have known thoroughly the division placements on the field or the commissary officers well. There is no other mention of him. With regard to Col. G.G. Pride, who was actually an engineer, there is another mention of him, a year later, coincidentally at the same time that Grant was pursuing the discrediting of General Lew Wallace. At the time Col. Pride was resigning, Grant sent him a courtesy letter that read: "At Pittsburg Landing on that memorable 6th of April 1862, when our men were being forced back from their first line were left without ammunition, except the supply in their cartridge boxes, by your foresight and energy in superintending in person, you kept up the supply from a single ordnance boat and over roads impassable."[29]

A surface consideration would cause a person to think that Col. G.G. Pride had everything under control. The content of this courtesy commendation, however, is quite revealing. Grant describes "when our men [by] being forced back from their first line were left without ammunition." Why were the men without ammunition? It is because the chief quartermaster was not there. Grant says Pride took charge "when our men were being forced back from their first line." Grant was nowhere near the Union first line when it was forced back. It can only be conjectured where he meant in this letter to Colonel Pride. The battle had been going on for four hours by the time he appeared on the field, so his perception of "first line" is far off base and only predicated on his personal experience when he finally showed up on the field. There is conviction of the huge mistake he made in sending Captain Baxter away revealed in the expression, "when our men were left without ammunition." Why were they left without ammunition? The chief of supply at the time, Captain A.S. Baxter, was somewhere in transit to merely deliver a message. His explanation of the vital role Col. G.G. Pride filled was in a private letter. It is one of the curiosities of Grant's report that in mentioning volunteer aide Col. G.G. Pride he does not say what function Pride performed other than he "accompanied me on the field." To have said in his official report that a "volunteer aide" was performing the function of overseeing the ammunition supply officially in charge of the quartermaster department and its general A.S. Baxter would have drawn attention to the mistake. Coupled with the fact he does not mention Captain A.S. Baxter at all, it is a conviction that Grant purposely hid the mistake of cutting off the head of his supply and transportation corps.

The Actual Delivery of the Order

The momentous ride back to Crump's Landing for Captain Baxter must have been anxiety-ridden with an elevated heart rate. The message itself was simple enough to deliver, it was important to get the message to General Lew Wallace, but what about his own quartermaster corps? He had seen and had been dealing with the conditions at the landing and its horrendously chaotic state, thousands of stragglers huddling beneath the bluffs while teamsters, quartermasters, commissary staff cavalry and artillerymen stalwart enough to buck the growing crowd tried to get their tasks done. Yet, there amidst that chaos, he had been singled out and taken away from the corps of men who needed his direction. The order was coming from the commanding General Grant. The question was, did Rawlins have to pick him? That point was moot, and Captain Baxter was not one to question orders. All he could do was be about the matter as urgently as possible.

Earlier that morning, what took place shows General Lew Wallace was in readiness:

> In anticipation of an order from General Grant to join him at that place, the equipage of the several brigades loaded in wagons for instant removal to my first camp at the river. The First and Third Brigades were also ordered to concentrate at the camp of the Second, from which proceeded the nearest and most practicable road to the scene of battle. At 11:30 o'clock the anticipated order arrived, directing me to come up and take position on the right of the army and form my line of battle at a right angle with the river. As it also directed me to leave a force to prevent surprise at Crump's Landing, the Fifty-sixth Ohio and Sixty-eighth Ohio Regiments were detached for that purpose, with one gun from Lieutenant Thurber's battery. Selecting a road that led directly to the right of the lines as they were established around Pittsburg Landing on Sunday morning, my column started immediately, the distance being about 6 miles.[30]

Of the quoted times in all of the commentary about the delivery of the message transmission, "11:30 o'clock" is the most plausible. At the time Wallace had no ax to grind or cross to bear in regard to accusations against him. None had been made. It also gives evidence that a watch was on his person or that of his staff. Based on all the writings of Lew Wallace, he was a man particular of detail.

On April 25, 1863, more than a year after the battle, Grant wrote: "Certainly not later than 11 A.M. the order reached General Wallace to March by a flank movement to Pittsburg Landing." Even by Grant and Rawlins's prejudiced reckoning, Captain Baxter would still have taken two hours to get to Wallace.[31] Therefore the round trip took four hours. This still put the chief quartermaster away from the field most of the day.

Baxter testified decades later: "On meeting General Wallace I gave the order verbally, also handed to him the written order. General Wallace said he was waiting for orders, had heard the firing all morning and was ready to move with his command immediately — knew the road and had put it in good order."[32]

His return trip would be at least another two hours. Without arguing any other time factors, Chief Quartermaster Baxter was gone four hours according to times supplied by Grant and Rawlins. That has to mean he returned to Pittsburg Landing around 1:00 P.M. At that time the Union right was beaten back to Jones Field that lay along the Savannah–Pittsburg Landing Road. It coincides with the time frame that Lt. Col. Enos P. Wood states in his report that he decided "to move off closer to the river for ammunition. This was about noon."

Allowing enough time for Lt. Col. Enos P. Wood to make his way over almost impassable roads, choked with ambulances, artillery caissons and teamster wagons, a distance of one and a half miles to the vicinity of the quartermaster activities, Wood rendezvoused with Captain Baxter at the time he returned, no doubt close to 1:00 P.M. The consequences of the time that Baxter, the district quartermaster, had been gone? Grant's words against Lew Wallace could be turned back upon him: "There is no estimating the difference this might have made in our casualties."

For one hundred and fifty years the public has been led to believe by U.S. Grant's overwhelming influence that the high casualties at the Battle of Shiloh would not have happened if only General Lew Wallace's division had showed up and fought the first day.[33] The fact is, General Lew Wallace and his division did show up the first day of the Battle of Shiloh. He and his division were brought to the place that had been prepared beforehand. The fact is, he did not take a "wrong road." The road he took was "the most practicable" and had been discussed by two division generals, Lew Wallace and W.H.L Wallace. The indications are that General Sherman of the 5th Division also knew which road was being prepared. It was General U.S. Grant himself who had instigated preparations in the direction toward Purdy, with segments called the Shunpike. It was not the matter of the road taken, *it was the matter of the courier chosen to take the message.*

With this in view, a discussion of marches and countermarches by General Lew Wallace will likely only keep the status quo, because it focuses on the road taken. Emphasis on the Lew Wallace march is obfuscation. In the appendix of this volume are the official reports that are pertinent to the Grant–Wallace matter. The reader may pursue them at leisure, minding that they are filled with contradictions and personality clashes. They are a tangled web. It is time to bring justice to the issue. No better a person than Captain Algernon Sydney Baxter could give the final word: "My stay with Lew Wallace did not exceed three minutes, I had no further conversation with him, and I returned immediately to Pittsburg Landing."[34] It is time to de-emphasize the route General Lew Wallace took to get to Shiloh battlefield and return to Pittsburg Landing for a close personal look at the casualties.

16

The Cost

There are defining events in the history of the United States that have had such an impact as to resonate like a clanging bell long after the clapper has stopped hitting metal. Mention the sinking of the *Titanic*, and people generations later are enthralled. Call to mind December 7, 1941, "a date which will live in infamy," and Pearl Harbor's grief and outrage still lingers. And, alas, there is 9/11. The Battle of Shiloh was also such an event when it first happened. The nation was so shocked at the tremendous number of dead, wounding and missing in the Battle of Shiloh, that it kept reeling until Antietam, Chickamauga, Gettysburg and a couple of dozen equally costly battles numbed the nation so as not to be able to sort out which was the worst.

It is important to get the conglomerate numbers of both sides of the Battle of Shiloh; they were, after all, both American. The total number of casualties, of men dead, wounded and missing, was about 24,000. Casualties at the battle of Shiloh involved deaths in forms so diverse that the macabre encounters with the dead bodies and parts of bodies left the observers both fascinated and ever changed. William Dean Howell, friend of General and future President James Garfield, who witnessed Shiloh's carnage, stated the way Garfield reacted: "At the sight of these dead men whom other men had killed, something went out of him, the habit of a lifetime, that never came back again: the sacredness of life and the impossibility of destroying it." Shiloh was the first great battle of the Civil War, and as more great battles came, a North Carolina soldier described the men killing other men as "majestic murder."[1] Some wounded very often survived, only to have the missiles and debris that disabled them be the ultimate cause of death years later. An example was Lt. Colonel Fairchild of the 16th Wisconsin. After his wounding at Shiloh in some of the first assaults by the Confederates, he returned home with the ball in his upper thigh. He recovered to the extent that he continued as commander until the war was over. A year later and two weeks into his marriage, he served as a pallbearer for a friend. The weight of carrying his friend's coffin cracked his pencil-thin thigh bone, which severed an artery, and he died from the wound he received at Shiloh.[2] The country became filled with common sights of the disfigured veterans and sometimes stumpy torsos of once vital men and some women. As to the missing, that is a varied tale. Most disappeared because of desertion or were captured and placed into a prisoner of war camp. Others simply disappeared because artillery left nothing of them to bury, or they died in the woods while taking refuge and were never found.

It is not just the totality of numbers in a newspaper that stays with a society; it is when every community is touched in some way by a death or wounding or someone missing. The communities that deserve the most attention in this book are those of the 6th Division, but especially of the 16th Wisconsin. It is a member of that division, Lt. Richard P. Derickson, who was instrumental in the researching of this book. Especially does his home Company K deserve not simply a numeration of those dead, wounded or missing, but of names that humanize those statistics.

The Microcosm of Co. K 16th Wisconsin

The voice of 16th Wisconsin veteran Daniel E. McGinley rings through the decades as he sentimentally remembers his Company K of the 16th Wisconsin after many of them had passed away. This excerpt is taken from *The Port Washington Star*, June 20, 1896:

In September, 1861, Geo. C. Williams, a lawyer of Port Washington, secured a commission and commenced recruiting the "Ozaukee Rifles," which subsequently became Company "K," of the Sixteenth Regiment of Wisconsin Volunteer Infantry. With but a very few exceptions the members of the "Rifles" were splendid specimens of the American soldier, were brimming over with patriotism, and entered the service with the determination to sacrifice, if need be, their fortunes, health, limbs and lives for their country. If the history of this company was properly written it would be very interesting as it saw a great deal of hard service, lost heavily in battle and by disease, and was very unfortunate in other ways, but nevertheless made a record of which its surviving members are justly proud.

At the time the "Rifles" came into existence, the war had become a much graver reality than most people had supposed it would when Ft. Sumter's guns bade defiance to rebellion. The boys who enlisted then knew full well that their work at the front would be anything but a holiday parade, as some of the earlier volunteers had expected theirs would be. The Union defeats at Bull Run and Wilson's Creek had shown the Federal government that its small army was totally unable to cope with the gigantic rebellion, and had warned the North and the world that the slaveholders were in earnest, and that the war would be a long, bloody and costly one.

An intense excitement or patriotic fervor was pervading our state at this time, the shrill music of the fife and the roll of the drum were resounding along the streets of the cities, on the village greens, and through the country lanes; and although they were aware that the chances were greatly against their safe return, thousands of young men and boys were hurrying to the front in response to the calls for volunteers to serve "three years or during the war." Previous to this time, Ozaukee boys had left the county, singly and in small squads, to enlist in organizations from other counties, but now when a movement was on foot to raise a whole company within the county, local pride was touched and the boys flocked so quickly around the standard of the "Ozaukee Rifles" that it was nearly full at the end of four weeks. The first members of the "Rifles" were sworn in on September 19, and enough had been enrolled by October 15, to warrant the acceptance of the company by the Governor.

The headquarters of the Rifles were in the old Arcade Hall, Port Washington, and the members were quartered in different hotels, and boarding houses. Enough of musicians were soon enrolled to form a fife and drum corps, and the inspiring music to which the boys marched proudly and enthusiastically made their enthusiasm being very catching as many a recruit could aver. Here is an example. James Wilson, a young, married Irishman, then living in the town of Scott, came to Port Washington on business. On his way home he saw the "Rifles" marching into town after an afternoon's drill, and was so captivated by the martial music, flaunting colors and the fine appearance of the company, that he fell in love with it on the spot, and hurrying home he told his wife that he must go to the war in that company. Next day he became one of the Rifles, and gave his life for his adopted country, at the front May 23, 1862. The vacant lots which then abounded in the outskirts of the town made very good drill and parade grounds, where the company spent many long hours learning the rudiments of the drill, so essential in the education of the soldier. Sometimes they took long marches out into the country for the two-fold purpose of becoming accustomed to marching and of gathering in recruits.

In the second week of October the company elected its officers. The commissioned officers chosen were:

Geo. C. Williams, of Port Washington, Captain.
Rich. P. Derrickson, of Grafton, 1st Lieutenant.
David F. Vail, of Port Washington, 2nd Lieutenant.

The sergeants: John L. Derrickson, of Grafton; Edward D. Bradford, of Fredonia; John Gough, of Saukville; Lorenzo D. Osgood, Milo M. Whedon, of Port Washington.

The corporals: Ephriam Cooper, of Grafton; Louis C. DeCoudres, Sam'l Gunther and Thomas E. Wildman, of Port Washington; John Goggin and John P. McGinley, of Saukville; Geo. W. Hedding and Orlando J. Valentine, of Fredonia.

The privates enrolled previous to the departure of the company for the state camp were: John Bristol, Jerome Case, John and Wm. Clark, John Cody, Robt. A. and Wm. W. Coleman, Anth. Collins, Wm. and Geo. D. Cooper, A.J.

Cowen, Stewart Daniels, Wallace W. Davis, Chr. Benson, Allen Godfrey, F.C. Kerner, Nils Livson, Thos. Manning, John Murphy, Lars Nelson, Ole Oleson and James Wilson No. 1, of Grafton.

Nic. Colling, Edmund Gee, John Hennessey, G. Janish, Jos. Johann, R.C. Kann, Dennis Mangin, Corn. Murphy, Wm. E. Pierce, Wm. Richards, Tax. W. Shaw, Ogden Tomlinson, Wm. A. and Stoel H. Tousley, James Toole, Pat. Walsh No. 1, L.W. White and Samuel H. Wildman, of Port Washington.

Pat. Carroll, Chas. W. and Lyman W. Chapman, Rich. Goggin, Robt. B. Ingersoll, Pat. Keogh, Thos. Murphy, James O'Hare, Samuel Orcutt, Wm. H. Pawlett, D.B. Raynor, James Reeves, Chas. and Henry Thomas and Pat. Walsh No. 2, of Saukville.

Peter Beckus, Chas. W. Brott, Augustus Hyde, Rich. Kershaw, Edward M. O'Neill, Jacob Smith and Benj. Walker of Fredonia.

James Wilson No. 2, of Scott; Rich. J. Powers of Milwaukee; Jonathan W. Pulford of Plymouth; and Chas. H. Townsend of Mequon.

The privates enrolled after the company reached the camp were: Chas. A. Ayres, Isaac G. Kendall and E.D. King, of Grafton; E.B. Brewster, David Porter, Henry C. Ramsey, Selby Trumbull and Thomas Wildman, Sr., of Port Washington; Charles Gatfield of Fredonia; Wm. Goggin, of Saukville; John Beard, Mansel Barnes, Hiram Franklin, Steph. Golather, James H. Rooney, John Turner and Louis Wert, of Dane county; A.B. Hunt, of Beloit; John R. Burge, of Farmington; Philander Watkins, of Saxeville; and O.B. Underhill and John J. Vincent, whose residence was not given.

There were 104 in all, 66 of whom were born in the United States, 11 in Germany, 9 in Ireland, 8 in the British Dominions, 4 in Norway, two in England, one in Scotland and the nativity of three is unknown. Their ages ranged from 15 to 55, and averaged 26 years. The married members numbered 32, 16 of whom were killed or died in the service, while others died after the war of diseases contracted in the army.

On the 22nd of November, 1861, the Ozaukee Rifles left the county under orders to report at Camp Randall, Madison, Wis. The company was conveyed to Milwaukee by the ill-fated steamer Sea-Bird and thence by rail to its destination. One member deserted at Port Washington and one in Milwaukee, but neither of their names appears in the foregoing roster of the company.

In that terrible harvest of death on the first day of the Battle of Shiloh, the Sixteenth had lost 80 killed, 152 wounded and a few missing. Of that number the Ozaukee Rifles had lost more than its share: Brave, heroic Ephriam Cooper and William Clark, both of the town of Grafton, had said that they would never turn their backs to the foe in battle, and they both kept their word, dying in the first line. John Hennessey was also killed on that line while bravely doing his whole duty. In those never-to-be-forgotten struggles on the parade ground and in the rear of the camp three more of the Ozaukee boys gave their lives for their starry banner. They were the portly English gentleman and sterling patriot Thomas Manning, of the town of Grafton, and the heroic Americans, William A. and Stoel H. Tousley, father and son, of Port Washington. There were five mortally wounded, the brave, patriotic young German, Samuel Gunther, of Port Washington, and four noble, heroic young Americans, little more than boys in years, Orlando J. Valentine, and Ed. M. O'Neil of Fredonia, John Murphy, of Port Washington, and Elijah D. King of Port Ulao. There were 16 others of the Rifles wounded, Capt. Williams, very slightly; Lieut. David F. Vail severely in leg; Sergeants, John L. Derrickson and Ed. D. Bradford; Corporals, Selby Trumble, Geo. W. Hedding and Thos. E. Wildman, privates, Ben. Walker, James Reeves, John Clark, Anthony Collins, Wm. Cooper, Cornelius Murphy, Lars Nelson, Gregory Janish and Robert H. Ingersoll. Thus we find that the loss of the Rifles was 6 killed and 21 wounded, 5 mortally. These figures speak louder than words and prove with what heroism, devotion and endurance our gallant Ozaukee boys fought on Shiloh's storied field on that memorable Easter Sunday of 1862 [*sic*: Easter was two weeks later]. The friends of the members of the heroic band have ever been proud of that organization since that eventful day, and every citizen of the county can now point with pride to the record made by its company when it grappled with the foe and helped to turn defeat into a great victory on Shiloh's "dark and bloody ground."[3]

Lt. Richard P. Derickson kept his documents, some seen in this book, but among them are no personal letters. Fortunately one of his letters was recorded in his hometown newspaper, the *Ozaukee Advertiser and Democrat,* so his own voice testifies to the state of affairs while the battle was still raging on the second day. He writes to his friend and the brother of Company K, 16th Wisconsin 2nd Lt. Daniel Vail:

> On Board Steamer Galena
> Pittsburg, Tenn.
> April 6, 1862

J.W. Vail:- Sir — I write you amidst great excitement, but will give you correct information in so far as it goes. The fight, of which you will receive telegraph news before you receive this, commenced yesterday morning about daylight. The first attack was made on our right, which was badly cut up. Col. Allen and Lieut. Colonel Fairchild are both badly wounded.

Killed: Capt. Saxe Company A, E. Cooper, Wm. Clark, Henry Thomas, B. Walker, of Company K, Lieut. Vail Company I.

Badly Wounded: D. Vail, in thigh; J. Clark, in head; Thos. Manning, O.J. Valentine, Wm. Cooper, Bradford O'Neil, and S. Gunther.

Slightly Wounded: Captain Williams; J. Derickson in hand.

I do not give names of all, but such as occur to me now.

The following were safe up to 10:00 today: H. Ramsey, R. Cowen, John Burge, C. Gatfield, Joseph Johann, Wm. Richards, Hedding, George Cooper, John Gough, P. Cahoe, McGinley, Ingersoll, the two Chapmans, and Charles Thomas.

This morning, we could not find more than thirty of our company, but it is quite probable that more will come in soon. I acted as aid to Gen. Prentiss yesterday, until our Division was broken up and Gen. P. taken prisoner. Today I am acting as Q.M. Gen of the Sixth Division.

I have taken Henry Ramsey and most of the boys into my service, so they are comparatively out of danger. Our company have done enough fighting for one time.

I will say for the comfort of all but that one coward was found in the company, and he is not from Ozaukee.

Your brother is now in Savanah and is comparatively easy and comfortable.

Fighting goes on most terribly today, but I think we will whip them yet.

In Haste,

R.P. Derickson[4]

The last statement that Derickson makes here echoes the famous statement, "We will whip them tomorrow," that Grant made to Sherman on the night of April 6. It is possible that Derickson was in proximity of the statement when it was made. The role Derickson played upon the return of Captain Baxter suggests that he came under General Grant's observation. Since Baxter was Grant's staff quartermaster, and Derickson was an immediate subordinate in Baxter's corps as the quartermaster general of Prentiss' Division, it appears that Grant took note of Derickson. By Grant's order on April 10 after the battle, Derickson was given authority to "impress all teams necessary into his service in bringing in the wounded and taking provisions to the regiments in the advance." Those loyal to Grant were rewarded during his presidency. After the war Grant appointed Richard P. Derickson as tax assessor and collector for the district about Chicago. Derickson also served as a congressman in Illinois. Although war numbed the compassion of many, in Derickson it may have been cathartic, for he also served as the third president of the Illinois Humane Society.

On the Southern Side

In the estimation of General U.S Grant, "the Confederate assaults were made with such disregard of losses on that our line of tents fell into their hands."[5] There is much truth to that statement. About the time Baxter was returning to Pittsburg Landing from delivering the order to General Lew Wallace, Confederate chief commander General Albert Sidney Johnston was living out the last hour of his life. He had said regarding the Union troops at Pittsburg Landing that he "would fight them if they were a million."[6]

From 12: 00 M (noon) until 2:00 P.M. a relative stalemate was fought in the region of the Hornet's Nest, the peach orchard, and east of the Hamburg road. Seeing this, Johnston sought to direct troops to the Union left. It was part of his battle plan. He had wanted to push the Federals away from the river and cut them off from being re-enforced. He considered this so important that when seeing his men becoming impotent in that sector he began behaving like a brigade commander rather than the chief of the Army. The Tennessee and Arkansas men were stagnated. Even after sending Isham Harris, the Tennessee governor, to get them going, they could not be moved. Finally Johnston personally rode up and down their lines giving a stirring speech that encouraged them to move. Taking the little cup he had said was part of his spoils, he touched individual bayonets and told them how noble they were. His men were moved, and his encouragement indeed caused them to have courage and mount a successful attack.[7] Then Johnston cantered off to the far right to observe the progress and for a time he was alone. His horse was hit by a ball. Then a projectile hit the heel of his boot. At the same time something had hit him behind the knee. He was unaware for a time that it had happened. Soon he began to swoon, his boot having filled with blood loss from a severed artery. He had made the humane mistake of sending his surgeon away to care for the wounded of his enemy, and when his aide Isham Harris returned, he found General Johnston reeling in the saddle. Harris reached out to steady him, asking if he was hurt. "Yes ... and I fear seriously," were his last conscious words. Harris could not help. Another officer and a relative by marriage, Col William Preston, rode up, and between the two of these men, they eased Johnston to the ground and carried him to a ravine for cover. Searching for torso damage and finding none, with the mortal wound covered by his tall boot, they had no idea where to apply a tourniquet, not realizing the location of the damage. Johnston's life ebbed from him in a few minutes, and he died about 2:30 P.M.[8]

It was during this period that the infantry of Cummings and Maney that had been with Colonel Nathan Bedford Forrest and Wirt Adams moved up from Greer's Ford after several hours guarding that "damned creek." Maney's Brigade proved to be a decisive factor in breaking the Federal line in Sara Bell's cotton field nearing the peach orchard. Maney is credited with a canny tactic of causing his men to lie down amidst the smoke of the battle, fire a volley, then wait for Federal response. Seeing the flash of their muskets when the Northerners returned fire, it enabled Maney and his brigade to determine direction and strength of the Federal line. They jumped up, charged headlong and reckless into the Federal fire of Colonel Pugh's brigade.[9] What Maney did not know was that he had serendipitously hit the very area that was especially practicing economy of firing by the Federals. Pugh, Colonel John Logan and the other officers in that area knew of no arrangements for resupply of cartridges.[10]

Soon Colonel Forrest's and Wirt Adams's Cavalry joined the fray, largely keeping to the woods in front of the Hornet's Nest. Normally serving as the eyes and ears of the army, Forrest was transforming his command into more of a guerrilla-style fighting force, more accurately performing as mounted infantry. They tried to take a Federal battery but were repulsed.[11] Recoiling, Forrest fell back, and there is little record of the part his men played through the afternoon, but there can be no doubt they were actively seeking the weak points of the Federal lines. Oral accounts in the author's family state that Wirt Adams's Cavalry then became associated with Jackson's Brigade. It was one of few to penetrate the farthest into the Union positions just across the Dill Ravine at Pittsburgh Landing.[12]

Private Sam Watkins with Maney's Brigade in the 1st Tennessee took part in the successful attack upon the Federals and unknowingly witnessed a scene he only deduced the meaning of later. In the jubilation of the moments of success he states: "Advancing a little further on, we saw General Albert Sidney Johnson surrounded by his staff and Governor Harris, of Tennessee. We saw some little commotion among those who surrounded him, but we did not know at the time that he was dead. The fact was kept from the troops."[13]

In the minds of most Southerners, the loss of Albert Sidney Johnston was the cause of the Confederate failure at the Battle of Shiloh, even the whole war, but the failure of the Battle of Shiloh was not about who won or lost. There was no clear winner of the Battle of Shiloh, if that can competently be ascertained by some yardstick. As Sam Watkins stated: "Now, those Yankees were whipped, fairly whipped, and according to all the rules of war they ought to have retreated. But they didn't."[14]

Both sides were losers with the casualty counts unimaginably high. Union general Rosseau gave the assessment that it was little credit to the Federals for a victory. "It must not be forgotten that we fought this battle some miles within the lines of the encampment of General Grant's army and in the camps occupied by his troops, and it was thereby rendered apparent to the most ignorant soldier that the army had been driven in by the enemy till within a few hundred yards of the river and that the work before us was by no means easy."[15]

However, the Confederates had not driven the Federals out of Tennessee. That was the tactical loss for the Confederates. Then began a search for the scapegoat to salve the loss. General G.T. Beauregard became that scapegoat.

Inadequacy of Description

The above anecdotes do not begin to approach the totality of the losses that were being suffered on the fields of Shiloh by both sides. Trying to give the full impact of the individual stories of all the men at Shiloh would be like giving short biographies of every person listed in the phone book. It has not been the purpose of the book to resemble the more comprehensive studies of the Battle of Shiloh. The recapitulation by Major D.W. Reed in *The Battle of Shiloh and the Organizations Engaged* (revised 1909 edition) shows the five divisions of the Union Army that were engaged at Pittsburgh landing on April 6 sustained the following casualties. Out of 39,830 Federals on fighting on the fields of Shiloh, there were 1,473 killed, 6,202 wounded, and 2,818 missing, for a total of 10,493 Union casualties on the first day of the battle of Shiloh.[16]

On the Confederate side, reports do not allow a separation of the two days of battle. The total number of troops engaged given in Reed's book were 43,968. Casualties for both days were 1,728 killed, 8,012 wounded, and 959 missing, for a total of 10,699 Confederate casualties over both days of battle.[17]

The grand total of both Union and Confederate Armies involved both days, after reinforcements, was 111,511 engaged, with 3,482 killed, 16,420 wounded, and 3,844 missing, for a total of 23,746 American casualties.[18]

The Death of Compromise

What is one of the root causes that drove all these Americans to kill and maim one another? The cause is alluded to by General Lew Wallace in a letter he wrote to Secretary of War Stanton on August 25, 1862. At the time he wrote the letter, he had been shelved by General U.S. Grant while on a home leave, and his whole division had been dissolved. Trying any way he could, as an unattached major general in Lexington, Kentucky, to get back into action, he wrote this letter on behalf of the grandson of Henry Clay, the "Great Compromiser." Addressing Stanton, he requested, "I beg leave to present the name of my young friend, Thomas H. Clay of this City for appointment to the Staff. Mr. Clay is a grand son of Henry Clay.... The Government will lose nothing by having such names enlisted on its side in the struggle...."[19]

When compromise is abandoned, the brush strokes of the tongue use pigments only of black and white. One with the ability to effect compromise is an artist with a many-colored palette. In the antebellum world, Henry Clay was one of these rare men. With similarities to Abraham Lincoln, but an elder generation than he, Clay crafted his negotiation skills in sparse rural settings with the aim of influencing heavier concentrations of human minds in the population centers and the ruling complex of Washington, D.C. A story told about him, which is hard to verify, states that as a teen he would retreat to the family barn under lantern light and give great discourses to the attention of barnyard animals that represented his imaginary audience. There in the

ON FAME'S ETERNAL CAMPING-GROUND,
THEIR SILENT TENTS ARE SPREAD,
AND GLORY GUARDS WITH SOLEMN ROUND
THE BIVOUAC OF THE DEAD.

The words of Shiloh veteran Theodore O'Hara at the National Cemetery at Shiloh (photograph by the author).

solitude, among the smells of bovine and swine manure, he mastered not only golden tones of his larynx, but an understanding that each quarter of creation deserved a hearing and careful attention no matter the stink. When Henry Clay died, there was no successor with his skills in the halls of government to influence public opinion. The harsh extremes of the mid-nineteenth century social structure caused voices of levity to quickly sink into the mire. Rare was the clergyman who preached the lesson of Solomon, where the woman who was the true mother of the baby gave it up to the other woman so it would not be hurt. When the secession crisis came, both sides claimed the "baby" of sovereign rights but allowed for unimaginable bloodshed in their efforts to keep the baby as their own.

As has been stated, there is a temptation to paint other people with broad brush strokes. It is this tendency, in its worst manifestations, that leads to the idea that war is the only answer. What enables a nation or a person to go to war does not happen with the drop of a hat. There is a formula for getting to war. At the National Museum of Nuclear Science and History is a display that shows the path to get to war. Examining these principles exposes what brought on the Civil War. The formula comprises these steps: Assertion, Bandwagon, Card Stacking, Glittering Generalities, Lesser of Two Evils, Name Calling, Pinpointing the Enemy, Plain Folks, Testimonials and Transference.

Assertion often implies that the statement requires no explanation. *Bandwagon* is an appeal to follow the crowd, to join because others are doing so as well, hence "Get on the bandwagon." *Card Stacking* can also be termed selective omission. It involves only presenting information positive to an idea or proposal and omitting information contrary to it. *Glittering Generalities* are words that have positive meaning for an individual, but are linked to highly valued concepts. When used, they demand approval without thinking, simply because such an important concept is involved. *Lesser of Two Evils* is a matter of adding blame to an enemy country or political group as if it is the only option or path. *Name Calling* involves the use of derogatory language or words that carry a negative connotation when describing an enemy. It arouses prejudice, labeling the subject something the public dislikes, especially in cartoons or writings. *Pinpointing the Enemy* is the attempt to simplify a complex situation by presenting one specific group or person as the enemy, reducing it to black and white, as if it simply is a matter of clear-cut right and wrong. *Plain Folks* is an attempt to convince the public that the view reflects that of the common person, and that they are also working for the benefit of the common person. The speaker will often use the accent of the audience, specific idioms or jokes, and will increase the illusion through imperfect pronunciation, stuttering or a limited vocabulary. This makes the plea sound more sincere and spontaneous, and is often a companion of *Glittering Generalities*. *Testimonials* connect a famous or respectable person with the product or item, in this case the need to go to war. *Transference* is an attempt to make the subject view a certain item in the same way as they view another item, to link the two in the subject's mind. It can transfer a negative or positive most often used to transfer blame and bad feelings.

Once the war began, pragmatic destructionists like U.S. Grant and Robert E. Lee, and war-machine realists like W.T. Sherman and Nathan Bedford Forrest, took over. These gladiators did their jobs with unsentimental determination. Idealists, intellectual minds and pacifists could only enter the coliseum and watch. Some individuals reconciled themselves to combat by blending warfare with romanticism and religion, like a knight in shining armor who kills to get to the Holy Grail. Lew Wallace falls into this category. His later novel, *Ben-Hur: A Tale of the Christ*, reflects both his romantic bent, but perhaps the postwar realization that the Last Supper drinking cup, called the "Holy Grail," was not the thing of value; the thing of value was the example of the man who drank out of it.

17

Elephants

During the Civil War the expression to "see the elephant" meant to experience the impact of the battlefield. It was not the first time the elephant had been used as an analogy. "Seeing the elephant" appeared as a metaphor during the Mexican War. California gold miners and westward wagon trains experienced such great travails as to describe their experience as "seeing the elephant." The expression may go back as far as Alexander the Great in India, where he encountered the horror of monstrous elephants in battle, or the revolt against Rome by Hannibal, who took elephants through the Alps. In this examination the elephant analogy will be applied to important but unacknowledged things.

Black Americans on the Field at Shiloh

Surely at Shiloh the participants saw the elephant of battle, but there are mere passing mentions in the historical accounts this early in the war about the participation of black Americans. Their mention remains peripheral in some respects to the very battles that took place as a result of the abolitionist vs. states' rights arguments. It is not possible to determine how many black people witnessed or participated in the Battle of Shiloh. There were surely hundreds stoking the boilers of the scores of steamships that brought the combatants to the field. A number of regiments at Shiloh had colored cooks. The CWSS (Civil War Soldiers and Sailors database) reveals the 21st Missouri apparently had colored cooks in all of its companies, and other regiments had black personnel. These African Americans were at special risk if the units were taken prisoner. The 21st Missouri did have many prisoners taken at the Battle of Shiloh. The fate of these colored cooks is uncertain. If taken they would have been treated as plundered property, or worse, killed for rising up against white supremacy. Even the North referred to escaped

189

Colonel Madison Miller and his body servant James Milton Turner, who went to Shiloh with Miller, one of an undetermined number of African Americans who had a part in the battle. He escaped capture, unlike the man he served, and claimed he helped bring whiskey to General Grant (Library of Congress).

blacks as "contrabands," a word that still viewed them from an ownership perspective.

Slaves were definitely present in the communities around Pittsburg Landing. The owner of the Cherry Mansion was a slaveholder. With a little over 11,000 residents, approximately 15 percent of Hardin County was composed of slaves. This lends credence to Union reconnaissance reports of slaves reporting the presence of the Confederates on April 5.[1] There are mentions of Southern officers who brought black servants to the battlefield. Sam Watkins of the 1st Tennessee says: "The negro boys, who were with their young masters as servants, got rich. Greenbacks were plentiful, good clothes were plentiful, rations were not in demand. The boys were in clover."[2] A somewhat humorous incident of a slave donning a Union officer's uniform in a captured Union camp seems to indicate he made a getaway while some Confederates were drunk on captured whiskey. To witness the incident, if true, would have shown the talent of obsequious art that had been developed by blacks under oppression. One might picture the slave seeing his opportunity amidst the bizarre revelry of the taken Union battle camp. While the jubilant rebels forgot themselves in the moment, the slave picked up the uniform and clowned. Then, seeing his moment, he danced out of sight.

There were Union officers who brought black servants with them as well.

Colonel Madison Miller was one of those who brought a black man as his body servant to the field of Shiloh, James Milton Turner. Turner went on to become a leader in establishing civil rights and education for blacks after the war.[3]

Shiloh, however, was a major event that led to blacks fighting in combat for themselves. Shiloh was actually an accident of what was officially the Tennessee River Campaign against Corinth. Corinth, with its railroad crossroads, was the object of the Union thrust. Had the Confederates not decided to strike, coming out from behind their defenses at Corinth, the casualties of Shiloh would have come at that Mississippi town instead, and it would have had a bigger name in history than it has today. Corinth should be a more recognizable name in black history because it was at Corinth, after the Union established its presence there, that large numbers of blacks were drawn to a "contraband" camp, and where subsequently great numbers of them were recruited as United States Colored Troops.[4]

More Than One Church at Shiloh

Everyone knows that the log meeting house gave Shiloh its name. While Shiloh Church is most often dealt with delicately as a holy site, its name supposedly meaning "Place of Peace," that church's theology figured in the conflict. It is another figurative elephant on the literal battlefield that to this day receives a roundabout. The theology of the southern Methodists who met in that little church advocated slavery. In the years following the civil war, a mythical folderol came into being about the meeting house. In an attempt to put a different face on the horror, a plaque at this historical site proclaims that Shiloh means "place of peace." In Biblical history the Israelite town Shiloh was a "place of peace" only at times (Judges 21:19, Joshua 18:1; Joshua 22:10–34). It was also a place of disgrace in other Biblical quotations (Psalms 78:60, 61; 1 Samuel 4:21, 22; Jeremiah 7:12, 14; 26:6, 9). The word Shiloh itself is not translatable as "House of Peace" or "Place of Peace." The Southern Methodist Episcopal chapel at the time of the battle made it appropriately a symbol for the real issues: a war being fought about black people and states' rights to determine their fate.

That little log meeting house existed because its members favored slavery and some members were slaveholders. They had not wished fellowship with those who were against slavery. People of that West Hardin County community had once worshipped together at what was called Union Church. Its 19th century location was near the present Michigan Monument, where the Pittsburgh-Corinth and Purdy-Hamburg roads meet. It was not called the Union

Church because of being Unionist. It was merely called that because it was sited at the union of roads. It is not clear whether that Union Church building was still in existence at the time of the battle.[5] The small community above Pittsburg Landing was a true mirror of the struggles of the nation.

Shiloh is not translated correctly as "Place of Peace." The true meaning is: "He Whose It Is; He to Whom It Belongs," that is, the person to whom the right of kingship belongs. It is one of the names signifying Christ or Messiah.[6] The professors of Christianity lost a lot at Shiloh. Palm Sunday came a week after the battle, April 13, historically observed as the day Christ rode into Jerusalem on a colt as the son of David and Prince of Peace. Irony does come into play. Calling the battle "Shiloh" was like casting off the rider of the colt, the Prince of Peace. The carcasses of colts were still burning that Palm Sunday. Robert Ingersoll or Henry Morton Stanley would decry the religious involvement is this kind of thing. The stench of the battlefield rose in the nostrils of those gathered for Easter Services the next week, April 20, while chaplains blessed the affected consciences of former choir boys and believers trying to reconcile what they had done.[7] Many never would have time to reconcile their experiences at Shiloh, like Lt. Oliver Perry Newberry, who died young, self-medicating with alcohol, suffering what today would be called post-traumatic stress.[8]

As for the church buildings on the Shiloh battlefield, there was another one that would have been more to cynic Mark Twain's liking. Near Lick Creek was Shake-a-Rag Church. It was near here that Jackson's Confederate Brigade followed General Chalmers in early action at the behest of Supreme Commander Albert Sidney Johnston himself. The church was located across Locust Creek ravine near General Prentiss's headquarters. During the battle Girardey's Georgia battery was set up by the church and shelled the Union camps of Colonel Stuart.[9] It is a church that remains somewhat a mystery with its unusual name, though there are clues to its nature. There are almost no recorded facts that tell who its adherents were, but its name suggests it was a segregated church used by slaves who lived around those fields. It is well-known that many slavery-favoring churches held a double standard of education. Laws were passed against educating slaves, but churches also preached that "these poor pitiful souls" needed saving by "The Lord."

Inferior as they were considered, many slaveholders made provision for blacks to be taught what the master understood as Christianity; however, the worship services of slaves were kept separate, and this allowed for the development of a totally unique form of Christianity that had fusions of African culture. The name Shake-a-Rag is very visual and points to an intensely animated form of worship using the waving of scarves, which for black slaves meant a rag of cloth, while shouting praises, still common in many black churches today. There are communities in Tennessee and Arkansas that preserve this same name Shake-a-Rag, and their historical records show them to have been predominantly black communities. Also, the affectations of Pentecostal Church–style services are attributed to being the same as those that happened during the Biblical celebration of the Jewish festival of Pentecost in the book of Acts. This event is a Christian hallmark, the Bible describing "tongues of fire" that sat upon the heads of the 120 participants, and the members began speaking in "tongues." Anthropologists and missionaries working in Africa have chronicled identical displays among animist worshipping tribes. Pentecostal glossalalia, that is speaking in an unknown tongue, as well as other demonstrative manifestations of worship, have come into American prevalence with some roots in African experience.[10]

It is also to be noted that the form of music known as "ragtime" originated in the black community. The name Shake-A-Rag is suggestive of the music that evolved into secular jazz and the blues. The struggles within the black church over that musical evolution lasted late into the twentieth century in conservative black churches. Some regarded it as Devil's music.[11] Whatever eventual discoveries are made about the Shiloh Shake-a-Rag Church, General Sherman would agree with what conservative black congregations believed in one respect. Sherman found General Grant late on the rainy night of the 6th and said, "We have had the Devil's own day."

Was Grant Drunk at Shiloh?

For those who have experienced alcoholism or have lived with an alcoholic, the situation often becomes a pink elephant in the room. Everybody knows that it is there, but nobody will acknowledge the elephant's existence. Of all the controversies about General U.S. Grant, those about his drinking have lingered the most. Some who admire the very man become much like John A. Rawlins, Grant's friend and adjutant general throughout the war, and do not want to admit to the idea that he was alcoholic. It is not the purpose of this work to fully explore the matter of Grant's drinking. It is simply to say that the idea that alcoholics are incapable of functioning professionally is wrong. It may catch up with them one day, but common knowledge can bring to mind heavy drinkers who have played significant roles in important work. Ulysses S. Grant was probably a functioning alcoholic, but it did not affect his performance as a soldier. The blistering temperance attitudes of the time could hurt a famous man's career, so Rawlins took it on himself as part of his duties to deny and cover any incidence that would take away from Grant's reputation. In turn, Rawlins basked in the warmth of the older man's heterosexual, male-bonding attention. The gaping wound of his father's disappearance was succored by Grant, who did not condescend because of Rawlins's younger age, but admired him and treated him like a son. For the entire period of Rawlins's association with Grant, Rawlins worried over Grant as his father figure and fiercely covered his drinking and other short-comings.[12]

That being said, there are interesting things to relate about U.S. Grant's drinking as it relates to Shiloh. Of the reliable voices of Shiloh, James Milton Turner has escaped notice. He was a remarkable black man who negotiated his way not only through the Civil War but the Jim Crow era as well. He did it with such aplomb and shrewdness, he was appointed the first black American ambassador to any foreign country, Liberia. The voice in which he speaks cannot be discounted. He was the body servant of Colonel Madison Miller at the battle of Shiloh. He relates in a newspaper article:

> I was the body servant to the Colonel of a Missouri Regiment and on the morning of the battle fled across country eight miles to escape the confederates. Once I lay in the muddy water of a creek, submerged to the chin, and thanked Heaven I was black. Had I been white I surely would have been seen.... When I got near the river, the commander of a battery of artillery told me to go to the wharf and see whether Gen Grant had arrived. He had just come, and I showed him the way to the battery. You should have been here two hours ago, the commander shouted to Gen Grant. He replied slowly: I was fixing things for Sherman to turn the flank of the rebel charge. Have you got anything to drink? ... The artillery man told me to go to his tent and fill three quart bottles with white whiskey from the barrel. When I returned Gen Grant poured a pint of the liquid into a big cup and drank it in one draft.... Several newspaper correspondents were with Gen. Grant, and I saw them busily taking notes. One was Joseph B. McCullough of the St. Louis Globe-Democrat. I heard one of the correspondents say to him: "Give Grant H —l in your paper Joe." ... General Grant wanted me to carry whiskey for him whenever he wanted it from the river to the front, but I was too frightened by the grapeshot. Finally, he had one of his orderlies do it for him. Although General Grant drank quantities of whiskey, it did not seem to affect him in the least. To my knowledge, he was perfectly sober at the battle of Shiloh.[13]

It should also be kept in mind that this account is coming from a man who could speak with great elocution if given the circumstances for it. Turner was well educated, but in the vagaries of a black man making his way through a white man's world, the vernacular was not always precise.

Just eight years after his Shiloh experience, he was carrying the torch for his people, advocating black self-reliance and full participation in the political system. A rally was held in St. Louis to celebrate the adoption of the Fifteenth Amendment, which granted African American men the right to vote by declaring that the "right of citizens of the United States to vote shall not be denied or abridged by the United States or by any state on account of race, color, or previous condition of servitude." In a speech to those assembled, Turner's language reveals a man of intellect who spoke differently among white people so as to negotiate with obsequious diplomacy among them. James Milton Turner urged caution:

The spirit of self-reliance is the gem of all real growth in the individual, and wherever discovered in the masses it forms collective strength and contributes largely to the intelligent development of natural resources. I think it for us a fortunate circumstance that we are thus made to depend on our

James Milton Turner became ambassador to Liberia, civil rights champion and orator in the post–Civil War era (Kingdom of Calloway, Missouri).

own merit for the status we shall hold in the future. For in reading history, I find that whenever men or classes have been taught to recline dependently upon others, they have invariably lost their stimulus for active, self-reliant industry, and inertia has invariably ensued. The abstract fact of voting cannot elevate us.... I counsel individual improvement, personal effort to obtain education, wealth and every facility necessary to the citizen. I feel assured of success ultimately, provided we pursue this course.[14]

The particulars of Grant's drinking at the Battle of Shiloh may be debated, but the free black man, James Milton Turner, considered a peripheral player or "invisible elephant," is a valuable neutral witness. In Turner's Shiloh account, there is no way to know exactly who the artillery commander was or where the eight miles were that Turner says he ran. Surely this is his perception rather than the actual distance, but in other specifics Turner's account has as much semblance of truth as many other first-person accounts. Alcoholic or not, U.S. Grant or not, certainly the Battle of Shiloh was one in which many a man would have wished fortitude from a bottle.

18

The Ongoing Battle of Shiloh

The Prince Maker—John Aaron Rawlins

It can be argued that without John Rawlins, Grant's reputation as the general who won the Civil War would have not have been as sterling. Born out of an instinct for what had to be said and a determination to protect his commander and surrogate father, Rawlins enabled for 150 years the preservation of a more favorable slant on General U.S. Grant's legacy at Shiloh. The purpose of this book was to bring to light through the Derickson documents one of the strategic errors of Grant's command that has never been examined and the successful effort to pin blame on General Lew Wallace for the disaster of the first day.

It is instructive to examine the Machiavellian principles for princes coming to power during the Renaissance. These reveal a ruthlessness on the part of John Rawlins, an attorney in civilian life, which underlies his orchestration of the time-line of battle events and the subsequent dismissal of Lew Wallace as a threat. How appropriate that Machiavelli, the Italian diplomat who instructed the rulers of Italy and Europe in the art of war and government, descended from a family of attorneys who were instrumental in shaping the justice system of the country. After the expulsion of the Medicis, at only 29, he became the architect of how to forge political and military alliances among countries striving for dominance in a tumultuous grab for power and influence. He gained a reputation as a skilled negotiator, one especially adept at diplomacy in military affairs. His insights into how a new prince must stabilize the city-state in order to build an abiding political system is presented in his most famous work, *Il Principe* (*The Prince*). The adage "The end justifies the means" sums up Machiavelli's understanding that a ruler had to subjugate moral considerations in the pursuit of a stable society. For the new prince, a separation from personal morality in favor of a secure political organization ensured the stability of the governing authority. The occasional need for heartless methods and subterfuge in order to preserve a reputation and a country were sometimes necessary.

Machiavellian Principles

- Whoever conquers ... and does not demolish ... commits a great error and may expect to be ruined himself.
- War should be the only study of a prince. He should consider peace only as a breathing-time, which gives him leisure to contrive, and furnishes an ability to execute military plans.
- War is just when it is necessary; arms are permissible when there is no hope except in arms.
- To understand the nature of the people one must be a prince, and to understand the nature of the prince, one must be of the people.
- There is no avoiding war; it can only be postponed to the advantage of others.
- The promise given was a necessity of the past: the word broken is a necessity of the present.
- The new ruler must determine all the injuries that he will need to inflict. He must inflict them once and for all.
- Men are so simple and yield so readily to the desires of the moment that he who will trick will always find another who will suffer to be tricked.
- Men ought either to be indulged or utterly destroyed, for if you merely offend them they take vengeance, but if you injure them greatly they are unable to retaliate, so that the injury done to a man ought to be such that vengeance cannot be feared.
- Men rise from one ambition to another: first, they seek to secure themselves against attack, and then they attack others.
- Men should be either treated generously or destroyed, because they take revenge for slight injuries — for heavy ones they cannot.
- One change always leaves the way open for the establishment of others.
- One who deceives will always find those who allow themselves to be deceived.
- Politics have no relation to morals.
- Severities should be dealt out all at once, so that their suddenness may give less offense; benefits ought to be handed out drop by drop, so that they may be relished the more.

- Since it is difficult to join them together, it is safer to be feared than to be loved when one of the two must be lacking.
- Tardiness often robs us of opportunity, and the dispatch of our forces.
- The distinction between children and adults, while probably useful for some purposes, is at bottom a specious one, I feel. There are only individual egos, crazy for love.
- The fact is that a man who wants to act virtuously in every way necessarily comes to grief among so many who are not virtuous.
- A prince never lacks legitimate reasons to break his promise.
- A wise ruler ought never to keep faith when by doing so it would be against his interests.
- For among other evils caused by being disarmed, it renders you contemptible; which is one of those disgraceful things which a prince must guard against.
- Men are so simple and so much inclined to obey immediate needs that a deceiver will never lack victims for his deceptions.

It is likely that John A. Rawlins was familiar with Machiavelli, especially since he was a lawyer. The classic literature of the Renaissance was staple reading for educated 19th-century Americans. Whether or not he intentionally followed the principles in *The Prince*, he proved to use many of them. This review exposes John A. Rawlins not only as a fierce defender of U.S. Grant, but as the prince-maker he was at the expense of Lew Wallace and Algernon Baxter.[1]

After Shiloh

It is more than a postscript to find out why Captain Baxter was unavailable to General Grant or his closest aide John Rawlins for the scapegoating of General Lew Wallace. Here is what the official record says about what happened to A.S. Baxter: "Baxter, Algernon Sydney, Vt. Ill. Vt. Capt. a q m vols. 23 Nov 61, resigned 27 April, 1862."[2]

Notice that Baxter's resignation date was while still on the field of Shiloh. This is the last known official record of the captain. In Baxter's obituary his resignation is attributed to illness.[3] This is very possible because of the massive numbers of men who were very sick at Shiloh. An unprovable irony would be the possibility that Lt. Col. Enos P. Wood, who so bravely sought out ammunition for the Union right, transmitted illness to A.S. Baxter, as he stood shivering with the ague, requesting that ammunition; but there were plenty of sources of contagion, and Captain Baxter was more exposed than most because of his duties. There are other hidden reasons that may have caused Baxter to quietly disappear from the military scene.

When Baxter was appointed to his position by Grant, Grant spoke of hidden enemies.[4] They came in all forms. A major enemy of U.S. Grant was the perfidy of General H.W. Halleck. When Halleck finally arrived on the battlefield April 11, 1862, he immediately took over field operations, an area in which he had no practical experience. He officially backed and exonerated General Grant from any blame, but in subterfuge and jealousy over one more "success" of Grant, he made Grant second in command, with no real power to affect strategy. In realty it left Grant without any true command.[5] Halleck brought with him his own department quartermaster. That put Captain Baxter out of a job, much as had happened with General Grant.

In the reorganization of the Army in the West that occurred after the Battle of Corinth in October of 1862, there was a tremendous upset among all veterans of the Shiloh battle. Animosity occurred at every level because of the loss of promotion opportunities. An example was Company K of the 16th Wisconsin. Due to decimation, the regiment consolidated companies after Corinth. Its Colonel Benjamin Moore, Captain Williams and Lt. Richard P. Derickson were held in disdain by many members of the regiment with claims of promotion and ambitions for higher rank.[6] Major General Lew Wallace, after almost two years of war, requested a home leave and it was granted by Grant. Grant, no doubt with the counsel of counselor John Rawlins, dissolved Lew Wallace's whole division and promoted many of its prime officers to positions that effectively made them less accessible to Lew Wallace for what ensued. Especially of interest is General Lew Wallace's own adjutant general Captain Kneffler. He was most privy to the contents of the order through Baxter, and he was the one who lost it. It seems as purposeful as anything, since Kneffler got a regiment of his own and promotion to colonel far away, with command of the 79th Indiana Regiment.[7] As General Lew Wallace languished with no command, he realized what had been done to him. When he requested restoration to a command, Grant, in a shrewd and pragmatic way for his own conformability, said only "if he had less rank" there be room for Wallace. Grant had enough major generals under his command. He had effectively recommended promotion for other officers that would prevent Wallace from returning to his camps. Though he wrote to the War Department that he could use Wallace "if he had less rank," it seems disingenuous to say the least, but Machiavellian in practice.[8]

There are a couple of last observations to be made about Captain A.S. Baxter. He was an exceptional businessman. For this reason, Grant had chosen him as his chief quartermaster because of his acquaintance in St. Louis. With no evidence of corruption of any kind on the part of Baxter, because he was chosen for that quality, it is likely that Algernon Sydney Baxter was really just sick of the chicanery in army and politics. Walt Whitman put this kind of thing this way: "Future years will never know the seething hell and the black infernal background of the countless minor scenes and interiors, (not the official surface-courteousness of the Generals, not the few great battles) of the Secession war; and it is best they should not — the real war will never get in the books."[9] Baxter had early on been led to believe he would get promotion to higher rank. Every aide under General Grant got promotions soon after the Battle of Shiloh, except A.S. Baxter.[10] In the midst of all the putrid horror of the battlefield of Shiloh, he was the head of the transportation corps responsible for transferring the horribly wounded. As district quartermaster he administered the removal and burial of the ghastly corpses on the field. The silence of the former Captain Baxter makes a strong case that he, more than most, could have been a victim of post-traumatic stress, and would have excused himself from any later mention of the Battle of Shiloh. He returned to New York, where he made a fortune on the stock exchange. Grant himself later became a partner in a Wall Street brokerage, but there is no record that Grant and Baxter had any association during that period.[11]

But it is easy to paint people with a broad brush stroke. That is also true of specific events one hundred and fifty years after the Battle of Shiloh. Giving the fairest of evaluations to get at the truth is always an extreme challenge. Old maxims and proverbs serve well when looking at the men and the vagaries of what happened at Shiloh. There are two sides to every coin. There are many facets to a diamond. Especially important for the modern examiner of the Battle of Shiloh is the recognition that *we were not there*. Even so, the soldiers themselves on the field when it happened could not completely comprehend except in the narrow scope of their field of vision. As Private Sam Watkins, who had waited with Forrest and Adams Cavalry near Lick Creek, stated:

> I was but a private soldier, and if I happened to look to see if I could find out anything, "Eyes right, guide center," was the order. "Close up, guide right, halt, forward, right oblique, left oblique, halt, forward, guide center, eyes right, dress up promptly in the rear, steady, double quick, charge bayonets, fire at will," is about all that a private soldier ever knows of a battle. He can see the smoke rise and the flash of the enemy's guns, and he can hear the whistle of the minnie [*sic*] and cannon balls, but he has got to load and shoot as hard as he can tear and ram cartridge, or he will soon find out, like the Irishman who had been shooting blank cartridges, when a ball happened to strike him, and he halloed out, "Faith, Pat, and be jabbers, them fellows are shooting bullets."[12]

The specifics of personalities of the St. Louis and Galena gang of Grant's could be called into question. Especially Captain John Rawlins can be selectively criticized for his actions, just as he did to General Lew Wallace. But at

Shiloh everybody was in the meat grinder. Understating it, war is not a compassionate environment. But a compassionate look at John Rawlins reveals that under the surface bluster, he was a hurting man. He was a man who had risen from literal ashes in the lead mining district of Galena, Illinois. His father had a business rendering virgin hardwood logs into charcoal that he sold for firing the lead-smelting furnaces of Galena. John Rawlins worked for his often inebriated father in hard labor conditions. In 1849 his father disappeared somewhere in the gold fields of California, leaving with promises typical of end-of-the-rainbow searches. At seventeen John Rawlins took over his father's charcoal business and continued to provide for his father's family. Determined to get out of it and make a better life, he saved enough to get schooling in law. His determination after getting his law license elevated him to a different stratum in Galena. In 1861 he lost his wife to tuberculosis. He was in grief at Shiloh. He was also was carrying in his body at Shiloh the bacteria his wife had transmitted to him. Pictures of Rawlins show a waxing and waning of physical appearance. His rancor at Lew Wallace may not have been only a deep-seated dislike of Wallace, but could have been a projection of the physical exertion tuberculosis sufferers experience just to stay alive and function. The former common name of tuberculosis was consumption; the symptomatic weight loss gave the appearance that the sufferer was being mysteriously consumed. John Rawlins was being consumed and was fighting on a number of fronts at Shiloh.[13]

As for U.S. Grant, he was almost penniless days before his death. Had it not been for Mark Twain, the former steamboat captain, he would have died that way. Mark Twain got the memoirs published and made more money from the publication of U.S. Grant's memoirs that he ever made from his own writings. The publication of Grant's memoirs left his widow wealthy. But how many people read Grant's memoirs today? Mark Twain is still beloved for his stories. Lew Wallace is beloved for *Ben-Hur*. No one can be summed up in a sentence or two, and neither can the events of Shiloh.

Shiloh's Legacy

Shiloh courses through the veins of this author. Samuel Asbury Garrett was his great-great grandfather. However, he despises what Samuel A. Garrett went through in many respects, for he feels the conflict was passed on through successive generations to him. After Shiloh, both by choice and the coercion of the Jefferson Davis administration, Sam rode long and lean through the rest of the war in the combined cavalry forces under Nathan Bedford Forrest in the major shuddering threat that the Confederacy produced in the West.

Sam Garrett saw many reorganizations of command structure in the units he served with in the South. This started with his participation at Shiloh with Wirt Adams's cavalry. There were numerous units organized as 1st regiments, all thinking they had been the first to answer their state's call. Wirt Adams's Cavalry claimed to be the 1st Mississippi Cavalry, but there was another 1st Mississippi Cavalry at Shiloh. The confusion continued as Wirt Adams's Cavalry was transformed into Woods's Regiment, and somewhere Samuel Asbury Garrett became part of the 5th Mississippi Cavalry Regiment. Before Shiloh, what had been promised to these partisan units of volunteers was that they could come and go to their farms in the fight, but that policy was reversed in favor of a prohibition to leave service, and these volunteers were inducted into a permanent Confederate States of America army. With that development immediately after Shiloh, it became clear to vast numbers of Southern fighters that it was a rich man's war and a poor man's fight. Plantation owners holding 20 slaves were exempted from actual fighting. Of the notable generals, Braxton Bragg continued his ruthless ways of pouring out the blood of Southern men like it was water, and added to it the execution of freedom-loving men called deserters for wanting to check on their farms and families. Nathan Bedford Forrest finally refused to serve with Bragg.

With the vast amount of blood shed at Shiloh and in the fall at Antietam, the participants in the war were numbed by fields of corpses and filled with vengeance in their hearts. Within two years' time of the start of the Civil War, tens of thousands of blacks joined the Union ranks as United States Colored Troops, and the reversal in traditional ideas curdled Southern men's minds. Samuel Asbury Garrett saw his dreams disappear. The Southwest theater of battles had turned into a wasteland. In April of 1864, two years after Shiloh, Samuel Asbury Garrett was present at the extermination of the largely black garrison at Ft. Pillow.

The Loss of Compromise

> For want of a nail the shoe was lost.
> For want of a shoe the horse was lost.
> For want of a horse the rider was lost.
> For want of a rider the battle was lost.
> For want of a battle the kingdom was lost.
> And all for the want of a horseshoe nail.

This nursery rhyme outlines the demise of a kingdom because one thing was lost. The "nail" that was lost, leading to the Civil War, was the influence of sane voices to engage in problem resolution. Slavery and expansionism were at the heart of these problems. Henry Clay was foremost among these sane voices. So adept was he at finding middle ground that he became known as the Great Compromiser. When he died, the raging sea of radical abolitionists and fire-eating secessionists took over. With the debates left to them, a bloodless outcome was impossible. Strong similarities are apparent in today's political atmosphere.

For the vast majority who saw and participated in the war, they simply could not talk about it, victims of what is today called post-traumatic stress. That was a major loss for them and the generations following. Among literary veterans like Ambrose Bierce, Henry Morton Stanley, Mark Twain and others, their losses are shown by disdain for the Deity. Their disgust of the carnage emerged in ironic literature. To them, hypocritical and justifying arguments offered up by men of the cloth on both sides were like bellows super-heating coals. The "God is on our side" theology to them was a manipulation of spirituality that is peculiar to mankind.

The lack of compromising discourse that led to the Civil War was like the way the pounding of cold iron lines up molecules all in the same direction. Without compromise, the cold iron pounding over and over on the same emotional points led to an inevitable magnetizing polarization. The splitting of the metal of the nation created two poles; for five years the two parts of the nation behaved as magnets. The intense feelings of nationality on both sides were like the familiar physics demonstrated when the same poles are facing one another: they push one another apart. Irrefutable is the point that slavery was wrong, but a few, like some Quakers and small religious movements, clung to nonviolent professions of resolution. However, instead of being drawn to the Bible admonitions against taking up the sword lest it lead to perishing by the sword, or beating swords and spears into implements of peace, most churches gravitated toward militant messages perceived in Scripture. It is hardly any wonder that the novel ideas of Charles Darwin took root in the same age. Thinking people were looking for reasons for the way man was the way he was. But the theory that man was descended from a common ape ancestor in an evolution to a higher form of life was ironic. The apes and other beasts did not go to church or develop songs that fed a bloody kind of patriotism. Never were the apes heard singing "Mine eyes have seen the glory of the coming of the Lord/He is trampling out the vintage where the grapes of wrath are stored." The deists, atheists and agnostics sprouted from "flanders" fields of lost comrades, fathers, brothers, sisters, aunts, uncles, cousins. The argument against Darwin's theory could be made in a nonreligious way, also. There was no evolution; there was devolution. The argument might be made that the apes were superior.

Shiloh: A Requiem (April 1862)

Skimming lightly, wheeling still,
The swallows fly low
Over the field in clouded days,
The forest-field of Shiloh —
Over the field where April rain
Solaced the parched ones stretched in pain
Through the pause of night
That followed the Sunday fight
Around the church of Shiloh —
The church so lone, the log-built one,
That echoed to many a parting groan
And natural prayer
Of dying foemen mingled there —
Foemen at morn, but friends at eve —
Fame or country least their care:
(What like a bullet can undeceive!)
But now they lie low,
While over them the swallows skim,
And all is hushed at Shiloh.

— Herman Melville

Today Shiloh National Military Park does have a hushed atmosphere for its visitors. The hush could be viewed as the calm of a hurricane's eye by the wise. The circling whirlwinds of war came again and again after Shiloh. To many, Shiloh Military Park is more than a tourist attraction. For those aware of ancestral participants in the battle with specific connections to their forebears, a variety of emotions surge through them. Some feel a specific pull to whichever pole the old magnet draws them, North or South, to research their ancestors and return to the folderol and incantations of glory, honor and gallantry. They renew the arguments of which God, country and flag the participants invoked. There can be a confusing sense of obsession. Obsession: the way Lew Wallace was obsessed by the accusations of causing the casualties, the way Ambrose Bierce and Henry Morton Stanley were obsessed by their own participation and disgust in how these events were facilitated through politics and religion, the way that Robert Ingersoll was driven to agnosticism, and Mark Twain was driven to cynicism.

Legions of other Americans, however, might feel the pull of Shiloh in their veins without knowing the source, since over a hundred thousand participated and went on to father children, grandchildren, great-grandchildren, and the fourth generation from Shiloh, great-great-grandchildren. To the reflective visitor, one who meditates, a spirit lingers over the ground where men died and reaches up to brush living ankles, sometimes to bend knees in the cemetery and press upon the heart, thinking of the men whose blood ebbed into the ground to nourish the trees that now stand where they fell. The dead men that died returned to dust and mulch, feeding the trees and the grasses of the meadows. When you see the trees, you are seeing the soldiers now in peace.

There are newer scientific explanations of the causes of war and the traumas it sets in motion. The discoveries confirm the ripple effect of war on following generations, like the rings emanating from a boulder cast into a pond. Atheists, agnostics, and religionists might be able to come together with these new scientific discoveries. Right-wing evangelists and left-wing liberals can come together on an innate principle stated with the Ten Commandments. Curiously, the Bible, carried by hundreds of thousands of soldiers into battle during the Civil War, stated a dispassionate scientific truth that now is emerging in the field of epigenetics. Among the Bible commands, it infers fratricidal murder results in post-traumatic stress disorder as far distant as the great-great-great-grandchildren, the fourth generation. The latter part of verse 34:7 in Exodus (King James Version) hints at molecular biology, basically stating that when Jehovah's laws are broken, there is a consequence of "visiting the iniquity of the fathers upon the children, unto the third and to the fourth generation."[14]

Michael Skinner, a molecular biologist at Washington State University, as quoted in an article called "Sins of the Grandfathers," presents his genetic discoveries of the ancient Biblical principle, scientifically explaining them this way: "The life experiences of grandparents, even great-grandparents, alter sperm and eggs so indelibly that the change is passed on to their children, grandchildren, and beyond. It's called transgenerational epigenetic inheritance: the phenomenon in which something in the environment alters the health not only of the individual exposed to it, but also of that individual's descendant." In the article the journalist comments,

> The astounding part of Skinner's statement is that this altered inheritance does not occur the way generations of biologists have been taught. Instead of changing the DNA sequences that make up the genes that ancestors pass down to the descendants — the A's, T's, C's and G's that spell out the genetic code — something more occurs in epigenetic inheritance. A life experience — in Skinner's study, exposing rats to a fungicide called vinelozolin — alters the on-off switches that control DNA in sperm or eggs. Biologists have long known about the switches, which are clusters of atoms called methyl groups. The cluster can silence a gene it attaches to; when the cluster is removed, the gene is active again. (This silencing is why the DNA for, say, insulin, is turned off in brain cells but active in pancreas cells.) But biologists believed that when sperm and eggs grew up, as it were , and created an embryo, the tags were reset, nature's

Reunion of Shiloh survivors, North and South, in 1894. Note three black veterans at the right, one with his hand on his heart. The effects of the Battle of Shiloh veterans' descendants are still felt (*The Graphic Chicago*).

way of scrubbing the sins of the fathers and mothers before they could afflict the next generation.

Skinner's discovery that not all those marks are erased, but are instead permanently modified (at least as far out as he bred his rats: four generations), has challenged the decades-old tenet of reproductive biology ... which, when brought to his attention, he acknowledges with an *Oh, right:* "The 'permanently' does astonish me," he concedes. "I guess it's why we get such a push back from the medical community."[15]

Skinner's findings are far from anomalous. For one thing they are not confined to rats or to the fungicide he fed them. Other labs, too, are finding that experiences — everything from a lab animal being exposed to a toxic chemical to a person smoking, being malnourished in childhood, or even overeating — leaves an imprint on sperm and eggs, an imprint so tenacious that it affects not only those individual's children but their grandchildren as well.[16]

This author can attest to the repeated manifestation of bipolar disorder and PTSD in his own family going back generations. He has felt the pull of the blood spilled and the massive release of adrenaline that trauma on the Shiloh fields precipitated in the same way it affected his forebears, for he suffers from PTSD with its inexpiable outbursts of anger. Consider: there were over a hundred thousand men in and around Shiloh. According to epigenetic findings, the logarithms of population growth mean that the Battle of Shiloh affects millions today at a biological level. Extrapolations of emerging science point out that life experiences of the forebears continue to affect the descendants at a genetic level. The subtitle of *Blue and Gray* magazine, "For those Who Still Hear the Guns," becomes more than a literary allusion. It points to a partial explanation of why we live in such a violent society. Every time a war takes place, it imprints itself upon the mechanisms in the genes.

At present thousands of American veterans of many wars take their own lives each year, and it is only the tip of the iceberg as it pertains to the general population, who may not have been in the actual conflict of these veterans, yet live with these veterans, and the ramifications of war go unchecked.[17] When the attacks of 9/11 succeeded, once again came the call for vengeance and glory, God and country. More war came out of it. New veterans of new wars will perpetuate the curse of epigenetics.

It may be simply stated: As the findings of epigenetics continue to add knowledge, they point to the issue of post-traumatic stress disorder not being just the problem of soldiers. Even the protest songs of the 1960s pleaded in their eloquent and powerful lyrics. They asked when the lessons would be learned, or, regarding war, what good is fighting with guns and other weapons? Who benefits? War is not good for anyone. With it the flower of mankind only returns to flowers.

More than lip service is needed for peace. "Those who do not remember the past are condemned to repeat it," as George Santayana observed. Cries of "Never again!" go on ad nauseum. Peace requires that individuals understand more than the romantic reasons the Civil War "made us who we are." Each individual must beat his sword into a plowshare and his spear into a pruning hook. Whether pursued religiously, philosophically or scientifically, peace will only happen when the true peaceful meaning of Shiloh is understood.

Appendix A:
The Derickson Documents

Documents of 1st Lieutenant Richard P. Derickson, Company K, 16th Wisconsin Infantry and staff quartermaster of Brigadier General Benjamin M. Prentiss, commanding the 6th Division of the Union Army of West Tennessee under Major General Ulysses S. Grant, commanding.

These documents were discovered at an auction by the author several years ago. Originals may be viewed by arrangement with the author. Copies supplied to Shiloh National Military Park, Hardin County, Tennessee, and U.S. Grant Association, Mississippi State University.

DERICKSON DOCUMENT 0024
Derickson receives his orders and promotion as quartermaster.

Headquarters 6th Division, A. of W. Tenn
In the field near Pittsburg Tenn
3rd April 1862

General Order}
No. 5 }

        x   x   x   x   x   x

2. Lieut Richard P. Derickson of Company "K
16th Wisconsin Infantry is detail, to act until
otherwise ordered as Assistant Quartermaster He
will report to these headquarters for instructions

By order of Brig. Gen. B.M. Prentiss
Henry Binmore
Asst. Adjutant General

DERICKSON DOCUMENT 0025

First Document: Captain A.S. Baxter, district quartermaster (U.S. Grant's Chief supply and transportation officer). A.S. Baxter is ordered to commandeer steamer *Iatan* as commissary and quartermaster boat by General Grant's orders:

District of West. Tennessee
Pittsburg April 4, 1862

Lt, R. P Derickson
A A Q Master
6th Division

The Steamer "Iatan" is
Assigned to the 6th Division for Commissary &
Quartermaster Boat, and the Capt. of Boat
Will furnish you with suitable quarters to
Conduct you business

Respty Yours
A.S. Baxter
A. Q. Master

Captain of Steamer "Iatan"
Your boat is assigned to
Genl Prentiss Division and under control of Quartermaster
& Commissary of Said Division
Per Order of Genl Grant
S. Baxter
Dist Quartermaster

DERICKSON DOCUMENT 0026

Requisition for Forage for Public Horses and Mules in the Service of the 2nd Brigade
of 6th Division U.S. Army for Five days, commencing the 3 of April, 1862, and ending
on 7th of April, 1862, at In the Field near Pittsburg Landing West Tennessee.
Document shows 20 horses, 120 mules, with a total of 140 animals.
Needing five day supply of 700 rations. Allowance for each animal is 1209 pounds of
corn, 1209 pounds of oats, 14 pounds of hay, for a total allowance of 3300 pounds of
corn, 3300 pounds of oats, 9800 pounds of hay.

Order Requested by Colonel Madison Miller Commanding 2nd Brigade 6th Division.
Received of Richard P. Derickson only 3300 pounds of corn and 3300 pounds of oats.

Signed by D.A. Cudworth
Acting Brigade Q.M. of 2nd Brigade
6th Division

DERICKSON DOCUMENT 0027

List of Quartermaster's Stores, &c., *transferred by* A.S. Baxter *Captain and Assistant Quartermaster U.S. Army,* to Lieut. Richard P. Derickson A.A. q.m. *U.S. Army* at Pittsburgh [*sic*] Landing, Tennessee on the 5th day of April 1962

145600—One Hundred
Forty Five Thous—
and Six Hundred-Pounds Corn ... good condition ...
1046 and 140#- One Thousand &
Forty Six Gunny Bags ... new

I Certify that I this day delivered to Lieut Richd P. Derickson A.A Quartermaster U.S. Army, at Pittsburgh [*sic*] Landing, Tenn, the articles specified in the foregoing list.

A.S. Baxter
A. Quartermaster

DERICKSON DOCUMENT 0028

Early Morning of the day of the outbreak of the Battle of Shiloh, unaware of what is
taking place in the far fields, Lt. Derickson makes this request that was never received.
Corporal Valentine was mortally wounded.

Head Quarters Q.M 6th Division
on Board Steamboat Iatan Pittsburgh [*sic*]
Landing West Tennessee April 6th 1862

Genl B. BM Prentiss

I request for
the Public Service Corporal O. J
Valentine of Sixteenth Regt. Company
K Wisconsin Volunteers forth with
R P Derickson
A A. Q. M

DERICKSON DOCUMENT 0029

This document is the most important of the Derickson documents because it transmits the character, style of writing and protocol that Captain A.S. Baxter used. This order was written immediately on his return to Pittsburg Landing after delivering the order to General Lew Wallace. This is as close as we can come to what the character of the order taken to General Lew Wallace would have been. That order was lost. The EPW in the order is Lt. Col. Enos P. Wood of the 17th Illinois regiment, subsequently McClernand's 3rd Brigade Commander after the death of Colonel Julius Raith. This order violates chain of command and represents a shift of supply away from the Hornet's Nest.

Lt. Derickson

> Send all teams available
> to Steamer Rocket to haul ammunition
> to the field immediately

> > By order of
> > Capt. A.S. Baxter- aqm
> > E P. W line officer

Pittsburgh [*sic*] April 6

DERICKSON DOCUMENT 0030

This document attests to the pandemonium at Pittsburg Landing at noon on April 6, 1862. Unauthorized seizure of the corn that is recorded in the earlier Derickson documents takes place. Evidence shows the corn was taken by members of Silversparre's Battery. It is one of only three instances where breastworks were implemented at the Battle of Shiloh.

12M
The "Iatan" Apr 6th 1862

Lt. Derickson
         Sir

              Your Presence
     is required *immediately* here.
     Many requisitions are made which
     we cannot fill. & The Corn is being
     taken & no one will give vouchers.

(In haste)   John Ryan

DERICKSON DOCUMENT 0031
After battle on Monday night, a surgeon makes a desperate request.

No. 40

Special Requisiton

For Use of Hospital on board *Steamer Iatan*

Two Bales of Blankets

I certify that the above requisition is correct and that the articles specified are absolutely requisite for the public service rendered so by the following circumstances, for the sick and wounded and rebel prisoners on board *S. B. Iatan*

Lieut R. P. Derickson Acting Asst. Quartermaster U. S. Army

Will issue the articles specified in the above requisition

R.H. Wyman Surg

21st Reg Mo. Vol

Received at Pittsburg Landing Tenn. the 7th of April 1862 of Lieut. R.P. Derickson Acting Asst. Quartermaster U. S Army

Two Bales of Blankets in full of the above requisition

R.H. Wyman Surg

Signed Dupicates   21st Reg Mo Vol

DERICKSON DOCUMENT 0032

Captain A.S. Baxter demonstrates his style of order once again, emphasizing the nature of the order that would have been sent to General Lew Wallace. Lt. Derickson is given even greater responsibility with authority by Major General Grant to commandeer all supply teams.

Dist Quartermaster Office
Pittsburgh [sic] April 10, 1862

Lt. RP Derickson
A.A. QMaster 6th Division

You will impress, if necessary,
what teams you require for your service in the bringing in
bringing in the wounded, & carrying provisions to
the regiments in the advance

By order of
Maj Genl Grant
A.S. Baxter Dist. QMaster

DERICKSON DOCUMENT 0033

A promoted but stunned Lt. O.P. Newberry requests basic covering as most regiments have lost everything.

No. 40
Special Requisition
2 Bales (For the 25th Regt. Mo. Vol.
280 Two Hundred and Eighty Blankets

I certify that the above requisition is correct
And that the articles specified are absolutely requisite for
the public service rendered so by the following circumstances.
That the Blankets of the Regiment were taken
by the enemy in the engagement of the 6th of April 1862

Lt. O.P. Newberry
R. Q. M 25th Rgt Mo Vol

Received at Pittsburg Landing the 10th day of April 1862
of _____Assistant Q.M. U.S.A.
the following articles Two Hundred and eighty
blankets in full of the above requisition

Lt. O.P. Newberry
A.R. Q.M 25th Rgt. Mo Vo.

No. 43.—[VOUCHER TO ABSTRACT L.]

List of Articles Lost or Destroyed in the public service at *Pittsburgh Landing*, while in the possession and charge of *R. B. Denickson*, in the month of *April* 186*2*.

Number or Quantity.	Articles.	Circumstances and Cause.
1.35.140	Pounds of Corn	Taken from Pittsburg Landing April 6th 1862 to Build breastworks near Pittsburg Landing

I certify the above mentioned Corn was taken by United States Forces to me unknown on the day mentioned above and for the purposes named to the best of My Belief

Sworn and subscribed to before me this fourteenth day of April 1862 at Pittsburgh Landing, Tennessee

John M. Wootten
Brig Gen Vols

I certify that the several articles of Quartermaster's stores above enumerated, have been unavoidably lost or destroyed while in the public service, as indicated by the remarks annexed to them respectively.

R. B. Denickson
A A Quartermaster.
Sixth Division

Approved, _____

_____ Commanding.

DERICKSON DOCUMENT 0034
An accounting had to be made for the seized corn lost during the battle.

List of Articles Lost or Destroyed in the public service at *Pittsburgh* [*sic*] *Landing,* while in the possession of *R. P. Derickson*, in the month of April 1862.
135140 Pounds of Corn Taken from Pittsburg Landing April 6th 1862 to build breastworks near Pittsburg Landing

> I certify the above mentioned Corn
> Was taken by United States Forces to me unknown
> on the day mentioned above and for the Purposes
> Named to the best of my Belief

Sworn and Subscribed to before me this fourteenth
Day of April 1862 at Pittsburgh [*sic*]
Landing Tennessee
John McArthur

> Brig Gen Com
> 2nd Div U.S. A

R.P. Derickson
A A Quartemaster Sixth Division

Appendix B: Pertinent Complete Reports from *The Official Records of the War of the Rebellion*

These reports are related to the U.S. Grant/Lew Wallace "Wrong Road Controversy" and other matters in the text of this book.

O.R.— SERIES I — VOLUME X/1 [S# 10]
April 6–7, 1862.— Battle of Pittsburg Landing, or Shiloh, Tenn.
No. 1.— Reports of Maj. Gen. Henry W. Halleck, U.S. Army, commanding the Department of the Mississippi.

SAINT Louis, *Mo., April* 8, 1862.

The enemy attacked our works at Pittsburg, Tenn., yesterday, but were repulsed with heavy loss. No details given.

H.W. HALLECK,
Major-General

Hon. E.M. STANTON.

———

HEADQUARTERS DEPARTMENT OF THE MISSISSIPPI,
Pittsburg, Tenn., April 13, 1862.

SIR: It is the unanimous opinion here that Brig. Gen. W.T. Sherman saved the fortune of the day on the 6th instant, and contributed largely to the glorious victory on the 7th. He was in the thickest of the fight on both days, having three horses killed under him and being wounded twice. I respectfully request that he be made a major-general of volunteers, to date from the 6th instant.

Very respectfully, your obedient servant,

H.W. HALLECK,
Major-General, Commanding.

Hon. E.M. STANTON,
Secretary of War.

222

WAR DEPARTMENT, *April* 23, 1862.
The President desires to know why you have made no official report to this Department respecting the late battle at Pittsburg Landing, and whether any neglect or misconduct of General Grant or any other officer contributed to the sad casualties that befell our forces on Sunday.

EDWIN M. STANTON,

Secretary of War.
Major-General HALLECK,
Pittsburg Landing.

———

PITTSBURG LANDING, *April* 24, 1862.
The sad casualties of Sunday, the 6th, were due in part to the bad conduct of officers who were utterly unfit for their places, and in part to the numbers and bravery of the enemy. I prefer to express no opinion in regard to the misconduct of individuals till I receive the reports of commanders of divisions. A great battle cannot be fought or a victory gained without many casualties. In this instance the enemy suffered more than we did.

H.W. HALLECK,

Major-General.

Hon. E.M. STANTON.

———

PITTSBURG LANDING, *May* 2, 1862.
Reports of the battle of the 6th and 7th are received, and copies forwarded as rapidly as possible. The newspaper accounts that our divisions were surprised are utterly false. Every division had notice of the enemy's approach hours before the battle commenced.

H.W. HALLECK,

Major-General.

Hon. E.M. STANTON.

———

CORINTH, *MISS., June* 15, 1862.
SIR: I transmit herewith a topographical map of the plain of Shiloh showing the various positions occupied by our troops between Shiloh Church and Pittsburg Landing in the battle of April 6 and 7 last. This map has been made from careful surveys, and the positions of the various divisions are designated in the precise places which they occupied on the ground at the times indicated. It will enable the reader to understand the official reports of the battle which have already been forwarded to the War Department.

It is not my object in this communication to offer any comments on the battle, beyond the remark that the impression which at one time seemed to have been received by the Department that our forces were surprised in the morning of the 6th is entirely erroneous. I am satisfied from a patient and careful inquiry and investigation that all our troops were notified of the enemy's approach some time before the battle commenced.

Again, our loss was overstated in the official reports, very many of those reported missing having subsequently reported for duty. The number taken prisoners by the enemy was also greatly exaggerated. There seems to have been a morbid desire on the part of some of our officers to make the loss of their particular commands much greater than it really was.

Very respectfully, your obedient servant,

H.W. HALLECK,

Major-General, Commanding.

Hon. E.M. STANTON,
Secretary of War, Washington, D.C.

O.R.—SERIES I—VOLUME X/1 [S# 10]
April 6–7, 1862.—Battle of Pittsburg Landing, or Shiloh, Tenn.
No. 3.—Reports of Maj. Gen. U.S. Grant, U.S. Army, commanding Army of the Tennessee, with abstracts from the field returns of the several divisions, April 4–5 and April 10–15, 1862.

PITTSBURG, *April 7,* 1862.

Yesterday the rebels attacked us here with an overwhelming force, driving our troops in from their advanced position to near the Landing. General Wallace was immediately ordered up from Crump's Landing, and in the evening one division of General Buell's army and General Buell in person arrived. During the night one other division arrived, and still another to-day. This morning, at the break of the day, I ordered an attack, which resulted in a fight which continued until late this afternoon, with severe loss on both sides, but a complete repulse of the enemy. I shall follow to-morrow far enough to see that no immediate renewal of an attack is contemplated.

U.S. GRANT,

Major-General.

Maj. Gen. H.W. HALLECK,
Saint Louis, Mo.

———

PITTSBURG, *TENN. (via SAVANNAH), April 8,* 1862.

Enemy badly routed and fleeing towards Corinth. Our cavalry, supported by infantry, are now pursuing him, with instructions to pursue to the swampy grounds near Pea Ridge. I want transports sent here for our wounded.

U.S. GRANT.

———

HEADQUARTERS DISTRICT OF WEST TENNESSEE,

Pittsburg, April 9, 1862.

CAPTAIN: It becomes my duty again to report another battle fought between two great armies, one contending for the maintenance of the best government ever devised, the other for its destruction. It is pleasant to record the success of the army contending for the former principle.

On Sunday morning our pickets were attacked and driven in by the enemy. Immediately the five divisions stationed at this place were drawn up in line of battle, ready to meet them. The battle soon waxed warm on the left and center, varying at times to all parts of the line. The most continuous firing of musketry and artillery ever heard on this continent was kept up until night-fall, the enemy having forced the entire line to fall back nearly half way from their camps to the Landing.

At a late hour in the afternoon a desperate effort was made by the enemy to turn our left and get possession of the Landing, transports, &c. This point was guarded by the gunboats Tyler and Lexington, Captains Gwin and Shirk, U.S. Navy, commanding, four 20-pounder Parrott guns and a battery of rifled guns. As there is a deep and impassable ravine for artillery or cavalry, and very difficult for infantry, at this point, no troops were stationed here, except the necessary artillerists and a small infantry force for their support. Just at this moment the advance of Major-General Buell's column (a part of the division under General Nelson) arrived, the two generals named both being present. An advance was immediately made upon the point of attack and the enemy soon driven back. In this repulse much is due to the presence of the gunboats Tyler and Lexington, and their able commanders, Captains Gwin and Shirk.

During the night the divisions under Generals Crittenden and McCook arrived. General Lewis Wallace, at Crump's Landing, 6 miles below, was ordered at an early hour in the morning to hold his division in readiness to be moved in any direction to which it might be ordered. At about 11 o'clock the order was delivered to move it up to Pittsburg, but owing to its being led by a circuitous route did not arrive in time to take part in Sunday's action.

During the night all was quiet, and feeling that a great moral advantage would be gained by becoming the attacking party, an advance was ordered as soon as day dawned. The result was a gradual repulse of the enemy at all parts of the line from morning until probably 5 o'clock in the afternoon, when it became evident the enemy was retreating. Before the close of the action the advance of General T.J. Wood's division arrived in time to take part in the action.

My force was too much fatigued from two days' hard fighting and exposure in the open air to a drenching rain during the intervening night to pursue immediately.

Night closed in cloudy and with heavy rain, making the roads impracticable for artillery by the next morning. General Sherman, however, followed the enemy, finding that the main part of the army had retreated in good order.

Hospitals of the enemy's wounded were found all along the road as far as pursuit was made. Dead bodies of the enemy and many graves were also found.

I inclose herewith report of General Sherman, which will explain more fully the result of this pursuit.

Of the part taken by each separate command I cannot take special notice in this report, but will do so more fully when reports of division commanders are handed in.

General Buell, coming on the field with a distinct army long under his command, and which did such efficient service, commanded by himself in person on the field, will be much better able to notice those of his command who particularly distinguished themselves than I possibly can.

I feel it a duty, however, to a gallant and able officer, Brig. Gen. W.T. Sherman, to make a special mention. He not only was with his command during the entire two days' action, but displayed great judgment and skill in the management of his men. Although severely wounded in the hand the first day his place was never vacant. He was again wounded, and had three horses killed under him.

In making this mention of a gallant officer no disparagement is intended to the other division commanders, Maj. Gens. John A. McClernand and Lewis Wallace, and Brig. Gens. S.A. Hurlbut, B.M. Prentiss, and W.H.L. Wallace, all of whom maintained their places with credit to themselves and the cause.

General Prentiss was taken prisoner in the first day's action, and General W.H.L. Wallace severely, probably mortally, wounded. His assistant adjutant-general, Capt. William McMichael, is missing; probably taken prisoner.

My personal staff are all deserving of particular mention, they having been engaged during the entire two days in conveying orders to every part of the field. It consists of Col. J.D. Webster, chief of staff; Lieut. Col. J.B. McPherson, chief engineer, assisted by Lieuts. W.L.B. Jenney and William Kossak; Capt. J.A. Rawlins, assistant adjutant-general; Capts. W.S. Hillyer, W.R. Rowley, and C.B. Lagow, aides-de-camp; Col G.G. Pride, volunteer aide, and Capt. J.P. Hawkins, chief commissary, who accompanied me upon the field.

The medical department, under the direction of Surgeon Hewitt, medical director, showed great energy in providing for the wounded and in getting them from the field regardless of danger.

Colonel Webster was placed in special charge of all the artillery and was constantly upon the field. He displayed, as always heretofore, both skill and bravery. At least in one instance he was the means of placing an entire regiment in a position of doing most valuable service, and where it would not have been but for his exertions.

Lieutenant-Colonel McPherson, attached to my staff as chief engineer, deserves more than a passing notice for his activity and courage. All the grounds beyond our camps for miles have been reconnoitered by him, and plats carefully prepared under his supervision give accurate information of the nature of approaches to our lines. During the two days' battle he was constantly in the saddle, leading troops as they arrived to points where their services were required. During the engagement he had one horse shot under him.

The country will have to mourn the loss of many brave men who fell at the battle of Pittsburg, or Shiloh, more properly. The exact loss in killed and wounded will be known in a day or two. At present I can only give it approximately at 1,500 killed and 3,500 wounded.

The loss of artillery was great, many pieces being disabled by the enemy's shots and some losing all their horses and many men. There were probably not less than 200 horses killed.

The loss of the enemy in killed and left upon the field was greater than ours. In wounded the estimate cannot be made, as many of them must have been sent back to Corinth and other points.

The enemy suffered terribly from demoralization and desertion.

A flag of truce was sent in to-day from General Beauregard. I inclose herewith a copy of the correspondence.

I am, very respectfully, your obedient servant

U.S. GRANT,

Major-General, Commanding.

Capt. N.H. McLEAN,
A.A.G., Dept. of the Miss., Saint Louis, Mo.
[**Inclosures.**]
HEADQUARTERS ARMY OF THE MISSISSIPPI,
Monterey, April 8, 1862.

SIR: At the close of the conflict of yesterday, my forces being exhausted by the extraordinary length of time during which they were engaged with yours on that and the preceding day, and it being apparent that you had received and were still receiving re-enforcements, I felt it my duty to withdraw my troops from the immediate scene of conflict.

Under these circumstances, in accordance with usages of war, I shall transmit this under a flag of truce, to ask permission to send a mounted party to the battlefield of Shiloh for the purpose of giving decent interment to my dead.

Certain gentlemen wishing to avail themselves of this opportunity to remove the remains of their sons and friends, I must request for them the privilege of accompanying the burial party, and in this connection I deem it proper to say I am asking only what I have extended to your own countrymen under similar circumstances.

Respectfully, general, your obedient servant,

G.T. BEAUREGARD,
General, Commanding.
Maj. Gen. U.S. GRANT, U.S.A.,
Commanding U.S. Forces near Pittsburg, Tenn.

———

HEADQUARTERS ARMY IN THE FIELD,
Pittsburg, April 9, 1862.

Your dispatch of yesterday is just received. Owing to the warmth of the weather I deemed it advisable to have all the dead of both parties buried immediately. Heavy details were made for this purpose, and now it is accomplished. There cannot, therefore, be any necessity of admitting within our lines the parties you desire to send on the grounds asked.

I shall always be glad to extend any courtesy consistent with duty, and especially so when dictated by humanity.

I am, general, very respectfully, your obedient servant,

U.S. GRANT,
Major-General, Commanding.
General G.T. BEAUREGARD,
Comdg. Confederate Army of the Mississippi, Monterey, Tenn.

———

GENERAL ORDERS No. 34.
HDQRS. DISTRICT OF WEST TENNESSEE,
Pittsburg, April 8, 1862.

The general commanding congratulates the troops who so gallantly maintained, repulsed, and routed a numerically superior force of the enemy, composed of the flower of the Southern Army, commanded by their ablest generals, and fought by them with all the desperation of despair.

In numbers engaged, no such contest ever took place on this continent; in importance of results, but few such have taken place in the history of the world.

Whilst congratulating the brave and gallant soldiers, it becomes the duty of the general commanding to make special notice of the brave wounded and those killed upon the field. Whilst they leave friends and relatives to mourn their loss, they have won a nation's gratitude and undying laurels, not to be forgotten by future generations, who will enjoy the blessings of the best government the sun ever shone upon, preserved by their valor.

By order of Maj. Gen. U.S. Grant:

JNo. A. RAWLINS,

Assistant Adjutant-General.

[Addenda.]

Abstracts from the field returns of the several divisions of the Army of the Tennessee, Maj. Gen. U.S. Grant commanding.

APRIL 4–5, 1862.

O Officers.   **A** Aggregate.   **M** Men.   **P** Pieces of artillery.

— — — —Present for duty.— — —-

Command.	O	M	A	P	Notes by the compiler.
First Division:					From "statement of effective force" April 5. Pieces of artillery not reported on original.
1st Brigade	125	2,531	2,656	....	
2d Brigade	77	1,769	1,846	....	
3d Brigade	110	2,118	2,228	....	
Unattached	9	289	298	....	
	321	6,707	7,028	....	
Total First Division.					
Second Division:					Return dated April 5.
1st Brigade	108	1,996	2,104	6	
2d Brigade	123	2,603	2,726	6	
3d Brigade	180	3,517	3,697	....	
Unattached	8	173	181	12	
	419	8,289	8,708	24	
Total Second Division.					
Third Division:					Return dated April 4; the division not in the battle of April 6.
1st Brigade	65	1,933	1,998	....	
2d Brigade	103	2,133	2,236	....	
3d Brigade	111	2,430	2,541	....	
Unattached	35	754	789	12	
	314	7,250	7,564	12	
Total Third Division.					
Fourth Division:					Return dated April 5.
1st Brigade	99	2,416	2,515	6	

2d Brigade	113	2,698	2,811	4
3d Brigade	87	1,739	1,826	....
Unattached	7	143	150	....
	306	6,996	7,302	10

Total Fourth Division

Fifth Division: Return dated April 5.

1st Brigade	79	2,050	2,129	6
2d Brigade	90	1,936	2,026	4
3d Brigade	110	2,331	2,441	....
4th Brigade	103	2,131	2,234	6
	382	8,448	8,830	16

Total Fifth Division

Sixth Division: Return dated April 5; strength of two regiments and one battery not reported on the original.

1st Brigade	119	2,671	2,790	....
2d Brigade	85	1,689	1,774	....
Unattached	41	858	899	....
	245	5,218	5,463	....

Total Sixth Division.
Grand total

	1,987	42,908	44,895	62

Division staff not included in this abstract.

APRIL 10–15, 1862.

O   Officers.   A   Aggregate.   M   Men.

— — Present for duty. — —

Command.	O	M	A
First Division:			

From statement April 15 of "effective force."

1st Brigade	81	1,763	1,844
2d Brigade	55	1,260	1,315
3d Brigade	75	1,575	1,650
Artillery	14	230	244
Cavalry	12	246	258
	237	5,074	5,311

Total First Division

Second Division: Return of April 13.

1st Brigade	42	860	902
2d Brigade	81	1,979	2,060
3d Brigade	100	2,031	2,131
Artillery	18	301	319
Cavalry	4	186	190
	245	5,357	5,602

Total Second Division

Third Division: Return of April 10: Brigade organization not indicated; casualties noted are 39 killed, 253 wounded, and 1 missing.

Infantry	226	4,791	5,017
Artillery	11	289	300
Cavalry	14	263	277
	251	5,343	5,594

Total Third Division

Fourth Division:

Return of April 10: The casualties noted are 296 killed, 1,436 wounded, and 144 missing.

1st Brigade	61	1,715	1,776
2d Brigade	71	1,929	2,000
3d Brigade	65	1,226	1,291
Artillery	4	127	131
Cavalry	36	655	691
	237	5,652	5,889

Total Fourth Division

Fifth Division:

Return of April 10: The casualties noted are 314 killed, 1,242 wounded, and 475 missing.

1st Brigade	67	1,337	1,404
2d Brigade	74	1,328	1,402
3d Brigade	66	1,669	1,735
4th Brigade	82	1,823	1,905
Artillery	12	303	315
Cavalry	27	449	476
	328	6,909	7,237

Total Fifth Division

Sixth Division:

Return of April 13: the casualties noted are 35 killed, 53 wounded, and 52 missing.

1st Brigade	57	1,666	1,723
2d Brigade	52	1,028	1,080
Unattached	77	1,693	1,770
	186	4,387	4,573

Total Sixth Division

Grand total   1,484   32,722   34,206

O.R. — SERIES I — VOLUME X/1 [S# 10]
April 6–7, 1862. — Battle of Pittsburg Landing, or Shiloh, Tenn.
No. 34. — Reports of Maj. Gen. Lewis Wallace, U.S. Army, commanding Third Division, with communications in reference thereto.

HDQRS. THIRD DIVISION, *UNITED STATES FORCES,*
Pittsburg Landing, Tenn., April 12, 1862.

SIR: Sunday morning, 6th instant, my brigades, three in number, were encamped, the first at Crump's Landing, the second 2 miles from that Landing, the third at Adamsville, 2½ miles farther out on the road to Purdy. The Eleventh Indiana, Col. George F. McGinnis; Eighth Missouri, Lieut. Col. James Peckham, and Twenty-fourth Indiana, Col. Alvin P. Hovey, composed the First Brigade, Col. Morgan L. Smith commanding. The First Nebraska, Lieut. Col. W.D. McCord; Twenty-third Indiana, Col. W.L. Sanderson; Fifty-eighth Ohio, Col. V. Bausenwein, and Fifty-sixth Ohio, Col. P. Kinney, composed the Second Brigade, Col. John M. Thayer commanding. The Third Brigade consisted of the Twentieth Ohio, Col. M.F. Force; Seventy-sixth Ohio, Col. Charles R. Woods; Seventy-eighth Ohio, Col. M.D. Leggett, and Sixty-eighth Ohio, Col. S.H. Steedman; Col. Charles Whittlesey commanding. To my division were attached Lieutenant Thurber's Missouri battery and Capt. N.S. Thompson's Indiana battery; also the Third Battalion Fifth Ohio Cavalry, Maj. C.S. Hayes, and the Third Battalion Eleventh Illinois Cavalry, Maj. James F. Johnson.

Hearing heavy and continuous cannonading in the direction of Pittsburg Landing early Sunday morning, I inferred a general battle, and, in anticipation of an order from General Grant to join him at that place, had the equipage of the several brigades loaded in wagons for instant removal to my first camp at the river. The First and Third Brigades were also ordered to concentrate at the camp of the Second, from which proceeded the nearest and most practicable road to the scene of battle. At 11.30 o'clock the anticipated order arrived, directing me to come up and take position on the right of the army and form my line of battle at a right angle with the river. As it also directed me to leave a force to prevent surprise at Crump's Landing, the Fifty-sixth Ohio and Sixty-eighth Ohio Regiments were detached for that purpose, with one gun from Lieutenant Thurber's battery. Selecting a road that led directly to the right of the lines as they were established around Pittsburg Landing on Sunday morning, my column started immediately, the distance being about 6 miles. The cannonading, distinctly audible, quickened the steps of the men. Snake Creek, difficult of passage at all times, on account of its steep banks and swampy bottoms, ran between me and the point of junction. Short way from it Captain Rowley, from General Grant, and attached to his staff, overtook me. From him I learned that our lines had been beaten back; that the right, to which I was proceeding, was then fighting close to the river, and that the road pursued would take me in the enemy's rear, where, in the unfortunate condition of the battle, my command was in danger of being entirely cut off. It seemed, on his representation, most prudent to carry the column across to what is called the "River road," which, following the windings of the Tennessee bottoms, crossed Snake Creek by a good bridge close to Pittsburg Landing. This movement occasioned a counter-march, which delayed my junction with the main army until a little after night-fall. The information brought me by Captain Rowley was confirmed by Colonel McPherson and Captain Rawlins, also of the general's staff, who came up while I was crossing to the River road. About 1 o'clock at night my brigades and batteries were disposed, forming the extreme right, and ready for battle.

Shortly after daybreak Captain Thompson opened fire on a rebel battery posted on a bluff opposite my First Brigade, and across a deep and prolonged hollow, threaded by a creek and densely wooded on both sides. From its position and that of its infantry support, lining the whole length of the bluff, it was apparent that crossing the hollow would be at heavy loss, unless the battery was first driven off. Thurber was accordingly posted to assist Thompson by a cross-fire and at the same time sweep the hiding place of the rebels on the brow of the hill. This had the desired effect. After a few shells from Thurber the enemy fell back, but not before Thompson had dismounted one of their rifled guns. During this affair General Grant came up and gave me my direction of attack, which was forward at a right angle with the river, with which at the time my line ran almost parallel.

The battery and its supports having been driven from the opposite bluff, my command was pushed forward, the brigades in echelon — the First in front, and the whole preceded by skirmishers. The hollow was crossed and the hill gained almost without opposition. As General Sherman's division, next on my left, had not made its appearance to support my advance, a halt was ordered for it to come up. I was then at the edge of an oblong field that extended in a direction parallel with the river. On its right was a narrow strip of woods, and beyond that lay another cleared field, square and very large. Back of both fields, to the north, was a range of bluffs overlooking the swampy low grounds of Snake Creek, heavily timbered, broken by ravines, and extending in a course diagonal with that of my movement. An examination satisfied me that the low grounds afforded absolute protection to my right flank, being impassable for a column of attack. The enemy's left had rested upon the bluff, and, as it had been driven back, that flank was now exposed. I resolved to attempt to turn it. For that purpose it became necessary for me to change front by a left half-wheel of the whole division.

While this movement was in progress, across a road through the woods at the southern end of the field we were resting by, I discovered a heavy column of rebels going rapidly to re-enforce their left, which was still retiring, covered by skirmishers, with whom mine were engaged. Thompson's battery was ordered up, and shelled the passing column with excellent effect; but while he was so engaged he was opened on by a full battery, planted in the field just beyond the strip of wood on the right. He promptly turned his guns at the new enemy. A fine artillery duel ensued, very honorable to Thompson and his company. His ammunition giving out in the midst of it, I ordered him to retire and Lieutenant Thurber to take his place. Thurber obeyed with such alacrity that there was scarcely an intermission in the fire, which continued so long and with such warmth as to provoke an attempt on the part of the rebels to charge the position. Discovering the intention, the First Brigade was brought across the field to occupy the strip of woods in front of Thurber. The cavalry made the first dash at the battery, but the skirmishers of the Eighth Missouri poured an unexpected fire into them, and they retired pell-mell. Next the infantry attempted a charge. The First Brigade easily repelled them. All this time my whole division was under a furious cannonade, but being well masked behind the bluff, or resting in the hollows of the wood, the regiments suffered but little.

A handsome line of battle now moved forward on my left to engage the enemy. I supposed it to be Sherman's troops, but was afterwards otherwise informed. Simultaneously mine were ordered to advance, the First Brigade leading. Emerging from the woods, it entered the second field I have mentioned, speedily followed by the Second Brigade, when both marched in face of the enemy, aligned as regularly as if on parade. Having changed front, as stated, my movement was now diagonal to the direction originally started on, though the order was still in echelon, with the center regiment of each brigade dropped behind its place in line as a reserve. While thus advancing Colonel Whittlesey, as appears from his report, in some way lost his position, but soon recovered it. The position of the enemy was now directly in front at the edge of the woods fronting, and on the right of the open field my command was so gallantly crossing. The ground to be passed getting at them dipped gradually to the center of the field, which is there intersected by a small run, well fringed with willows.

Clearing an abrupt bank beyond the branch, the surface ascends to the edge of the wood held by the enemy, and is without obstruction, but marked by frequent swells, that afforded protection to the advancing lines, and was the secret of my small loss. Over the branch, up the bank, across the rising ground, moved the steady First Brigade; on its right, with equal alacrity, marched the Second — the whole in view, their banners gaily decking the scene. The skirmishers, in action all the way, cleared the rise, and grouped themselves behind the ground swells within 75 yards of the rebel line. As the regiments approached them suddenly a sheet of musketry blazed from the woods and a battery opened upon them. About the same instant the, regiments supporting me on my left fell hastily back. To save my flank I was compelled to order a halt. In a short time, however, the retiring regiments rallied and repulsed the enemy, and recovered their lost ground. My skirmishers meanwhile clung to their hillocks sharpshooting at the battery. Again the brigades advanced, their bayonets fixed for a charge; but, pressed on their flank and so threatened in front, the rebels removed their guns and fell back from the edge of the woods. In this advance Lieut. Col. John Gerber was killed, and it is but justice to say of him, "No man died that day with more glory; yet many died, and there was much glory." Captain McGuffin and Lieutenant South-wick, of the same regiment, also fell — gallant spirits, deserving honor: able recollection. Many soldiers equally brave perished or were wounded in the same field.

It was now noon, and, the enemy having been driven so far back, the idea of flanking them further had to be given up. Not wishing to interfere with the line of operations of the division to my left, but relying upon it for support, my front was again changed — the movement beginning with the First Brigade, taking the course of attack precisely as it had been in the outset. While this maneuver was being effected a squadron of rebel cavalry galloped from the woods on the right to charge the flank temporarily exposed. Colonel Thayer threw forward the Twenty-third Indiana, which, aided by an oblique fire from a company of the First Nebraska, repelled the assailants with loss. Scarcely had the front been changed when the supporting force on the left again gave way, closely followed by masses of the enemy. My position at this time became critical, as isolation from the rest of the army seemed imminent. The reserves were resorted to. Colonel Woods, with his regiment, was ordered into line on the left. The remnant of a Michigan regiment, sent me by General McClernand, was dispatched to the left of Woods.' Thurber galloped up, and was posted to cover a retreat, should such a misfortune become necessary. Before these dispositions could be effected the Eleventh Indiana, already engaged with superior numbers in its front, was attacked on its left flank; but, backward wheeling three companies of his endangered wing, Colonel McGinnis gallantly held his ground. Fortunately, before the enemy could avail themselves of their advantage by the necessary change of front, some fresh troops dashed against them, and once more drove them back. For this favor my acknowledgments are especially due Col. August Willich and his famous regiment.

Pending this struggle, Colonel Thayer pushed on his command and entered the woods, assaulting the rebels simultaneously with Colonel Smith. Here the Fifty-eighth Ohio and Twenty-third Indiana proved themselves fit comrades in battle with the noble First Nebraska. Here also the Seventy-sixth Ohio won a brilliant fame. The First Nebraska fired away its last cartridge in the heat of the action. At a word the Seventy-sixth Ohio rushed in and took its place. Off to the right, meanwhile, arose the music of the Twentieth and Seventy-eighth Ohio, fighting gallantly in support of Thurber, to whom the sound of rebel cannon seemed a challenge no sooner heard than accepted.

From the time the wood was entered "Forward" was the only order; and step by step, from tree to tree, position to position, the rebel lines went back, never stopping again. Infantry, horse, and artillery — all went back. The firing was grand and terrible. Before us was the Crescent Regiment of New Orleans. Shelling us on the right was the Washington Artillery of Manassas renown, whose last stand was in front of Colonel Whittlesey's command. To and fro, now in my front, then in Sherman's, rode General Beauregard, inciting his troops and fighting for his fading prestige of invincibility. The desperation of the struggle may be easily imagined. While this was in progress far along the lines to the left the contest was raging with equal obstinacy. As indicated by the sounds, however, the enemy seemed retiring everywhere, cheer after cheer ringing through the woods. Each man felt that the day was ours.

About 4 o'clock the enemy to my front broke into rout and ran through the camps occupied by General Sherman on Sunday morning. Their own camp had been established about 2 miles beyond. There, without halting, they fired tents, stores, &c. Throwing out the wounded, they filled their wagons full of arms (Springfield muskets and Enfield rifles) ingloriously thrown away by some of our troops the day before, and hurried on. After following them until nearly nightfall I brought my division back to Owl Creek and bivouacked it.

The conduct of Col. M.L. Smith and Col. John M. Thayer, commanding brigades, was beyond the praise of words. Colonel Whittlesey's was not behind them. To them all belong the highest honors of victory.

The gratitude of the whole country is due Col. George F. McGinnis, Lieut. Col. James Peckham, Col. Alvin P. Hovey, Lieut. Col. W.D. McCord, Col. W.L. Sanderson, Col. Valentine Bausenwein, Lieut. Col. M.F. Force, Col. Charles R. Woods, Col. M.D. Leggett, and their field, staff, and company officers. Aside from the courage they all displayed one point in their conduct is especially to be noted and imitated — I mean the skill each one showed in avoiding unnecessary exposure of his soldiers. They are proud of what the division achieved, and, like myself, they are equally proud that it was done with so little loss of their brave men.

Of my regiments I find it impossible to say enough. Excepting the Twenty-third and Twenty-fourth Indiana and the Twentieth Ohio they had all participated in the battle of Donelson; but this was a greater battle than Donelson, and consequently a more terrible ordeal in which to test what may be a thing of glory or shame — the courage of an untried regiment. How well they all behaved I sum up in the boast, not one man, officer or soldier, flinched. None but the wounded went to the Landing. Ohio, Indiana, Missouri, and Nebraska will be proud of the steadfast Third Division, and so am I.

Captain Thompson and Lieutenant Thurber and their officers and men have already been spoken of.

My acknowledgments are again given the gallant gentlemen of my staff, Capt. Frederick Knefler and Lieutenants Ross and Ware. To them I add Capt. E.T. Wallace, of the Eleventh Indiana Regiment, acting aide. The courage and judgment of all were many times severely tried.

After the battle of Donelson I took pleasure in honorably mentioning two of my orderlies. One of them, Thomas W. Simson, of Company I, Fourth U.S. Cavalry, I again call attention to. His gallantry is deserving reward. Along with him I placed Albert Kauffman, a sergeant in the same company, who was of great service to me, and has every quality that goes to make a practical officer. Finally, it is so rare to find one of his grade in the constant and full performance of his peculiar duties that, as a matter of justice, a passing tribute is due the Rev. John D. Rogers, chaplain of the Twenty-third Indiana. After the battle he was unwearied in his attention to the wounded, and that the resting places of the dead of his regiment might not be forgotten he collected their bodies and buried them tenderly, and with prayer and every religious rite; and in this, as far as my knowledge goes, he was as singular as he was Christian.

Herewith you will find a statement of the dead and wounded of my division.

Very respectfully, sir, your obedient servant,

LEW. WALLACE,

General, Third Division.

Capt. JOHN A. RAWLINS,
Assistant Adjutant-General.

Return of casualties in the Third (Wallace's) Division, at the battle of Pittsburg Landing, April 7, 1862.

O	Officers.	A	Enlisted men missing.
M	Enlisted Men.	B	Aggregate.
K	Killed	W	Wounded

Command.	--K-- O	M	--W-- O	M	A	B
1st Brigade, Col. M. L. Smith	3	18	3	120	....	144
2d Brigade, Col. J. M. Thayer	....	20	....	105	5	130
3d Brigade, Col. C. Whittlesey	....	2	....	29	....	31
Total	3	40	3	254	5	305

[Indorsement.]

HEADQUARTERS ARMY OF THE TENNESSEE,
Pittsburg, April 25, 1862.

Respectfully forwarded to headquarters of the department.

I directed this division at about 8 o'clock A.M. to be held in readiness to move at a moment's warning in any direction it might be ordered. Certainly not later than 11 A.M. the order reached General Wallace to march by a flank movement to Pittsburg Landing. Waiting until I thought he should be here, I sent one of my staff to hurry him, and afterwards sent Colonel McPherson and my assistant adjutant-general.

This report in some other particulars I do not fully indorse.

U.S. GRANT,

Major-General.

———

WASHINGTON CITY, *March* 14, 1863.
Maj. Gen. H.W. HALLECK:

GENERAL: I have heard of prejudices against me at your headquarters, relative to my failure to participate in the first day's battle at Pittsburg Landing. I have also heard that you yourself entertain them. For very obvious purposes, therefore, I respectfully submit to you the following explanation of that affair:

On Sunday morning (April 6, 1862) my division, consisting of eleven regiments of infantry, one battalion of cavalry, and two batteries, was posted on the road from Crump's Landing to Purdy; the First Brigade at the Landing; the Second Brigade 2½ miles out, and the Third Brigade at Adamsville, 5 miles.

Very early that morning I became satisfied that a battle was in progress at Pittsburg Landing, and at once prepared my command for moving instantly upon receipt of an order from General Grant, and as the general was then at Savannah, 4 miles below, my expectation was that he would give me marching orders as he passed up the river to the scene of action. Accordingly my Second and Third Brigades sent their baggage to Crump's Landing, where it could be guarded by a single detachment. The First and Third Brigades joined the Second at its encampment.

About 9 o'clock General Grant passed up the river. Instead of an order to march, he merely left me a direction to *hold myself in readiness for orders.*

At exactly 11.30 A.M. a quartermaster by the name of Baxter brought me an order in *writing unsigned* by *anybody.* It directed me to leave a detachment to guard the public property at Crump's Landing, then march my division and form junction with the right of the army; after junction I was to form line of battle at a right angle with the river. This order, Captain Baxter told me, was from General Grant; that it had been given him verbally, but that in coming down the river he had reduced it to writing, leaving it unsigned. As I had resolved to march toward the cannonading at 12 o'clock without orders, if by that time none came, and as I had so informed Col. (now General) John M. Thayer, commanding my Second Brigade, I made no point upon the informality of the order brought by Baxter, but was glad to receive it in any shape.

Half an hour was given the men to eat dinner. Then I started the column at exactly 12 o'clock to execute General Grant's order. After leaving two regiments and one gun at Crump's Landing the column consisted of nine regiments of infantry and the cavalry and artillery stated; and as the regiments averaged 500 effectives, the whole command did not exceed 5,000 men of all arms.

The route was well known to my cavalry, since, in anticipation of a necessity for my retiring upon the main army, it had, by my order, corduroyed the road to the very point of junction.

Why, then, did I not make the junction sooner? There are two reasons why:
1st. Because of the lateness of the hour I received the order to march —11.30 A.M.

2d. Arrived with my column within a short distance of the point of junction, I was overtaken by an aide of General Grant's, sent by him to tell me that our army had been beaten back from the position it held in the morning, and was then fighting a desperate and losing battle close about Pittsburg Landing. General Grant sent no additional order, and that brought me by Baxter made no provision for such a contingency. I was therefore left to my own judgment. Certainly General Grant did not intend I should continue my march and unsupported from line of battle on the ground his whole army had been beaten from; certainly he did not intend that with 5,000 men I should thrust myself into a position where, without possibility of help from the main army — which according to the account was then unable to help itself— I would, in [all] likelihood, be cut to pieces by the enemy's reserves and detachments. The point of junction to which I was proceeding was at least 2¼ miles from Pittsburg Landing. Could I have successfully cut my way through the enemy, fighting superior forces over that space, in what condition would my regiments have been to give the general the assistance he so much required?

In this dilemma I resolved, as the most prudent course, to carry out *the spirit of General Grant's order, and join the right of his army as it then rested.* That could only be done by carrying my column to the lower or river road from Crump's to Pittsburg Landing, by following which I could cross Snake Creek by a good bridge at the very point of junction. A counter-march was therefore ordered, which, in the absence of any cross-road, was necessarily continued to within half a mile of the camp I had started from. On the diagram, in red ink [dotted lines], my whole march is distinctly traced. A little after sunset I made the required junction.

At no time during that afternoon's march was my column halted longer than to allow it to be closed up; the column was brought in in perfect order and without a straggler; the length of its march in the time (from 12 M. to a little after sunset) was nearly 15 miles; certainly there could have been no idling on the way.

Next morning, on the extreme right in the order of battle, my division had the honor of opening the fight; at the close of the day it was the farthest advanced of any along the line.

For your better understanding of my explanation it is accompanied with a diagram showing the situation of my division on the morning of the first day's battle and its route to the battle-field after the order to march was received.

I submit this as an official explanation, solely to vindicate my conduct from unjust aspersions.

Most respectfully, sir, your obedient servant,

LEW. WALLACE,

Major-General.

Maj. Gen. H.W. HALLECK.

[Indorsement]

HEADQUARTERS ARMY,
March 14, 1863.

Respectfully submitted to Major-General Grant for his remarks.

By order of Major-General Halleck:

J.C. KELTON,

Assistant Adjutant-General.

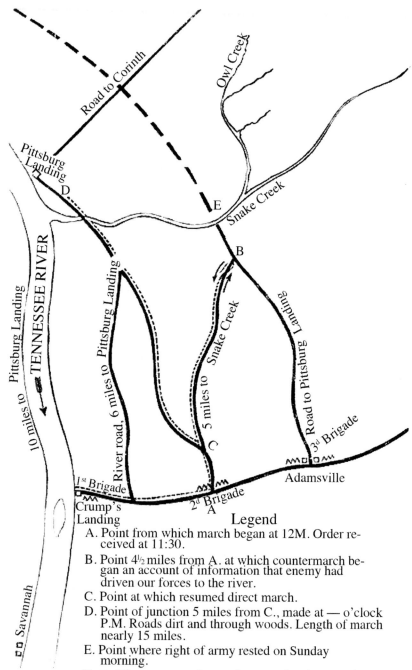

Legend

A. Point from which march began at 12M. Order received at 11:30.

B. Point 4½ miles from A. at which countermarch began an account of information that enemy had driven our forces to the river.

C. Point at which resumed direct march.

D. Point of junction 5 miles from C., made at — o'clock P.M. Roads dirt and through woods. Length of march nearly 15 miles.

E. Point where right of army rested on Sunday morning.

Dotted lines - route of my column on Sunday morning.

HEADQUARTERS DEPARTMENT OF THE TENNESSEE,
Before Vicksburg, April 13, 1863.

Col. J.C. KELTON,
Assistant Adjutant-General, Washington, D. C. :

COLONEL: I have the honor to acknowledge the receipt of a copy of a communication of Maj. Gen. Lewis Wallace to Major-General Halleck, of date March 14, 1863, relative to his failure to participate in the first day's fight at Pittsburg Landing, and submitted to me for my remarks.

Instead of making a detailed report myself in answer to said communication I called upon Maj. Gen. J.B. McPherson, Lieut. Col. John A. Rawlins, and Maj. W.R. Rowley, all of whom were members of my staff at that time and were cognizant of the facts, for their statements in reference to the same, and these I herewith respectfully transmit.

All these reports are substantially as I remember the facts. I vouch for their almost entire accuracy; and from these several statements, separate and independent of each other, too, a more correct judgment can be derived than from a single report.

Had General Wallace been relieved from duty in the morning, and the same orders communicated to Brig. Gen. Morgan L. Smith (who would have been his successor), I do not doubt but the division would have been on the field of battle and in the engagement before 10 o'clock of that eventful 6th of April. There is no estimating the difference this might have made in our casualties.

I am, colonel, very respectfully, your obedient servant,

U.S. GRANT,

Major-General, Volunteers.

[Inclosure No. 1.]

GALENA, *April* 4, 1863.

Col. JOHN A. RAWLINS,
Assistant Adjutant-General:

COLONEL: Yours, requesting a statement as to my knowledge of the part taken by General Lewis Wallace in the first day's fight at the battle of Shiloh, on the 6th of April, 1862, is just received.

In reply, I would state that at that time I was an aide-de-camp on the staff of General U.S. Grant, with the rank of captain, and on the morning of the 6th of April I accompanied the general together with the other members of his staff, from Savannah to Pittsburg Landing. When the steamer upon which we were embarked arrived near to Crump's Landing General Grant directed that it should be run close in to the shore, as he wished to communicate with General Wallace, who was standing upon the commissary boat lying at that place. General Grant called to General Wallace, saying, "General, you will get your troops under arms immediately, and have them ready to move at a moment's notice." General Wallace replied that it should be done, adding (I think) that the necessary orders had already been given. This was between the hours of 7 and 8 o'clock A.M. We passed on up the river, meeting the steamer Warner, which had been sent by General W.H.L. Wallace (as I understood) with a messenger to inform General Grant that a battle had been commenced. The Warner rounded to and followed us back to Pittsburg Landing.

Upon reaching the Landing General Grant immediately mounted his horse and rode upon the bank, and after conversing a moment with some officers turned to Captain Baxter, assistant quartermaster, and ordered him to proceed immediately to Crump's Landing, and direct General Wallace to march with his division up the river and into the field on the right of our line as rapidly as possible.

This order was given to Captain Baxter about the hour of 8 o'clock. I think not later than that. We immediately rode to the front. At about 11 o'clock General Grant expressed considerable solicitude at the non-appearance of General Wallace, and sent an orderly to the extreme right to see if he could see anything of him, remarking that it could not possibly be many minutes before he would arrive.

Shortly after the hour of 12 o'clock M., as we were riding towards the right of the line, a cavalry officer rode up and reported to General Grant, stating that General Wallace had positively refused to come up unless he should receive written orders. After hearing the report General Grant turned to me, saying, "Captain, you will proceed to Crump's Landing and say to General Wallace that it is my orders that he bring his division up at once, coming up by the River road, crossing Snake Creek on the bridge (which General Sherman would protect), and form his division on the extreme right, when he would receive further orders; and say to him that it is important that he should make haste." Adding, "It has just been reported to me that he has refused to come up unless he receives a written order. If he should require a written order of you, you will give him one," at the same time asking me if I had writing materials in my haversack. I started at once, when the general called to me again, saying, "You will take with you the captain (referring to the cavalry officer before mentioned, who was still sitting there on his horse — his name I do not recollect), and two orderlies, and see that you do not spare horse flesh." This was at the hour of 12.30 o'clock M., as near as I can recollect.

I proceeded at once to General Wallace's camp, back of Crump's Landing, and being well mounted, it took me but a short time to reach it. Upon arriving there I found no signs of a camp, except one baggage wagon that was just leaving. I inquired of the driver as to where General Wallace and his troops were; he replied that they had gone up to the fight. I inquired what road they took; to which he replied by pointing to a road, which I understand to be the Purdy road.

While sitting there upon my horse I could hear the firing upon the battle-field quite distinctly. I then took the road pointed out by the teamster and rode a distance of between 5 and 6 miles, as I judged, when I came up with the rear of General Wallace's division; they were at a rest, sitting on each side of the road, some with their arms stacked in the middle of the road. I passed the entire division (except the cavalry), all being at a halt. When I reached the head of the column I found General Wallace sitting upon his horse, surrounded by his staff, some of whom were dismounted and holding their horses by the bridles.

I rode up to General Wallace and communicated to him General Grant's orders as I had received them, and then told him that it had been reported to him (i.e., General Grant.) that he had refused to march without written orders; at which he seemed quite indignant, saying that it was a "damned lie!" that he had never refused to go without a written order, in proof of which he said, "Here you find me on the road." To which I replied that I had certainly found him on a road, but I hardly thought it the road to Pittsburg Landing. It certainly was not the road that

I had come down from there on, and that I had traveled farther since I had left his camp than I had in coming from the battlefield to the camp, and, judging from the sound of the firing, we were still a long distance from the battle-field. To which the general replied that this was the road his cavalry had brought him, and the only road he knew anything about. He then ordered one of his aides to ride ahead and bring the cavalry back. I then asked him where this road came into Pittsburg Landing; to which he replied that it crossed the creek at a mill (I think he called it Veal's Mill) and intersected the Corinth and Pittsburg Landing road in front of where General McClernand's camp was. I then told him that I thought it would be impossible for him to get in upon that road, as the enemy now had possession of those camps, and that our line of battle was to the rear of them. At this moment his cavalry came back and General Wallace rode forward to communicate with them. When he came back he remarked that it was true that the enemy was between us and our army; that the cavalry had been close enough to hear the musketry. The order was then given to counter-march; upon which I remarked to General Wallace that I would ride on and inform General Grant that he was coming; to which he replied, "No, captain; I shall be obliged to keep you with me to act as guide, as none of us know the River road you speak of." I accordingly remained.

The march toward the old camp was continued to a point about one-half mile north of it, where the troops filed to the right and came into the River road. At the point of filing off we were met by Lieutenant-Colonel (now Major-General) McPherson and Major Rawlins, members of General Grant's staff, who had also come to look after General Wallace. The march was continued up the River road until the battlefield was reached, which was just as it was getting dark and after the fighting for the day was over.

Of the character of the march after I overtook General Wallace I can only say that to me it appeared intolerably slow, resembling more a reconnaissance in the face of an enemy than a forced march to relieve a hard-pressed army. So strongly did this impression take hold of my mind, that I took the liberty of repeating to General Wallace that part of General Grant's order enjoining haste. The same idea seemed to have taken possession of the minds of Colonel McPherson and Major Rawlins, as on the march from the camp to the battle-field Major Rawlins on several occasions rode back for the purpose of trying to hurry up the troops and to ascertain what was the cause of the delay. I have no means of judging as to what distance General Wallace was from the battle-field when I found him, except that I could hear the firing much more distinctly at the camp he had left than I could at the point where I found him.

I remain, colonel, your obedient servant,

W.R. ROWLEY,

Major and Aide-de-Camp.

[Inclosure No. 2.]

HEADQUARTERS SEVENTEENTH ARMY CORPS,
DEPARTMENT OF THE TENNESSEE,
Lake Providence, La., March 26, 1863.

Lieut. Col. JOHN A. RAWLINS,
Assistant Adjutant-General:

COLONEL: I have the honor to submit the following in relation to the position of the troops and the battle of Shiloh:

When the troops first disembarked at Pittsburg Landing the Tennessee River was very high, the water backing up in all the streams, covering the bottoms in the vicinity of the river from 2 to 6 feet, rendering Lick and Snake Creeks impassable.

Four divisions of the army were encamped on the field of Shiloh in the relative positions indicated in the sketch, and one division (Maj. Gen. Lewis Wallace's) at Crump's Landing, about 6 miles below.

My attention was frequently called to the crossing of Snake Creek, on the direct road from Pittsburg Landing to Crump's, as it was considered very important that a line of land communication between the two portions of the army should be kept open.

As soon as the water subsided sufficiently the bridge across the creek was reconstructed, and a company of cavalry sent through to communicate with General Wallace's command. This was on Thursday, previous to the battle.

Sunday morning, the first day of the battle, I was with Brig. Gen. W.H.L. Wallace, who, in consequence of the severe illness of General C.F. Smith, commanded this division. It was well known the enemy was approaching our lines, and there had been more or less skirmishing for three days preceding the battle.

The consequence was our breakfasts were ordered at an early hour and our horses saddled, to be ready in case of an attack. Sunday morning, shortly before 7 o'clock, word came to the Landing that the battle had commenced. I immediately started, in company with General W.H.L. Wallace and staff; found his division in line ready to move out. At this time, not later than 7.30 A.M., General McClernand had moved a portion of his division up to support General Sherman's left. General Hurlbut had moved to the support of General Prentiss, and General W.H.L. Wallace's division was moved up to support the center and right. I was actively engaged on the field, and did not see General Grant until some time after his arrival, when I met him on the field, with Brig. Gen. W.H.L. Wallace. He informed me that when he came up from Savannah, at 7.30, he had notified Maj. Gen. Lewis Wallace, at Crump's Landing, to hold his command in readiness to march at a moment's notice, and that immediately on his arrival at Pittsburg Landing, finding that the attack was in earnest and not a feint, he had sent Captain Baxter, assistant quartermaster, with orders to him to move up immediately by the River road and take a position on our right. Shortly after this Captain Baxter returned, certainly not later than 10.30, and said that he had delivered the order.

At about 12 M., General Wallace not having arrived, General Grant became very anxious, as the tide of battle was setting against us, and shortly after dispatched Captain Rowley, one of his aides, to hasten up General Wallace. The battle still continued without cessation, our troops being forced back gradually at all points, though fighting most heroically. Two hours rolled around and no news from General Wallace, when at 2.30 P.M. General Grant directed me to go in search of him, report to him how matters stood, and hasten him forward, if possible. I asked Captain (now Lieutenant-Colonel) Rawlins to accompany me, and taking two orderlies, we started at a rapid pace on the River road, expecting to meet the command at every step; pushed on to the junction of the Purdy and Crump's Landing road; saw some soldiers, who could give us no information where General Wallace was;

galloped down toward the Landing a short distance and met a surgeon, who said he had started some time before with his command for Pittsburg Landing on a road branching off between Adamsville and the River road; pushed on in this direction, and at the point D met his Second Brigade returning, the rear of the First Brigade having just filed off on the road DA. We pushed on to the head of the column and found General Wallace, when I delivered my instructions, and told him for "God's sake to move forward rapidly."

I understood him to say that his guide had led him wrong, and I was most decidedly of the impression that he had mistaken the road, for his command had already marched a great deal farther than was necessary to reach the battle-field.

I told him, however, to hurry on and we might yet be there in time. I thought we could get there; sun three-quarters of an hour high. We did not, however, reach the ground until after dark.

After I had reached the head of the column I must say it seemed to me that the march was not as rapid as the urgency of the case required. Perhaps this arose in a great measure from my impatience and anxiety to get this force on the field before dark, as I knew very well unless we arrived before sunset we could be of no use in that day's battle and would not be able to retrieve the fortunes of the day.

Very respectfully,

JAS. B. McPHERSON,

Major-General.

[Inclosure No. 3.]
HEADQUARTERS DEPARTMENT OF THE TENNESSEE,
Before Vicksburg, April 1, 1863.

Maj. Gen. U.S. GRANT,

Commanding Department of the Tennessee:

GENERAL: I have the honor to submit the following statement of your orders to Maj. Gen. Lewis Wallace, who commanded the Third Division of the Army of the Tennessee on the 6th day of April, A.D. 1862, and the manner in which he obeyed them, together with facts and circumstances transpiring that day and the one immediately preceding, deemed necessary to a clear understanding of them: In pursuance of the following order—

GENERAL ORDERS No. 30.

HEADQUARTERS DISTRICT OF WEST TENNESSEE,
Savannah, March 31, 1862.

Headquarters of the District of West Tennessee is hereby changed to Pittsburg Landing. An office will be continued at Savannah, where all official communications may be sent by troops having easier access with that point than Pittsburg Landing.

By command of Major-General Grant:

JNo. A. RAWLINS,

Assistant Adjutant-General.—

I was in charge of the office at Savannah, Tenn., with instructions to make out the necessary orders, and send forward to Pittsburg Landing all troops arriving from below. Up to the 5th day of April, 1862, from the date of said order, you had

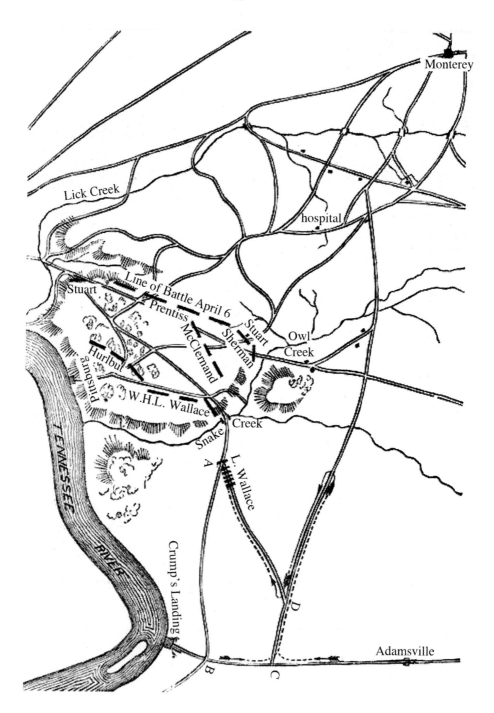

run up every morning to Pittsburg Landing and returned at night on the steamer Tigress, used for your headquarters boat, and on which boat steam was continually kept up.

The necessity for an office longer at Savannah having ceased, orders were issued for everything to be moved to Pittsburg Landing on Sunday, the 6th day of April, 1862, and arrangements were being made accordingly.

April 5, 1862, a dispatch was received from Maj. Gen. D.C. Buell, commanding the Army of the Ohio, dated Camp 3 miles west of Waynesborough, April 4, 1862, stating that he would be in Savannah, Tenn., with one and perhaps two divisions of his army the next day, and requesting to meet you there; to which you replied you would be there to meet him.

General Nelson's division of the Army of the Ohio reached Savannah on the afternoon of the 5th of April, but General Buell himself did not arrive; and supposing the must be near, you determined to ride out the next morning and meet him. That there might be no delay in getting off (and consequent detention in moving the office) to Pittsburg Landing, directions were given for breakfast and horses to be in readiness at an earlier hour than usual.

I was awakened by Capt. W.S. Hillyer, a member of your staff, who had arrived from Cairo on the boat that brought the mail from that place, about 3 o'clock A.M., and did not fall soundly to sleep again that morning. I got up at daylight, and in your private office was examining the mail, when you came down-stairs from your sleeping room. Your mail was handed you, and before you were through reading it Brig. Gen. John Cook, of Illinois, who had come in on a steamer during the night, reported to you in person his return from leave of absence for orders, and from that time until breakfast was announced, which was about 6 o'clock A.M., you were engaged in reading your mail and in conversation with General Cook.

While at breakfast, Edward N. Trembly, private Company C, First Regiment Illinois Artillery Volunteers, and on detached duty at headquarters, reported artillery firing in the direction of Pittsburg Landing. Breakfast was left unfinished, and, accompanied by your staff officers, you went immediately on board the steamer Tigress, then lying at the Landing. The horses being in readiness, as per orders of the night previous, were sent at once on the boat and orders given at once to start for Pittsburg Landing, delaying only long enough for you to write an order to General Nelson to move his division by the road from Savannah to the river opposite Pittsburg Landing, and a note to Maj. Gen. D.C. Buell, informing him of the supposed condition of affairs at or in the vicinity of Pittsburg Landing.

In passing Crump's Landing which is on the river between Savannah and Pittsburg Landing, and distant about 4½ miles from the former and 5½ miles from the latter place, and where was stationed the division commanded by Maj. Gen. Lewis Wallace, the Tigress ran close alongside the boat on which Major-General Wallace had his headquarters, and addressing him in person, you directed him to hold his division in readiness to move on receipt of orders, which he might expect when you ascertained the condition of affairs above, but in the mean time to send out and ascertain if there was any enemy on the Purdy road, apprehending, as you did, that the real attack might be intended against his position. His reply was that he was then in readiness, and had already taken the precautionary steps you directed as to the Purdy road. This was not far from 7 or 7.30 o'clock A.M.

From thence you continued direct to Pittsburg Landing, which place you reached about 8 o'clock A.M., and, with your staff, started immediately to the front. About half a mile from the river you met Brig. Gen. W.H.L. Wallace, who commanded Maj. Gen. C.F. Smith's Second Division of the Army of the Tennessee. From him you ascertained the particulars of the attack and how matters stood up to that time. You then directed me to return to the river and send Capt. A.S. Baxter, assistant quartermaster, U.S. Volunteers, and chief of the quartermaster's department in your district, on the steamer Tigress, without delay, to Crump's Landing, with orders to Maj. Gen. Lewis Wallace to bring forward his division by the River road to Pittsburg Landing to a point immediately in rear of the camp of Maj. Gen. C.F. Smith's division, and there form his column at right angles with the river on the right of our lines and await further orders.

In obedience to your command I proceeded to the river, and found Captain Baxter at the landing near where the Tigress lay, and communicated to him your orders, who, fearing lest he might make some mistake in the delivery of the orders, requested me to give him a written memorandum of them, and I went on board the steamer Tigress, where a pen and ink could be procured, and at my dictation he wrote substantially as follows:

Major-General WALLACE:

You will move forward your division from Crump's Landing, leaving a sufficient force to protect the public property at that place, to Pittsburg Landing, on the road nearest to and parallel with the river, and form in line at right angles with the river, immediately in rear of the camp of Maj. Gen. C.F. Smith's division on our right, and there await further orders.

Captain Baxter took this memorandum and started on the steamer Tigress to convey your orders to Maj. Gen. Lewis Wallace. This was not later than 9 o'clock A.M. Captain Baxter returned and reported before 12 o'clock M. his delivery of your orders to General Wallace, bringing at the same time from General Wallace to you the report of Col. Morgan L. Smith, that there was no enemy in the direction of Purdy; the result of his reconnaissance that morning. About an hour after Captain Baxter had gone down on the steamer Tigress to General Wallace an officer of the Second Illinois Cavalry, who was well acquainted with the road leading to Crump's Landing, was sent by you with a verbal message to Major-General Wallace to hurry forward with all possible dispatch. This officer returned between 12 o'clock M. and 1 o'clock P.M., and reported that when he delivered your message to Major-General Wallace he inquired if he had not written orders. He replied in the negative, and General Wallace said he would only obey written orders. He further stated that it had been more than one hour since he left General Wallace, and that his division was then all ready to move. He should have been by this time on the field. His presence then would have turned the tide of battle, which was raging with great fury; saved the lives of many brave men, and ere the setting of that crimson spring day's sun secured to us certain victory.

You then immediately dispatched Capt. William R. Rowley, of your staff, with orders to him, with the direction that, should General Wallace persist in requiring them to be in writing, he will write them out in full and sign them by your order. This was not later than 1 o'clock P.M.

You then rode back to the house near the river that had been designated for headquarters, to learn what word, if any, had been received from General Nelson, whose division you expected soon to arrive at the landing on the opposite side of the river; and you there met Maj. Gen. D.C. Buell, who had arrived at Savannah, and taken a steamer and come up to see you, and learn how the battle was progressing in advance of his force. Among his first inquiries was, "What preparations have you made for retreating?" To which you replied, "I have not yet despaired of whipping them, general;" and went on to state to him your momentary expectation of the arrival of General Wallace, to whom orders had been timely and repeatedly sent, and that General Nelson's division might soon be expected by the wagon road from Savannah. This was about 2 o'clock P.M.

You here inquired of Captain Baxter particularly what reply, if any, General Wallace made when he delivered him your orders. He said General Wallace appeared delighted; asked him for the written memorandum he had of the orders; read it; said it was all right, and put it in his pocket; ordered his horse at once, evincing the greatest alacrity in disposition to obey your orders; that he delivered him the orders about 10 o'clock A.M., and that General Wallace, from the time that had elapsed, must be at or near the point he was ordered.

You then directed Lieut. Col. J.B. McPherson, chief of engineers, and myself to go and meet him, supposing we would not have far to go, and conduct him to a certain position on the field you had pointed out to Lieutenant-Colonel McPherson, as we passed around the lines, in support of General Prentiss' division. We started, and before reaching the crest of the hill on the road between the river and Snake Creek, and over which General Wallace would be required to pass, the enemy's artillery was sweeping across it. We hurried on, anxiously expecting each moment to meet General Wallace.

We reached Snake Creek Bridge and crossed it — the foot of the hill beyond, but no General Wallace. We here pressed a citizen as guide, and continued on until we reached the road leading from Crump's Landing to Purdy. We here turned to the right and went toward the river until we met a surgeon of one of the regiments of General Wallace's division, who informed us General Wallace had taken the left-hand road leading from the camp of one of his brigades, which camp was between a quarter and half mile from the intersection of the main Pittsburg and Crump's Landing road with the Purdy road and towards Purdy, and about 4½ miles from Pittsburg Landing by the direct road. In company with this surgeon we proceeded on the road General Wallace was said to have taken in the forenoon of that day. About one-half mile from the camp we met Colonel Thayer's brigade of General Wallace's division, and Colonel Thayer informed us that the rear of Col. Morgan L. Smith's brigade had filed off on a cross road leading into the main Pittsburg Landing road, and that General Wallace was with the head of the column. Taking this cross road we came up with him about 3.30 o'clock P.M. General Wallace said his guide had misled him, and that he had marched about 10 miles. Capt. W.R. Rowley, of your staff, whom you had sent after him, was with him, and informed us that he had overtaken him about 5 miles from his camp and not on the road he was expected to take; that when he (Captain Rowley) informed him he was wrong, he sent forward and halted his cavalry, which was in the advance, and countermarched his command to within a half mile of where he had started in the forenoon. I here stated to General Wallace the report of the officer sent to him in the morning of his refusing to obey or receive any but written orders, which he denounced as wholly untrue, and manifested in his talk a great desire to get into the fight. Colonel McPherson, Captain Rowley, and myself represented to him how matters stood when we left. I urged upon him, with all the earnestness I possessed, the importance of his presence on the field; that General Nelson was expected, but might have difficulty in crossing the river. He said there was no danger; he would yet reach there in good season, and with his fresh division would soon end the fight in a victory for us.

General Wallace at this point expressed doubt as to our being on the road leading into the main Pittsburg and Crump's Landing road. Colonel McPherson went to a house near by, and, upon inquiry, ascertained that we were on the right road. After halting the head of his column for a considerable length of time, to enable it to close up and rest, he gave the order to march, and continued coolly and leisurely forward until we reached the main Pittsburg Landing road. Here Colonel McPherson suggested that to disencumber and facilitate the march, the artillery, which was immediately in the rear of the advance brigade, fall to the rear of the column, which suggestion was concurred in by General Wallace, and the artillery moved out of the road while the column filed by. This was an excuse for considerable delay—I should say for full half an hour-during which time he was dismounted and sitting down. From thence he continued his march until we reached the low bottom-lands through which runs Snake Creek, where we met some citizens, who informed us that the bridge across Snake Creek was in possession of the enemy. He then halted his column and sent forward his cavalry to ascertain if it was true.

Colonel McPherson and Captain Rowley went forward with the cavalry. I remained with General Wallace. In a few minutes a messenger came back from the cavalry with a message that the bridge was safe. General Wallace still remained stationary, waiting for his column to close up and his troops to rest. About this time the artillery firing at Pittsburg Landing became terrific, and we who had been there knew that it was our heavy guns, and that the enemy had attained a nearness to the river that filled our minds, situated as we were, with terrible apprehension for the fate of the brave army that had been fighting against such fearful odds and without intermission from early morning.

It seemed as though the enemy was immediately between where we were and the river, which seeming gained credence from the fact that as we passed out his artillery was sweeping the road in that direction.

General Wallace here asked, if such was the position of the opposing forces, what had best be done? Colonel McPherson said, "Fight our way through until communication can be had with General Grant"; to which General Wallace replied, "That is my purpose." Colonel McPherson and Captain Rowley again rode forward. General Wallace still gave no orders to move, but manifested the utmost coolness and indifference. I asked him if it would not be well to send forward a brigade to hold the bridge, lest the enemy should destroy it, and thus prevent his joining you? He replied that it was a "capital idea," and accordingly ordered Col. Morgan L. Smith, with his brigade, to move forward until the rear of his column rested on the further side of Snake Creek Bridge and there halt until he received further orders from you or himself.

Colonel Smith moved forward as ordered, and General Wallace, dismounting from his horse, seated himself on a log. I then rode forward until I came up with Colonel McPherson, to whom I communicated the order given by General Wallace to Colonel Smith, and submitted to him the propriety of giving the order, as from you to Colonel Smith, to push forward with his brigade. But he hesitated to take such a step. It was now near night; the firing ceased; the sun sank to rest, and darkness had spread her mantle over friend and foe, when a cavalryman brought the report that there was no enemy between General Wallace and the river; upon the hearing of which orders were given to move forward. Without opposition he reached the field of battle and received orders from you in person after night and about a mile from the steamboat landing at Pittsburg Landing.

The excuse that his guides misled him should avail nothing in extenuation of his want of knowledge of the road, for he had taken up his position at Crump's Landing on the 13th of March immediately preceding in the face of an enemy, and should have been perfectly familiar with all the roads leading to and from his camps.

Colonel McPherson and I came up to him about 3.30 o'clock P.M. He was then not to exceed 4 or 4½ miles from the scene of action; the roads were in fine condition; he was marching light; his men were in buoyant spirits, within hearing of the musketry, and eager to get forward. He did not make a mile and a half an hour, although urged and appealed to push forward. Had he moved with the rapidity his command were able and anxious to have moved after we overtook him, he would have reached you in time to have engaged the enemy before the close of Sunday's fight.

I am, general, very respectfully, your obedient servant,

JNo. A. RAWLINS,

Lieutenant-Colonel, Assistant Adjutant-General

CRAWFORDSVILLE, *IND., July* 18, 1863.
Hon. E.M. STANTON, *Secretary of War:*
SIR: Some months ago I discovered that Maj. Gen. U.S. Grant, in forwarding to your Department my official report of the battle of Pittsburg Landing, accompanied it with the following indorsement:

HEALQUARTERS ARMY OF THE TENNESSEE,
Pittsburg Landing, April 25, 1862.

I directed this division at 8 o'clock A.M. to be held in readiness to move at a momerit's warning in any direction it might be ordered. Certainly not later than 11 o'clock A.M. the order reached General Wallace to march by a flank movement to Pittsburg Landing. Waiting until I thought he should be here, I sent one of my staff to hurry him, and afterwards sent Colonel McPherson and my assistant adjutant-general.

This report in some other particulars I do not fully indorse.

Respectfully forwarded to headquarters of the department.

U.S. GRANT,

Major-General.

It will be observed that the indorsement contains several serious imputations against me, and in some particulars amounts to a denial of my official report.

1st. It says that at 11 o'clock A.M. I received an order to march by a flank movement to Pittsburg Landing. In my report, on the other hand, it is distinctly asserted that the order received by me came to hand at 11.30 A.M., and directed me to march to the right of the army and form junction there; a point nearly, if not quite, 3½ miles from Pittsburg Landing.

If General Grant's statement is true, then, in marching to a point so distant from Pittsburg Landing, I was guilty of a disobedience of orders, for which, in the disastrous turn of the battle at the time, there can be but slender apology. If his statement is true, then I am also guilty of making a false report in a very material matter.

2d. The indorsement says that "waiting until he should be here, I sent one of my staff officers to hurry him, and afterwards sent Colonel McPherson and my assistant adjutant-general." The imputations contained in the sentence quoted are of the gravest character. If they are true, I am unfit to hold a commission of any kind in the United States Army. The imputations can be easily shaped into charges of cowardice and treachery, and I regret to say such charges have been made and are yet existing against me in consequence of the time it took me to reach the battlefield from my position at Crump's Landing.

3d. General Grant, in his indorsement, further says that there are some other particulars in my official report which he cannot fully indorse. This amounts to saying that I have made a false report.

I have waited with all patience for the arrival of a period when the state of the war would permit me to ask a court of inquiry without detriment to the service. That time, in my judgment, has now come, and I therefore respectfully ask that such a court may be ordered, and that the scope of its investigation may cover my whole conduct in connection with the battle of Pittsburg Landing. That this investigation may be full and complete, I also request that Judge-Advocate General Holt may be specially charged with the duty of prosecution.

Very respectfully, sir, your friend and obedient servant,

LEW. WALLACE,

Major-General Volunteers.

[Indorsement.]

Respectfully referred to the General-in-Chief.
By order of the Secretary of War:

JAS. A. HARDIE,

A.A.G.

WAR DEPARTMENT, *July 24,* 1863.

———

CRAWFORDSVILLE, *IND., September* 16, 1863.

Hon. E. M. STANTON, *Secretary of War:*

DEAR SIR: You will please suspend action in the matter of my request for a court of inquiry until I communicate with you again on the subject. It is possible that I may satisfy General Grant upon the points involved and thus save further trouble. Meantime I hope you will consider me ready and anxious to go to any duty.

Very respectfully,

LEW. WALLACE,

Major-General.

O.R.—SERIES I—VOLUME X/1 [S# 10]

April 6–7, 1862.—Battle of Pittsburg Landing, or Shiloh, Tenn.

No. 14.—Report of Lieut. Col. Enos P. Wood, Seventeenth Illinois Infantry.

Early on the morning of the 6th of April heavy firing was heard in our front, but thinking it proceeded from our pickets, very little attention was paid to it, except to order the men to be ready to fall in at a moment's notice. About 7.30 A.M. notice came that we were really attacked, when our long roll beat, and the regiment, about 400 strong, fell in promptly. After waiting a time for orders, Acting Assistant Adjutant-General Ryan came with orders from Colonel Raith (who was in command of our brigade by seniority) to move to the left of Sherman's division, our regiment forming the right of the Third Brigade. In this position our regiment rested behind the encampment of an Ohio regiment, our left in a ravine. A section of some battery and a few skirmishers were already fighting in our front. After a time the enemy seemed to give back here, and we could see them on the opposite hill deploying men and forming heavy columns of regiments, which very soon commenced to advance.

Our front was now ordered to be changed obliquely on our right, throwing the entire left of our brigade back, so as to be clear of the ravine. Very soon the enemy made his appearance, and our boys opened fire on him, doing fine execution. Our fire seemed to check their advance for a short time, when they again advanced, and as they seemed to be flanking us on the left our regiment changed front again and moved obliquely to the left, the regiment on our right having given way and fallen entirely to our rear. The enemy now took possession of the battery in front of our left, about 200 yards distant, and planting their colors on one of the guns, Lieutenant Davis, of Company K, seized a musket, which had just fallen from the hands of one of his wounded men, aimed it at the rebel color-bearer and fired, when he fell to the ground; but the colors were soon replaced, and the enemy continued slowly to advance. At this juncture the order came to fall back and form a continuous line with the division on our right and about 50 or 60 yards in our rear, which was effected in good order, still pouring in a terrific fire on the advancing foe.

Major Schwartz now requested my regiment to support his battery, which we promptly did until he was obliged to limber up and moved off without losing a gun. In the mean time the regiments on our right and left had fallen back nearly a hundred yards, when I ordered my men to fall back and form in line again, this move being executed in good order. I found that we must move over the hill to have range on the enemy as they advanced up the opposite side. I consequently pushed my own regiment about 20 or 30 yards in advance of the line, where they could have full play as the enemy advanced. The regiments on our right failing to advance with us to our support, our boys stood their ground well and bravely, doing good execution with their fire until I found we were entirely unsupported both on our right and left, when I again gave the order to fall back.

As we came up to form in line the regiments on our right and left broke up in great confusion. Our ammunition being nearly gone, and having no support, I felt compelled to order a retreat. Facing by the rear rank we moved back near the first field, when I gave the order to move by the left flank, now become our right. The men not all understanding the order alike, here the regiment was for the first time thrown into some confusion. Having lost my horse in the early part of the engagement, and being on foot and also quite weak from previous illness, I could do but little to remedy this. I, however, ordered Major Smith to ride on in advance and halt and form our men at the first convenient place, and when I came up found the major had succeeded in getting most of our regiment into line. At this point I found Colonel Marsh, with the remnants of his regiment; also the remains of the Fifteenth Illinois and some batteries of artillery. Major Taylor not having men enough to work his guns, I detailed all that were left of Company G, of the Seventeenth, about 20 men, to assist his batteries, and after consulting with my officers decided to move off nearer the river and get a new supply of ammunition.

This was about noon. I now learned that Colonel Raith had been wounded and taken off the field, leaving me the ranking officer in the brigade, and consequently devoted my attention to gathering up all that remained of our command. At 2 o'clock I had succeeded in getting some 500 of the Seventeenth, Forty-ninth, and Forty-third together, and at the request of General Sherman moved them out and formed again on his extreme left. One of the Chicago batteries immediately took up position directly in front and opened fire upon the enemy's line, which we could distinctly see about 400 yards distant.

I now deployed my men down a ravine under the fire of our batteries, and formed them into line in a cross ravine, out of sight of the enemy, and advanced cautiously up the intervening ridge until I had them in full view. Here I got in a number of telling volleys, when you came down along our lines from the left and informed us we were unsupported on our left, and ordered us to retire in good order to our old position in rear of the Chicago battery and on General Sherman's left. The fight between the enemy and the battery in our front soon became quite exciting, but our battery seeming to get the worst of it and a number of their horses having been disabled, they were compelled to fall back and leave one of their guns, which was promptly and bravely brought off by our boys.

Thus ended the fight for the day as far as we were concerned. Our orders were to lay on our arms in our places, with which our men complied without a murmur.

About 10 o'clock P.M. I was taken with a severe ague chill, which obliged me to leave the field and seek assistance, leaving my command to Major Smith, who will report to you the labors of the second day.

Both men and officers behaved with great coolness and bravery through the whole day, remaining under the severe fire without flinching, and always promptly advancing at the word of command.

Respectfully,

E.P. WOOD,
Lieutenant-Colonel, Commanding Seventeenth Illinois Infantry.
General JOHN A. MCCLERNAND,
Comdg. First Division

O.R.—SERIES I—VOLUME X/1 [S# 10]
April 6–7, 1862.—Battle of Pittsburg Landing, or Shiloh, Tenn.

No. 83 — Report of Col. Benjamin Allen, Sixteenth Wisconsin Infantry.

SIR: Having heard various and conflicting reports in regard to the part taken in the engagement of the 6th and 7th of April by the regiments comprising General Prentiss' division, I deem it my duty to myself and command to submit a statement, which I should have done sooner but for the painfulness of a wound received on the battle-field. The regiment which I have the honor to command formed the left of Colonel Peabody's brigade, and was encamped on the south road leading from Pittsburg Landing to Corinth. On the evening of the 5th four companies of my regiment and two companies of the Twenty-first Missouri, under the command of George K. Donnelly, acting assistant adjutant-general, First Brigade, Sixth Division, was sent, by order of Colonel Peabody, on picket duty. At about 5.30 A.M. on the 6th a part of this force discovered some of the enemy's cavalry about 1½ miles in front and to the right of our camp, and while advancing upon them came upon a large force of the enemy concealed behind a fence and were fired upon by them. This was the first fire of the enemy. Captain Saxe and Sergeant Williams, of Company A, in my regiment, were killed, and Colonel Moore, who had just arrived with re-enforcements from the Twenty-first Missouri, was wounded. After firing they retreated, followed by our men, but they were soon re-enforced, and our men fell back toward our camp.

At about 6 o'clock I was ordered by General Prentiss to form my regiment and advance on the enemy. This I did, taking my position in a thicket of small timber about 80 rods in front of my camp. After remaining in this position about thirty minutes, waiting the approach of the enemy, I was ordered by General Prentiss to change front to the right, which I did, and in this position received the fire of the enemy, who appeared simultaneously on my front and left flank. We held this position, and delivered our fire with great effect, checking the advance of the enemy on our front, until we were ordered by General Prentiss to fall back, which I did, forming my second line about 40 rods in front of my camp. At this time the regiment on my right and left had fallen back, and we were entirely unsupported by any force. We maintained this position against a greatly superior force of the enemy until again ordered to fall back.

I made my next stand directly in front of our camp. While holding this position I was re-enforced by party of Company A, who were out on picket. A desperate conflict here ensued, in which Lieutenant-Colonel Fairchild was wounded in the thigh and carried from the field. I also had my horse shot under me, and my second horse was shot dead as I was about to remount. I was again ordered by General Prentiss to fall back, take to the trees, and hold the enemy in check as much as possible until re-enforcements could arrive. My men immediately took to the trees and fell back slowly, firing upon the enemy, until the advance of General Hurlbut's division made their appearance. I then fell back to the rear of his lines and formed my men, but finding them out of ammunition, I drew off for a fresh supply. My men were nearly exhausted, having been engaged since 6 o'clock without food or water, contesting the field inch by inch with a greatly superior force of the enemy.

After receiving a fresh supply of ammunition, and while waiting orders from General Prentiss, I was requested by a field officer to take the place of an Indiana regiment he said were out of ammunition and were falling back. I immediately complied with his request, and opened fire on the enemy. This position we maintained until we were flanked by the enemy on our left and were compelled to fall back. In this engagement I received a wound, the ball passing through my left arm, a little below the elbow, and I was obliged to leave the field about 3 P.M.

Of my regiment there were 46 killed, 176 wounded, and 23 missing. Of the wounded several have since died.

I cannot speak in too high terms of commendation of the bravery and endurance of both officers and men in my command, although never before in action. They with very few exceptions exhibited in an eminent degree the qualities of veteran soldiers, and in the last engagement I lost some of my brave and valuable men, among whom was Capt. O.D. Pease, of Company D, who received a wound that caused his death.

I have the honor to be, very respectfully, your obedient servant,

BENJ. ALLEN,

Colonel Sixteenth Regiment Wisconsin Volunteers.

Maj. Gen. U.S. GRANT.

Chapter Notes

Chapter 1

1. *The Papers of U.S. Grant*, U.S. Grant Association, Mississippi State University, vol. 4: 79–84.
2. Ibid. USG to A.Q.M. Capt. R.B. Hatch re: turn over all arms to Capt. Brinck, 180. Ordnance officer Capt. W.F. Brinck to USG re: faulty ammunition at Cairo, 399.
3. *Papers of U.S. Grant*, vol. 3: 22, 37, 43n, 209, 210n, 303n, 351, 352n.
4. *Papers of U.S. Grant*, vol. 4: 22–23.
5. Ibid., 37.
6. Ibid., 11, 37, 43n, 209, 210, 393n.
7. *Papers of U.S. Grant*, vol. 4: 97, 98, 98n, 207–208, 208n.
8. Augustus Chetlain, *Hamlin Garland Papers* (Doheny Library, University of Southern California), www.granthomepage.com/intchetlain.htm.
9. *Kennedy's 1860 St. Louis Directory*, http://www.rollanet.org.
10. James Grant Wilson and John Fiske, "Algernon Sydney Baxter," *Appleton's Cyclopedia of American Biography*, vol. 7 (New York: D. Appleton, 1901); "Horace Henry Baxter 1818–1884," *Rutland Historical Society Quarterly* 23, no. 3, http://vermontcivilwar.org.
11. *Papers of U.S. Grant*, vol. 3: 143, 148n.
12. *Papers of U.S. Grant*, vol. 4: 48, 50n, 72 and n, 77–78, 77n, 81n, 86n, 126–127, 127n, 192n, 302n, 359, 482, 484, 491.
13. Ibid., 50n, 127n, 209n.
14. *Papers of U.S. Grant*, vol. 4:220 and n, 234n, 237, 238, 230n, 241n, 478, 479.

Chapter 2

1. References to Pvt. Samuel Asbury Garrett come from oral family accounts of the author.

2. King James Authorized Version.
3. John Brazelton, *Brazelton's History of Hardin County* (self-published, 1885), Chapter 10: 1–12. http://www.tngenweb.org/hardin/hosey/bios/brazelton/brazelton.
4. James D. Brewer, *Tom Worthington's Civil War: Shiloh, Sherman, and the Search for Vindication* (Jefferson, NC: McFarland, 2001), 64–72.
5. Brewer, 85.
6. M.A. Dewolfe Howe, *Home Letters of General Sherman* (New York: Scribner's, 1909), 209.
7. Getchell Collection, copies available at Shiloh Military Park and the U.S. Grant Association.
8. Brewer, 71: Worthington diary entry, March 12, 1862.

Chapter 3

1. Albert Bigelow Paine, *Mark Twain's Autobiography: With commentary by Alfred Bigelow Paine* (New York: Harper & Brothers, 1924), Chapter XXIX, 12.
2. Mark Twain, "Private History of a Campaign That Failed," *American Claimant and Other Stories and Sketches* (New York: Scribner's, 1896).
3. "Charles Parsons Papers, 1808–1940: Steamboats Series, 1862–1864." Voucher No. 22 issued to *Iatan*, Capt. Albert Pearce (Missouri Historical Society).
4. Joseph G. Knapp, S.J., *The Presence of the Past: Beginnings of the Civil War in St. Louis* (St. Louis: St. Louis University Press, 1979), 1–7; W.T. Sherman, *Memoirs of General William T. Sherman* (New York: D. Appleton, 1889), vol. 1: 172; Bruce Catton, *The Coming Fury* (New York: Doubleday, 1961), 375.
5. Ibid.
6. *The War of the Rebellion: A Compilation*

of the Official Records of the Union and Confederate Armies (The Civil War CD-ROM, Oliver Computing LLC, 2006), vol. 3, no. 1: 183.

7. *Papers of U.S. Grant*, vol. 2: 177.

8. Stacey Allen, "If He Had Less Rank," in *Grant's Lieutenants: From Cairo to Vicksburg*, ed. Steven E. Woodworth (Lawrence: University of Kansas Press, 2001), 63; Robert E. Morseberger and Katherine M. Morseberger, *Lew Wallace: Militant Romantic* (New York: McGraw-Hill, 1980), 428, 429.

9. *Papers of U.S. Grant*, J.A.R. to L. Wallace, March 31, 1862.

10. *Papers of U.S. Grant*, vol. 4: 189, 189n, 191, 229.

11. *War of the Rebellion*, Series I, vol. X/1 [S#10], attached to No. 34 Report Major General Lew Wallace. Correspondence from U.S Grant Headquarters, before Vicksburg, April 13, 1863 (Inclosure No. 3), Headquarters Dept. of Tennessee, April 1, 1863, Lt. Col. John Rawlins to U.S. Grant, General Orders No. 30.

12. *War of the Rebellion,* Series I, vol. X/1 [S#10], Enclosure No. 3, USG from J.A.R, H.Q, Before Vicksburg, April 1, 1863, General Order No. 30, H.Q. District of Tennessee, Savannah, March 31, 1862.

13. *Papers of U.S. Grant*, vol. 5: 435n; U.S. Grant, *Personal Memoirs* (New York: Modern Library, 1999), No. 3: 172, 173; *War of the Rebellion*, 10, pt. 2.91.

14. *Papers of U.S. Grant*, vol. 5: 401–402, 402n–403n, 405n.

15. Ibid., vol. 4: 401, 402, 402n.

16. *Papers of U.S. Grant*, vol. 5: 401–2, 402n–403n, 405n.

17. Ibid., vol. 4: 404.

18. Ibid., 404n.

19. Ibid., 404n, 405n.

20. Ibid., vol. 4: 436, 437.

21. Ibid., vol. 05: 119. Special Orders No.47 Grant to Lagow to McArthur/Chetlain/ Morgan/ Reed/Gaddis.

22. Augustus L. Chetlain, *Memories of Seventy Years* (Galena, IL: Gazette, 1889), 71.

23. Dorothy Stanley, ed. *Autobiography of Sir Henry Morton Stanley* (Boston and New York: Houghton Mifflin, 1921), 175.

24. "Charles Parsons Papers," Asst. Q.M. Off., March 29, 1862.

25. Ibid. Pass issued H.Q. Fts. Henry & Heiman, April 1, 1862, from Lowe, Colonel of Curtis Horse, to Steamer *Iatan.*

26. Ibid. Voucher No. 22 issued to *Iatan* Capt. Albert Pearce.

27. *Papers of U.S. Grant*, Special Order No. 42, April 1, 1862.

28. Jack Hurst, *Nathan Bedford Forrest: A Biography* (New York: Vintage, 1993), 87, 88.

29. "Skirmish on Purdy Road," *War of the Rebellion*, vol. XI: 68 [S#10].

30. Ray E. Boomhower, *The Sword and the Pen: A Life of Lew Wallace* (Indianapolis: Indiana Historical Society Press, 2005), 16.

31. *Papers of U.S. Grant*, C.B. Lagow to L. Wallace, April 2, 1862.

32. Alfred Roman, *The Military Operations of General Beauregard* (New York: Harper & Brothers, 1884), ch. 22.

33. *Papers of U.S. Grant*, vol. 5, Sec. 036: 8.

34. Ibid., vol. 5, Sec. 034: 6, 6n, 7.

35. *War of the Rebellion*, Series I, vol. X/1 [S#10]: 170–190, No. 34. Reports of Maj. Gen Lewis Wallace, U.S. Army, commanding Third Division, with communications in reference thereto, enclosure No. 3 John A. Rawlins, Lt. Colonel, Assistant Adjutant General to Maj. Gen. U.S. Grant re: inquiries of Maj. Gen. Lewis Wallace to War Department.

36. *Papers of U.S. Grant*, John. A. Rawlins to A.S. Baxter.

37. *War of the Rebellion*, Series I, vol. X/1 [S#10]: 184, No. 34. Reports of Maj. Gen Lewis Wallace, U.S. Army, commanding Third Division, with communications in reference thereto, enclosure No.3 John A. Rawlins, Lt. Colonel, Assistant Adjutant General to Maj. Gen. U.S. Grant re: inquiries of Maj. Gen. Lewis Wallace to War Department.

38. Victor Davis Hanson, "Lew Wallace and the Ghosts of the Shunpike," in Robert Cowley, ed., *What Ifs? of American History* (New York: Berkley, 2003), 83–84.

Chapter 4

1. Beauregard narrative material and references based on Harry T. Williams, *P.G.T. Beauregard: Napoleon in Gray* (Baton Rouge: Louisiana State University Press, 1954); Roman, *Military Operations of General Beauregard*; Hamilton Basso, *Beauregard: The Great Creole* (New York: Scribner's, 1933).

2. Victoria E. Bynum, *The Free State of Jones: Mississippi's Longest Civil War* (Chapel Hill: University of North Carolina Press, 2001).

3. Jefferson Davis, "Proceedings of the First Congress," in *The Rise and Fall of the Confederate Government* (New York: D. Appleton, 1881), vol. 2: 132–133.

4. William Preston Johnston, *The Life of General Albert Sidney Johnston* (New York: D. Appleton, 1879), 582.

Chapter 5

1. O.P. (Oliver Perry) Newberry, *Oliver Perry Newberry Papers* (Chicago: The Newberry Library, Roger and Julie Baskes Department of Special Collections). Herein all quotes and references pertaining to O.P. Newberry come from this collection.

2. Miss Fanny Juda, "California Filibusters: A History of their Expeditions into Hispanic America," *The Grizzly Bear: Official Organ of the Native Sons and Native Daughters of the Golden West* 21, no. 4 (February 1919); James M. McPherson, *Battle Cry of Freedom: The Civil War Era* (Oxford: University of Mississippi Press, 1988) 110–116; Theodore Henry Hittell, *History of California* (San Francisco: N.J. Stone, 1898), 797.

3. *G.T. Beauregard Papers, 1839–1888*, Tulane University, Beauregard to Bowman, December 5, 1856; Williams, 42.

4. John G. Shea, *The American Nation: Lives of the Fallen Braves and Living Heroes* (New York: I. Farrell & Son, 1863), 355–57.

5. James G. Downhour, "Nathaniel Lyon," *Encyclopedia of the American Civil War: A Political, Social, and Military History*, ed. David S. Heidler and Jeanne T. Heidler (New York: W.W. Norton, 2000), 1233–1234.

6. W.A. Neal, *An Illustrated History of the Missouri Engineer and the 25th Infantry Regiments* (Chicago: Donnohue and Henneberry, 1889), 119–123.

7. *War of the Rebellion*, Series I, vol. 3: 183, No. 1, Siege of Lexington Miscellaneous Reports, September 12–23, Prentiss to Fremont, Brookfield, September 22, 1861.

8. Wiley Sword, *Shiloh: Bloody April* (Dayton, OH: Morningside House Press, 2001), 252.

9. Thomas Wentworth Higginson, *Harvard Memorial Biographies* (Columbia: Sever and Francis, 1866), 150–159.

10. *Oliver Perry Newberry Papers*.

11. Juda; Hittell, 797; McPherson, 110–116.

12. Charles Morton Stanley, "Opening of the Battle of Shiloh," War Paper No. 88 (New York: Commandery of the District of Columbia. Military Order of the Loyal Legion of the United States, 1907).

13. Neal, 119–123.

14. *War of the Rebellion*, Series I, vol. 10: 282, Report No. 10. Col David Moore.

15. Neal, 119–123.

16. *Papers of U.S. Grant*, vol. 1: 123n, 151n–152n, 169–177, including all notes.

17. Edward O. Cunningham, *Shiloh and The Western Campaign*, ed. Gary D. Joiner and Timothy B. Smith (New York: Savas Beatie, 2007, 2009), 72, 73.

18. Ibid., 137.

19. *Oliver Perry Newberry Papers*, O.P. Newberry to Mother; E.B. Quiner, "Newspaper Clippings" (Wisconsin Regiments, Wisconsin Historical Society), 212–250. One account in Quiner mentions three small drummer boys in 1st Brigade, in which the 16th Wisconsin served, with only one surviving. Newberry describes Major Powell's son as "the idol of the regiment" as a survivor.

20. Neal, 119–123.

21. John Robertson, *Michigan in the Civil War* (Lansing: W.S. George, 1882), 325.

22. Appendix: Derickson orders from Prentiss.

23. Quiner, "Newspaper Clippings," 214.

24. Thomas Lowry and William Davis, "The Worst Colonel I Ever Saw: Colonel Francis Quinn," in *Curmudgeons, Drunkards and Outright Fools* (Mechanicsburg, PA: Stackpole Books, 1997), chap. 41.

25. Quiner, "Newspaper Clippings," 214–250.

Chapter 6

1. John A. Wyeth, *That Devil Forrest: The Life of General Nathan Bedford Forrest* (New York: Harper & Brothers, 1899), 60; William Preston Diary, April 6, 1862, Misc. Collections Shiloh Military Park; Cunningham, 244.

2. Hurst, 22, 23–27. Hereafter most Forrest accounts relate to information in this biography.

3. Robert Selph Henry, *First with the Most: Nathan Bedford Forrest* (Bdd Promotional Books, 1991).

4. 1860 Census; Civil War Soldiers and Sailors System; oral transmission within author's family (source of all subsequent references to Samuel A. Garrett); John C. Rigdon, "Mississippi Civil War Soldiers Index," www.researchonline.net.

5. Allen Johnson, ed., *Dictionary of American Biography* (New York: Scribner's, 1936); Col. Charles E. Hooker, "Confederate Military History," in *A Library of Confederate States History* (Atlanta: Confederate Publishing, 1899), 385.

Chapter 7

1. *Papers of U.S. Grant*, April 5, 1862, JAR to B.M. Prentiss.

2. Ibid., April 4, 1862, W.R. Rowley for USG to SAH.

3. Ibid., April 5, 1862. W.R. Rawlins to Prentiss.

4. Ibid., April 5, 1862. SPO #45.

5. Ibid., April 5, 1862, Lew Wallace to W.H.L Wallace.

6. Brewer, 85.

7. *1860 Census*, Richard P. Derickson, Port Washington, Wisconsin.

8. Sword, 145, 149–153; Bradt, "Bradt Describes Waupace Men in Battle of Shiloh," *New London Press* (Waupaca, WI), March 11, 1925, 20.

9. Neal, 130; *War of the Rebellion*, vol. X, 282; Charles Morton, *A Boy at Shiloh* (New York: [s.n.], 1899), 58.

10. Sword, 145, 149–153; Bradt, 20.

11. Quiner Collection, 214.

12. Quiner Collection, 214; Quiner Collection, D.L. Jones, 56; *War of the Rebellion*, Series I, vol. 10: 282, 283.

13. Frederick Henry Dyer, "Part 3: History of the 3rd Iowa Regiment," in *A Compendium of the War of the Rebellion*, 3 vols. (New York: Thomas Yoseloff, 1959). http://www.civil-wararchive.com/regim.htm.

14. Quiner Collection.

15. *CWSS*, 21st Missouri Regiment.

16. *Papers of U.S. Grant*, April 5, 1862, CBL to Prentiss.

17. Gary R. Kremer, *James Milton Turner and the Promise of America: The Public Life of a Post–Civil War Black Leader* (Columbia: University of Missouri Press, 199), 16–17, 43, 121, 203.

18. Ibid., 1–24.

19. *Ozaukee Advertiser and Democrat,* April 7, 1862, Letter from Lt. Derickson, E.B. Quiner Collection, 213, 214.

20. *Oliver Perry Newberry Papers*, "Letter to Mother, about Shiloh"; E.B. Quiner Collection, 229, 230.

21. *War of the Rebellion*, vol. X/1: 305, 306.

22. Sword, 160, 161; "James Sligh Letters," letter written April 7, 1862, *New York Tribune*, April 21, 1862 (Michigan Historical Society).

23. Neal, 124–130.

24. Daniel McGinley, "Company K: 16th Wisconsin," *Port Washington Star*, 1897 (Wisconsin Historical Website).

25. Cunningham, 196, 197.

26. Lowry and Davis, 182–185.

27. E.B. Quiner Collection, 214–250.

Chapter 8

1. Dorothy Stanley, 3–204.

2. Ibid., 188, 189.

3. "Civil War Soldiers and Sailors System: 25th Missouri Regiment, Oliver Newberry"; Neal, 124–129, index; *Oliver Perry Newberry Papers*.

4. E.B. Quiner Collection, 224.

5. Dorothy Stanley, 195–197.

6. Ibid., 194–195.

7. Drew Gilpin Faust, *This Republic of Suffering: Death and the American Civil War* (New York: Vintage Books, 2008), 36.

8. Twain, "The Private History of a Campaign That Failed," 243–266.

9. Ambrose Bierce, *The Devil's Dictionary: Complete and Unabridged* (Mineola, NY: Dover, 2011), 256.

10. Ambrose Bierce, "What I Saw of Shiloh," in *The Collected Works of Ambrose Bierce* (New York: Neal Publishing, 1909), vol. 1: 261–262. http://www.online-literature.com/bierce/2037/.

11. Ibid., note 7, 196; Mark Twain, *Captain Stormfield's Visit to Heaven* (New York: Harper & Brothers, 1909), 1–121.

12. Robert Green Ingersoll, "Crumbling Creeds," in *The Works of Robert G. Ingersoll* (Dresden Memorial Edition), vol. 11: 463–470, http://www.positiveatheism.org/hist/ingban q.htm#CREEDS.

13. Ibid., "The Liberty of All."

14. Authorized King James Version.

Chapter 9

1. Bruce Catton, *Grant Moves South* (Boston: Little, Brown, 1960), 223.

2. Lew Wallace, *Lew Wallace: An Autobiography* (New York: Harper & Brothers, 1906), vol. 1: 397–399; ibid., note 1: 163; Gail Stephens, *Shadow of Shiloh: Major General Lew Wallace in the Civil War* (Indianapolis: Indiana Historical Society Press, 2010), 51.

3. *Papers of U.S. Grant*, vol. 1: 228n.

4. Peter Cozzens, "Who Kept Grant Sober?" http://www.historynet.com/who-kept -u-s-grant-sober.htm.

5. *Papers of U.S. Grant*, vol. 1: 116n–118n.

6. *War of the Rebellion*, Series I, vol. X/1: 178.

7. Ibid., 169, 170.

8. Robert Underwood Johnson and Clarence Clough Buel, *Battles and Leaders of the Civil War*, vol. 1 (New York: Thomas Yoseloff, 1956), 468.

9. *War of the Rebellion*, 250–51; Lloyd Lewis, *Sherman, Fighting Prophet* (Lincoln: University of Nebraska Press,1993), 213; James Lee McDonough, *Shiloh–in Hell before Night*

(Knoxville: University of Tennessee Press, 1977), 51, 52.

10. *War of the Rebellion*, vol. 10, part 2: 91, *Manning Force Papers* (Library of Congress), 133; *Papers of U.S. Grant*, vol. 5: 9, 10.

11. *Papers of U.S. Grant*, April 4, 1862, L. Wallace to W.H.L. Wallace.

Chapter 10

1. *War of the Rebellion*, 108.
2. Ibid.
3. Ibid., 109–111.
4. Ibid., 109.
5. Ibid., 178, 179.
6. Ibid., 178–180, Inclosure No. 1.
7. *Papers of U.S. Grant*, April 4, 1862, Grant to Sherman, vol. 5: 9.
8. *Papers of U.S. Grant*, April 5, 1862, L. Wallace to W.H.L. Wallace.
9. *War of the Rebellion*, 180–182, Inclosure No. 2.
10. Ibid., 185; Sword, 218, 219.
11. *War of the Rebellion*, 184, 188.
12. *Papers of U.S. Grant*, vol. 5: 6, April 3, 1862, USG to Commanding Officer, Paducah, KY.
13. http://aa.usno.navy.mil/cgi-bin/aa_pap .pl; http://www.usno.navy.mil/USNO/astron-omical-applications/data-services/rs-one-day-us.
14. Catton, *Grant Moves South*, 223; *War of the Rebellion*, vol. 10/1: 184; *War of the Rebellion*, vol. 10/1 Sec. 10: 276; Larry J. Daniel, *Shiloh: The Battle That Changed the Civil War* (New York: Touchstone, 1997), 174, note no. 29, 355.
15. Stanley, *Autobiography*, 189, 190.
16. Cunningham, 156, 157, notes; oral history of author's family living at Corinth.
17. *War of the Rebellion*, Series I, vol. 10/1: 179.
18. http://wiki.answers.com/Q/How_fast_ did_steamboats_go_in_the_1800s; http://voi ces.yahoo.com/steamboats-rise-cotton-kingd-om-robert-10753721.html.
19. *Papers of U.S. Grant*, vol. 8: 62n.
20. *War of the Rebellion*, Series I, vol. 10/1: 78.
21. *Papers of U.S. Grant*, Vol. 5:19n., Special Orders No. 47 April 6, 1862.
22. *War of the Rebellion*, Series I, vol. 10/1: 148.
23. *War of the Rebellion*, 147–148.
24. Ibid., 135.
25. Ibid., 156.
26. Ibid., 165.

27. Ibid., 238–240.
28. Ibid.

Chapter 11

1. *War of the Rebellion*, vol. 10/1: 454; General Clement A. Evans, ed., *Confederate Military History*, vol. 12, *Mississippi*, 235; Sword, 334; Hurst, 88, 89.
2. Author's oral family history.
3. Sam R. Watkins, *Company Aytch: Maury Grays, First Tennessee Regiment, or, A Side Show of the Big Show* (Columbia, TN: self-published, 1882); http://www.fullbooks .com/Co-Aytch-1.html.
4. Ibid.
5. Hurst, 89.
6. Watkins.
7. E.B. Quiner Collection, 214–250.
8. Ibid., note 6.
9. Hurst, 83, 84.
10. Cunningham, 13.
11. *Papers of U.S. Grant*, vol. 4: 218–219, Feb. 16, 1862, USG to Simon. B. Buckner.
12. Hurst, 71–74.
13. Evans, 385.
14. Robert S. Henry, *As They Saw Forrest* (Jackson, TN: Broadfoot, 1956) 93; Hurst, 88, 59.
15. Stanley, *Autobiography*, 194.
16. E.B. Quiner Collection, Derickson Official Order of Assignment, April 7, 1862. Lt. R.P. Derickson to J.W. Vail, 215.
17. E.B. Quiner Collection, 226, 227; *War of the Rebellion*, 285; Shiloh Military Park Marker 223.
18. *O.P. Newberry Papers*, Letter to Mother.
19. Kremer, *James Milton Turner*, 209.
20. Derickson Documents.
21. Ibid.
22. Ibid.
23. Derickson Documents.
24. Sword, 359; Daniel, 244, 245; *War of the Rebellion*, Report of 16th Wisconsin, Col. Benjamin Allen, 285; *War of the Rebellion*, 44th Indiana Report, Col. Hugh R. Reed, 285.

Chapter 12

1. *Papers of U.S. Grant*, vol. 2: 202n, 316n; Ibid., vol. 3: 182, 183n, 188n.
2. *War of the Rebellion*, Report of Lt. Col. Enos P. Wood; Ibid., 141, 142.
3. Major D.W. Reed, comp., *The Battle of Shiloh and the Organizations Engaged* (Washington, D.C.: Government Printing Office, 1909), Abstracts, 90–97.

4. Daniel, 177; *Papers of U.S. Grant*, vol. 4: 492.

5. *War of the Rebellion*, 139–140, Reports Lt. Abram Ryan and Col. Enos P. Wood , 141–142.

6. Derickson Documents.

7. *Map of the Battlefield of Shiloh*, 1904: Atwell Thompson, Engineer; D.W. Reed Historian.

8. *War of the Rebellion*, 141, 142, Report of Lt. Col Enos P. Wood.

9. "Grant County, Wisconsin, History." http://genealogytrails.com/wis/grant/history_overview.html.

10. "History of Mercer County, Ill., New Boston." http://freepages.history.rootsweb.ancestry.com/~mygermanfamilies/Part4.html.

11. *War of the Rebellion*, 248–250, Report of Brig. Gen. William T. Sherman.

12. Reed, 90.

13. *War of the Rebellion*, 141–142, Report of Lt. Col. Enos P. Wood.

14. *War of the Rebellion*, 141–142, Report of Lt. Col. Enos P. Wood; Daniel, 183, 184.

15. Ibid., 139–140, Report Lt. Abram. Ryan.

16. Shiloh Park Marker #417.

17. "German Settlers in Louisiana and New Orleans." http://www.hnoc.org/collections/gerpath/gersectl.html.

18. Stanley, *Autobiography*, 197.

19. Derickson Documents. See Appendix.

Chapter 13

1. Stacey Allen, "The Campaign and the First Day of Battle," *Blue and Grey Magazine: Shiloh!—A Visitor's Guide*, 18.

2. *War of the Rebellion*, 203–204, Report of Brig. Gen. Stephen A. Hurlbut, Commanding 4th Division.

3. Ibid., 278, Report of Brig. Gen. B.M. Prentiss, Commanding 6th Division.

4. E.B. Quiner Collection, 213, Lt. R.P. Derickson to J.W. Vail.

5. *War of the Rebellion*, 278, Report of Brig. Gen. B.M. Prentiss, Commanding 6th Division; Derickson Documents.

6. *War of the Rebellion*, 203–204, Report of Brig. Gen. Stephen A. Hurlbut, Commanding 4th Division.

7. Ibid., 214–215, Report of Colonel John Logan.

8. *War of the Rebellion*, 214–215, Report of Colonel John Logan.

9. Harvey Riley, *The Mule: A Treatise on the Breeding, Training and Uses to Which He May Be Put.* http://www.gutenberg.org/files/10878/10878-h/10878-h.htm.

10. Ibid., note 8.

11. Brewer, 85.

12. *War of the Rebellion*, 213, Report of Col. Armory K. Johnson, 28th Illinois.

13. *War of the Rebellion*, 215–216, Report of Colonel John Logan, 32nd Ill.; ibid., 216, Report of Captain Alfred C. Campbell 32nd Illinois.

14. Ibid.

15. *War of the Rebellion*, 217–218, Report of Maj. John Warner, 41st Illinois.

16. Ibid., 235–236, Report of Col. Charles Cruft, 31st Indiana Infantry.

17. *Papers of U.S. Grant*, vol. 5: 19n, April 6, 1862, General Orders No. 47, Clark B, Lagow.

18. *War of the Rebellion*, 238–239, Report of Col Hugh B. Reed, 44th Indiana; Sword, 359.

19. Ibid. 238–239.

20. Ibid.

21. Sword, 359.

22. Ibid., 359.

Chapter 14

1. *War of the Rebellion*, 179.

2. Ibid., 185.

3. Ibid.

4. Cunningham, 159.

5. Daniel, 175.

6. *War of the Rebellion*, 185.

7. Sword, 220–221.

8. Reed, 15; Shiloh Military Park, markers of 6th Division regiments.

9. *War of the Rebellion*, 108–111.

10. Ibid., 185.

11. *Papers of U.S. Grant*, vol. 4: 97–98, 98n, 491.

12. The Army Transportation Corps Creed (earlier version of Army Quartermaster Corps Creed), http://www.qmmuseum.lee.army.mil/index.html.

13. *War of the Rebellion*, 117.

14. Ibid.

15. Ibid., 117–118.

16. Ibid., 117.

17. Ibid., 118.

18. Ibid., 122.

19. Ibid., 124.

20. Ibid., 131.

21. Ibid., 134.

22. Ibid., 135.

23. Ibid., 136.

24. Ibid., 142.

25. Ibid., 139–140.

26. Ibid., 144–145.

27. Ibid., 146–147.
28. Ibid., 142.
29. Ibid., 152.
30. Ibid., 154.
31. Ibid., 155.

Chapter 15

1. *O.R.* Series I, vol. 10/1, 108.
2. *O.R.* Series I, vol. 10/1, 109.
3. *War of the Rebellion*, 119, McClernand's report; ibid., 251, Sherman's Report; Daniel, 280.
4. Johnson and Buel, vol. 1: 607, excerpt from the *New York Mail and Dispatch* for November 4, 1886.
5. *War of the Rebellion*, 184, 185.
6. *Papers of U.S. Grant*, April 4, 1862, W.R. Rowley for U.S Grant to Stephen A. Hurlbut; April 5, 1962, John A. Rawlins to B.M. Prentiss.
7. Gail Stephens, *Shadow of Shiloh*, 84–88.
8. Sword, 219.
9. Stephens, 84–88.
10. *Papers of U.S. Grant.* March 31, 1862, JAR to L. Wallace; April 3, 1862, Special Orders No. 44; April 5, 1862, John A. Rawlins to B.M. Prentiss.
11. *War of the Rebellion*, 179.
12. Ibid., 184–185; Johnson and Buel, vol. 1: 607, excerpt from the *New York Mail and Dispatch* for November 4, 1886.
13. *Papers of U.S. Grant*, vol. 4: 7.
14. Ibid., Special Order No. 44, April Papers of USG.
15. Grant, *Personal Memoirs,* 177.
16. *War of the Rebellion,* 184–185.
17. Ibid., 170.
18. Ibid., 181.
19. Ibid., 110.
20. *Papers of U.S. Grant*, vol. 5: 20n, 21, 47, 48n–49; vol. 4: 352n, 367n, 392n, 397, 451, 452n.
21. Cunningham, 387.
22. *War of the Rebellion*, 99.
23. Ibid., 110.
24. Ibid., 99.
25. Ibid., 174.
26. Ibid., 110.
27. Ibid.
28. Ibid., 61n.
29. *Papers of U.S. Grant*, vol. 8: 112–113.
30. *War of the Rebellion*, 170.
31. Ibid., 174.
32. Ibid., 184–185; Johnson and Buel, vol. 1: 607, excerpt from the *New York Mail and Dispatch* for November 4, 1886.

33. *War of the Rebellion*, 178.
34. Johnson and Buel, vol. 1: 607 excerpt from the *New York Mail and Dispatch* for November 4, 1886.

Chapter 16

1. Faust, 55; Gerald Linderman, *Embattled Courage: The Experience of Combat in the American Civil War* (New York: Your Free Press, 1987), 128.
2. "History of Dane County, Wisconsin, 1880," http://www.wisconsinhistory.org.
3. McGinley, Daniel E., "Ozaukee County's War History: Ozaukee Rifles," extracts from *Port Washington Star*, series issues May 6, 1896–July 18, 1896, http://www.rootsweb.ance stry.com/~wiozauke/WarHistory/OzRiflesCh1 .html.
4. E.B. Quiner Collection, 213.
5. Johnson and Buel, vol. 1: 414.
6. Johnston, 566–569.
7. Cunningham, 265.
8. Johnston, 614; Cunningham, 273–276.
9. Cunningham, 270–273.
10. *War of the Rebellion*, 214–215.
11. Hurst, 89.
12. Cunningham, 326.
13. Watkins, chapter 2: 3.
14. Ibid., 11–14.
15. *War of the Rebellion*, 310.
16. Reed, 98.
17. Ibid., 110.
18. Ibid.
19. Author's collection, Lew Wallace to Secretary Stanton, August 25, 1862.

Chapter 17

1. Sword, 117; Brazelton.
2. Watkins, chapter 2: 12.
3. Kremer, 16–17.
4. Corinth Contraband Camp, 902 North Parkway Corinth Mississippi, ph. (662) 287–9273, Corinth Area Convention and Visitors' Bureau.
5. Dr. Ronnie Fullwood, *Shiloh's House of Peace: The Church that Named the Battle* (Selmer, Tennessee: G.& P. Printing Services, 2003), 13.
6. F.C. Cook, "Speaker's Commentary on Genesis 49:10," in *Insight on the Scriptures* (Brooklyn, NY: Watchtower Bible and Tract Society of Pennsylvania, International Bible Students Association, 1988), vol. 2: 928–929.
7. Dorothy Stanley, 196–197.

8. Papers of Oliver Perry Newberry.

9. Reed, 75; Land Protection Plan Shiloh National Military Park, Tennessee–Mississippi (Biennial Review, 2002), Figure 1: Authorized Boundary of Shiloh National Military Park, as described in ...... on the bluff (roughly 400 yards west of the old Shake-A-Rag Church site) east ..., http://www.nps.gov/shil/park-mgmt/upload/lpp.pdf.

10. "Behavioral Science on the Nature of Glossolalia," http://www.asa3.org/ASA/PSCF/1968/JASA9–68Pattison.html; "The Linguis-cality of Glossolalia," http://www.asa3.org/ASA/PSCF/1968/JASA9–68Pattison.html; http:// "Speaking in tongues," www.spirithome.com/tongues1.html.

11. "The Social Acceptance of Ragtime," http://mickeymccord.com/RagtimeAcceptanc ethe Blues Devil's Music; *Is the Blues Devil's Music?* http://blues.about.com/od/earlyblues-essentials/tp/DevilMusic.htm

12. Cozzens, *Who Kept Grant Sober?*, http://www.historynet.com/who-kept-u-s-grant-sober.htm.

13. Kremer, 209–210.

14. Kremer, 46.

Chapter 18

1. Niccolo Machiavelli, *The Prince* (Selected Quotes), 1515, translated by W.K. Marriot; rendered into HTML by Jon Roland of the Constitution Society, http://www.constitution.org/mac/prince00.htm.

2. Frances Bernard Heitman, *Historical Register of the United States Army: from its Or-ganization, September 29, 1789, to September 29, 1889* (Washington, D.C.: The National Tribune, 1890).

3. Wilson and Fiske.

4. *Papers of U.S. Grant*, vol. 4, Jan. 8– Mar. 31, 1861, 97, 98, 98n, 207–208, 208.

5. *The Papers of U.S. Grant* Vol. 5, p.88/89.89n,168–169,169–170n,171,171n.,174n.

6. McGinley.

7. George W. Parker, *History of the Seventy-ninth Regiment Indiana Volunteer Infantry in the Civil War of Eighteen Sixty-one in the United States* (Indianapolis: Hollenbeck Press), 1899.

8. *O.R.* 52, pt. 1; 313–314; Woodworth.

9. Walt Whitman, *Prose Works,* excerpt from http://teachingamericanhistory.org/library/index.asp?document=1723.

10. *Papers of U.S. Grant*, vol. 5, 52–53, 53n, 73: promotions of Rawlins, LaGow, Hillyer, and Riggins.

11. Wilson and Fiske.

12. Watkins, chapter 2: Shiloh.

13. James Harrison Wilson, *The Life of John A. Rawlins* (New York: Neale Publishing, 1916).

14. Sharon Begley, "Sins of the Grandfathers," *Newsweek Magazine*, Nov. 8, 2010, 48–50.

15. Ibid.

16. Ibid.

17. http://www.nytimes.com/2012/04/15/opinion/sunday/kristof-a-veterans-death-the-nations-shame.html; http://www.armytimes.com/news/2010/04/military_veterans_suicide_042210w/—182k.

Bibliography

Allen, Stacy D. "The Campaign and the First Day of Battle." *Blue and Grey Magazine: Shiloh!—A Visitor's Guide.*
_____. "Crossroads of the Western Confederacy." *Blue and Gray Magazine: Corinth, Mississippi,—A Visitor's Guide.*
Balch, William Ralston. *Life of President Garfield.* Philadelphia: Hubbard Bros., 1831.
Basso, Hamilton. *Beauregard: The Great Creole.* New York: Scribner's, 1933.
Begley, Sharon. *Sins of the Grandfathers. Newsweek,* Nov. 8, 2010.
Bierce, Ambrose. *The Devil's Dictionary.* Mineola, NY: Dover, 2011. First published in *The Collected Works of Ambrose Bierce,* vol. 7, in 1911.
_____. "What I Saw of Shiloh." In *The Collected Works of Ambrose Bierce,* vol. 1. New York: Neal Publishing, 1909. http://www.online-literature.com/bierce/2037/.
Bonner, Robert E. *The Soldier's Pen: Firsthand Impressions of the Civil War.* New York: Hill & Wang, 2006.
Boomhower, Ray E. *The Sword and the Pen: A Life of Lew Wallace.* Indianapolis: Indiana Historical Society, 2005.
Bowman, Thornton H. *Reminiscences of an Ex-Confederate Soldier.* http://mississippiconfederates.wordpress.com/2011/12/21/reminiscences-of-an-ex-confederate-soldier-by-thornton-h-bowman-wirt-adams-cavalry/.
Bradt. "Bradt Describes Waupace Men in Battle of Shiloh." *New London Press* (Waupaca, WI). March 11, 1925. E.B. Quiner Collection.

Brazelton, John. *Brazelton's History of Hardin County.* First published by the author in Tennessee, 1885. http://www.tngenweb.org/hardin/hosey/bios/brazelton/brazelton (accessed August 18, 2012).
Brewer, James D. *Tom Worthington's Civil War: Shiloh, Sherman, and the Search for Vindication.* Jefferson, NC: McFarland, 2001.
Bynum, Victoria E. *The Free State of Jones: Mississippi's Longest Civil War.* Chapel Hill: University of North Carolina Press, 2001.
Catton, Bruce. *The Coming Fury.* New York: Doubleday, 1961.
_____. *Grant Moves South.* Boston: Little, Brown, 1960.
"Charles Parsons Papers, 1808–1940: Steamboats Series, 1862–1864." St. Louis, MO: Missouri Historical Society Archives.
Chetlain, Augustus L. *Memories of Seventy Years.* Galena, IL: Gazette, 1889.
"Civil War Soldiers and Sailors System." U.S. Department of the Interior: National Park Service, www.itd.nps.gov.
Cook, F.C. "Speaker's Commentary on Genesis 49:10." *Insight on the Scriptures,* vol. 2. Brooklyn, NY: Watchtower Bible and Tract Society of Pennsylvania, International Bible Students Association, 1988.
Cozzens, Peter E. "My poor little Ninth: The Ninth Illinois at Shiloh." *Illinois Historical Journal* 83, no. 1 (1990): 31–44.
_____. "Who Kept Grant Sober?" Historynet.com http://www.historynet.com/who-kept-u-s-grant-sober.htm.
Crowley, Robert, ed. *What Ifs? of American History.* New York: Berkeley, 2003.

Cunningham, Edward O. *Shiloh and the Western Campaign of 1862.* Gary D. Joiner and Timothy B. Smith, eds. New York: Savas Beatie, 2007, 2009.

Daily Missouri Republican, January 12–August 20, 1862. http://www2.uttyler.edu /vbetts/missouri_republican.htm.

Daniel, Larry J. *Shiloh: The Battle That Changed the Civil War.* New York: Touchstone, 1997.

Davis, Jefferson. "Proceedings of the First Congress." In *The Rise and Fall of the Confederate Government.* New York: D. Appleton, 1881.

Davis, William C. *The Orphan Brigade: The Kentucky Confederates Who Couldn't Go Home.* Baton Rouge: Louisiana State University Press, 1983.

Dillahunty, Albert. *Shiloh: National Military Park, Tennessee.* Washington, DC: Government Printing Office, 1955.

Downhour, James G. "Nathaniel Lyon." In *Encyclopedia of the American Civil War: A Political, Social, and Military History.* David S. Heidler and Jeanne T. Heidler, eds. New York: W.W. Norton, 2000.

Dyer, Frederick Henry. "Part 3: History of the 3rd Iowa Regiment." In *A Compendium of the War of the Rebellion.* 3 vols. New York: Thomas Yoseloff, 1959. http: //www.civilwararchive.com/regim.htm.

Eisenschiml, Otto. "An Historian Without an Armchair." http://www.archive.org/s tream/illustratedhisto00neal#page/n9/mo de/2up.

_____. *The Story of Shiloh.* Chicago: The Civil War Round Table, 1946.

"Epigenetics: DNA Isn't Everything." *ScienceDaily*, Apr. 13, 2009.

Evans, Gen. Clement A., ed. *Confederate Military History*, vol. 12: *Alabama*, by Lt. Gen. Joseph Wheeler, and *Mississippi*, by Col. Charles E. Hooker. Secaucus, NJ: Blue and Grey Press, 1899.

Faust, Drew Gilpin. *This Republic of Suffering: Death and the American Civil War.* New York: Vintage Books, 2008.

"5th Regiment, Mississippi Cavalry." https://www.familysearch.org/learn/wiki/ en/5th_Regiment,_Mississippi_Cavalry.

Fullwood, Ronnie, DD. *Shiloh's House of Peace: The Church That Named the Battle.* Selmer, TN: G&P Printing Services, 2003.

Garrison, Webb. *Civil War Curiosities: Strange Stories, Oddities, Events and Coincidences.* Nashville: Rutledge Hill Press, 1994.

_____. *Mutiny in the Civil War.* Shippensburg, PA: White Mane Books, 2001.

Grant, Ulysses S. *Personal Memoirs.* Caleb Carr, ed. New York: Modern Library, 1999. Reprinted from *Personal Memoirs of U.S. Grant.* New York: Charles Webster, 1885.

G.T. Beauregard papers, 1839–1888. Tulane University. http://specialcollections.tulan e.edu/archon/?p=collections/controlcard &id=55.

Halleck, H. Wager. *Elements of Military Art and Science*, 3rd ed. New York: D. Appleton, 1862.

Hardee, William Joseph. *Hardee's Rifle and Light Infantry Tactics.* 2 vols. Philadelphia: Lippincott, Grambo, 1855.

"Harrison County Missouri Biographies: Major General Benjamin Prentiss, 1819–1901." *Bethany Republican*, Feb. 13, 1901. http://genealogytrails.com/mo/harrison/b iographies_p.html.

Heitman, Frances Bernard. *Historical Register of the United States Army: from its Organization, September 29, 1789, to September 29, 1889.* Washington, DC: The National Tribune, 1890.

Henry, Robert Selph. *As They Saw Forrest: Some Recollections and Comments from Contemporaries.* Jackson, TN: Broadfoot, 1992.

_____. *First with the Most: Nathan Bedford Forrest.* New York: Bdd Promotional Books, 1991.

Hewitt, Janet B., ed. "O'Neal and O'Neils in the Civil War: The South Confederate O'Neals." *The Roster of Confederate Soldiers, 1861–1865.* Broadfoot and the National Archives Trust Fund Board. The Military Service Records from the National Archives and Records Administration — NARA, Submitted by Jerry Roebke. http://www.ronsattic.com/cw3.htm.

Higginson, Thomas Wentworth. *Harvard Memorial Biographies.* Cambridge: Sever and Francis, 1866.

Hittell, Theodore Henry. *History of California*. San Francisco: N.J. Stone, 1898.

Hooker, Col. Charles E. "Confederate Military History." In *A Library of Confederate States History*. Atlanta: Confederate Publishing, 1899.

"Horace Henry Baxter, 1818–1884." *Rutland (Vermont) Historical Society Quarterly* 23, no. 3: 1993. http://www.rutlandhistory.com/documents/RHSQVol.XXIIINo.31993.pdf.

Horwitz, Tony. *Confederates in the Attic: Dispatches for the Unfinished Civil War*. New York: Vintage Books, 1999.

Howe, M.A. Dewolfe. *Home Letters of General Sherman*. New York: Scribner's, 1909.

Hurst, Jack. *Nathan Bedford Forrest: A Biography*. New York: Vintage Books, 1994.

Ingersoll, Robert G. "Crumbling Creeds." In *The Works of Robert G. Ingersoll*. Dresden Memorial Edition. http://www.positiveatheism.org/hist/ingbanq.htm#CREEDS.

_____. "The Liberty of All." In *The Works of Robert G. Ingersoll*. Dresden Memorial Edition. http://www.positiveatheism.org/hist/ingbanq.htm#CREEDS.

"Iowa in the Civil War: Roster and Record of Iowa Soldiers in the War of the Rebellion, Together with Historical Sketches of Volunteer Organizations, 1861–1866." Des Moines: E.H. English, State Printer, E.D. Chassell, State Binder, 1908–11. http://iagenweb.org/civilwar/books/logan/logan.htm.

"James Sligh Letters." *New York Tribune*, April 21, 1862. Michigan Historical Society. www.hsmichigan.org.

Johnson, Allen, ed. *Dictionary of American Biography*. New York: Scribner's, 1936.

Johnson, Robert Underwood, and Clarence Clough Buel, eds. *Battles and Leaders of the Civil War*, vol. 1. New York: Thomas Yoseloff, 1956. Reprint of the *Century Magazine* 1887. www.betterworldbooks.com/dictionary-of-american-biography.

Johnston, William Preston. *The Life of General Albert Sidney Johnston, Embracing his Services in the Armies of the United States, the Republic of Texas, and the Confederate States*. New York: D. Appleton, 1879.

Jones, Archer. *Confederate Strategy from Shiloh to Vicksburg*. Baton Rouge: Louisiana State University Press, 1991.

Juda, Fanny. "California Filibusters: A History of their Expeditions into Hispanic America." In *The Grizzly Bear: Official Organ of the Native Sons and Native Daughters of the Golden West* 21, no. 4 (February 1919).

Keller, Rudi. "The Battle of Jefferson City: What if it happened?" *Columbia (Missouri) Daily Tribune*, Sunday, June 12, 2011. http://www.columbiatribune.com/news/2011/jun/12/battle-jefferson-city-what-if-it-happened/.

Kennedy's 1860 St. Louis City Directory.

Knapp, Joseph G., S.J. *The Presence of the Past: Beginnings of the Civil War in St. Louis*. St. Louis: St. Louis University Press, 1961, 1979.

Kremer, Gary R. *James Milton Turner and the Promise of America: The Public Life of a Post–Civil War Black Leader*. Columbia: University of Missouri Press, 1991.

Lewis, Lloyd. *Sherman, Fighting Prophet*. Lincoln: University of Nebraska Press, 1993.

Linderman, Gerald. *Embattled Courage: The Experience of Combat in the American Civil War*. New York: Your Free Press, 1987.

Logsdon, David R., comp. and ed. *Eyewitnesses at the Battle of Shiloh*. Nashville: Kettle Mills, 1994.

Lowry, Thomas, and William Davis. "The Worst Colonel I Ever Saw: Colonel Francis Quinn." In *Curmudgeons, Drunkards and Outright Fools: Courts-Martial of Civil War Union Colonels*. Mechanicsburg, PA: Stackpole, 1997.

Luvass, Jay, Stephen Bowman, and Leonard Fullenkamp, ed. *Guide to the Battle of Shiloh*. Lawrence: University Press of Kansas, 1996.

Machiavelli, Niccolo. *The Prince*. 1515. W.K. Marriot, trans. Rendered into HTML by Jon Roland of the Constitution Society. http://www.constitution.org/mac/prince00.htm.

McDonough, James Lee. *Shiloh—in Hell before Night*. Knoxville: University of Tennessee Press, 1977.

McGinley, Daniel. "Company K: 16th Wisconsin." *Port Washington Star*, 1897. Wisconsin Historical Society. wwwwisconsinhistory.org.

_____. "Ozaukee County's War History: Ozaukee Rifles." *Port Washington Star*, May 6, 1896–July 18, 1896. http://www.rootsweb.ancestry.com/~wiozauke/WarHistory/OzRiflesCh1.html.

McGregor, Malcolm G. *The Biographical Record of Jasper County, Missouri*. Lewis, MO: Lewis Publishing, 1901.

McPherson, James M. *Battle Cry of Freedom: The Civil War Era*. Oxford, MS: University of Mississippi Press, 1988.

Madison Miller Biography. Missouri History Museum. http://genealogytrails.com/mo/harrison/biographies_p.html.

"The March of Lew Wallace's Division to Shiloh." In *The Opening Battles*. Vol. 1 of *Battles and Leaders of the Civil War*. Robert Underwood Johnson and Clarence Clough Buel, eds. http://www.perseus.tufts.edu/hopper/text?doc=Perseus.

"Memorial to the Baxter Family." Internet Archive. http://www.archive.org/stream/memorialofbaxter00baxt/memorialofbaxter00baxt_djvu.txt.

Merry, Robert W. *A Country of Vast Designs: James K. Polk, the Mexican War and the Conquest of the American Continent*. New York: Simon & Schuster, 2010.

"Mississippi Units by County of Origin 1861–1865." http://humphreys1625.homestead.com/Unit Index.html.

Mitchell, Joseph B., Lt. Col. *Decisive Battles of the Civil War*. Greenwich, CT: Fawcett World Library, 1955.

Morseberger, Robert E., and Katherine M. Morseberger. *Lew Wallace: Militant Romantic*. New York: McGraw-Hill, 1980.

Morton, Charles. *A Boy at Shiloh*. New York: [s.n.], 1899.

Murray, R.L., ed. *Irish Brigade at Antietam*, vol. 2: *New Yorkers in the Civil War*. Wolcott, NY: Benedum Books, 2006.

Neal, W.A. *An Illustrated History, Missouri Engineer, 25th Regiments*. Chicago: Donnohue and Henneberry, 1889. http://www.archive.org/stream/illustratedhisto00neal#page/n9/mode/2up Index-Newberry p. 119–123 Donnohue and Henneberry, Chicago 1889 (accessed Aug. 22, 2012).

Newberry, Oliver Perry. *Oliver Perry Newberry Papers*. Chicago: The Newberry Library, Roger and Julie Baskes Department of Special Collections.

Northcott, Dennis. *Guide to Civil War Manuscripts in the Missouri Historical Society Archives*. http://www.mohistory.org/files/archivesguides/CivilWar.

_____. *Military Order of the Loyal Legion of the United States, Commandery of the State of Missouri, Records, 1885–1931*. Processed 2003. http://www.mohistory.org/files/archives_guides/MilitaryOrder.pdf.

The Online Archive of Terry's Texas Rangers. www.terrystexasrangers.org/index.html.

Paine, Albert Bigalow. *Mark Twain: A Biography. The Personal and Literary Life of Samuel Langhorne Clemens*. Adelaide: eBooks@Adelaide, 2010. http://www.adelaide.edu.au (accessed March 17, 2012).

_____. *Mark Twain's Autobiography: With Commentary by Alfred Bigelow Paine*. New York: Harper & Brothers, 1924.

The Papers of U.S. Grant. U.S. Grant Association, Mississippi State University. http://digital.library.msstate.edu.

Parker, George W. *History of the Seventy-ninth Regiment Indiana Volunteer Infantry in the Civil War of Eighteen Sixty-one in the United States*. Indianapolis: Hollenbeck Press, 1899.

Perret, Geoffrey. *Ulysses S. Grant: Soldier & President*. http://www.booknotes.org/Watch/91723–1/Geoffrey+Perret.aspx.

Petersen, William J. *Steamboating on the Upper Mississippi*. Iowa City: State Historical Society of Iowa, 1968.

Photographic History of the Civil War. 10 vols. New York: Review of Reviews, 1911. http://www.archive.org/stream/photographichist10mill#page/46/mode/2up.

Quiner, E.B. "Newspaper Clippings." Wisconsin Regiments, Wisconsin Historical Society. http://www.wisconsinhistory.org/.

Reed, Major D.W., comp. *The Battle of Shiloh and the Organizations Engaged*. Washington, DC: Government Printing Office, 1909.

"Records of United States Army Continental Commands, 1821–1920" (Record Group

393)1817–1940). National Archives (bulk 1817–1920). http://www.archives.gov/research/guide-fed-records/groups/393.html.

Rice, DeLong. *The Story of Shiloh.* 3rd ed. Memphis: Julia M. Rice, 1961.

Rich, Joseph W. *The Battle of Shiloh.* Iowa City: State Historical Society of Iowa, 1911.

Rigdon, John C. "Mississippi Civil War Soldiers Index." www.researchonline.net.

Riley, Harvey. "The Mule: A Treatise on the Breeding, Training, and Uses to Which He May Be Put." Washington, DC: 1867. Project Gutenberg. http://www.gutenberg.org/files/10878/10878-h/10878-h.htm.

Robertson, John. *Michigan in the Civil War.* Lansing: W.S. George, 1882.

Roman, Alfred. *The Military Operations of General Beauregard.* 2 vols. New York: Harper & Brothers, 1884.

"Roster of Wisconsin Volunteers." Online Collection: Wisconsin Historical Society. http://www.wisconsinhistory.org/roster/search.asp#regiment.

Rowland, Dunbar. *Military History of Mississippi, 1803–1898:1st Mississippi Cavalry.* Courtesy of H. Grady Howell's *For Dixie Land, I'll Take My Stand.* http://www.mississippiscv.org/MS_Units/1st_MS_CAV(AW).htm.

_____. *Military History of Mississippi, 1803–1898: Mississippi Minutemen (State Troops).* Courtesy of H. Grady Howell's *For Dixie Land, I'll Take My Stand.* http://www.mississippiscv.org/MS_Units/minute_men.htm.

Russell, William Howard, and Fletcher Pratt, ed. *My Diary North and South.* New York: Harper & Brothers, 1954.

"The Seizures in Missouri." *Missouri Democrat,* May 25, 1861. http://www.nytimes.com/1861/05/27/news/the-seizures-in-missouri.html.

Senatobia Centennial, Inc. *Senatobia Centennial: Celebrating 100 Years of Progress.* Senatobia, MS: 1960.

Sharra, Jeff. *A Blaze of Glory: A Novel of the Battle of Shiloh.* New York: Ballantine Books, 2012.

Shea, John G. *The American Nation: Lives of the Fallen Braves and Living Heroes.* New York: I. Farrell & Son, 1863.

Sherman, W.T. *Memoirs of General William T. Sherman,* 2 vols. 2nd revised edition. New York: D. Appleton, 1889.

Shiloh Battlefield Commission. *The Seventy-Seventh Pennsylvania at Shiloh.* Harrisburg, PA: Harrisburg Publishing, 1905.

Simon, John, ed. *The Papers of Ulysses S. Grant.* Vol. 8: April 1–July 6, 1863. http://books.google.com/books.

61st Illinois Infantry in the American Civil War, Report of the Adjutant General of the State of Illinois. Volume 4, Revised by Brigadier General J.N. Reece, Adjutant General, 1900. http://www.civilwarindex.com/armyil/61st_il_infantry.html.

Smith, Timothy B. "Shiloh's False Hero." http://www.historynet.com/shilohs-false-hero.htm.

_____. *This Great Battlefield of Shiloh: History, Memory, and the Establishment of a Civil War National Military Park.* Knoxville: University of Tennessee Press, 2004.

"Society at Home and Abroad, Social Standing shown, Engagement of Algernon Sydney Baxter's granddaughter." http://query.nytimes.com/mem/archive-free/pdf.

"Soldiers and Sailors Data Base." National Park Service. http://www.nps.gov/civilwar/soldiers-and-sailors-database.htm.

Stanley, Dorothy, ed. *The Autobiography of Sir Henry Morton Stanley.* Boston and New York: Houghton and Mifflin, 1921.

Stanley, Sir Henry Morton. "Opening of the Battle of Shiloh." *War Paper No. 88.* New York: Commandery of the District of Columbia. Military Order of the Loyal Legion of the United States, 1907.

State of Illinois. *Report of the Adjutant General of the State of Illinois,* vol. 3. Springfield: Baker, Bailhache, 1987.

"Steamboat Iatan. Involvement in Disaster of Steamboat Edna." *National Intelligencer,* July 14, 1842. http://news.google.com/newspapers.

Stephens, Gail. *Shadow of Shiloh: Major General Lew Wallace in the Civil War.* Indianapolis: Indiana Historical Society Press, 2010.

"A Stockbroker's Troubles." *New York Times,*

February 18, 1867. http://query.nytim es.com/mem/archive-free/pdf.

Sword, Wiley. *Shiloh: Bloody April*. Dayton, OH: Morningside House Press, 2001.

Twain, Mark. *Autobiography of Mark Twain*, vol. 1, Harriet Elinor Smith and other editors of the Mark Twain Project. Berkley: University of California Press, 2010.

_____. *Captain Stormfield's Visit to Heaven*. New York: Harper & Brothers, 1909.

_____. "Private History of a Campaign that Failed." *American Claimant and Other Stories and Sketches*. New York: Scribner's, 1896. http://www.archive.org /stream/photographichist10mill#page/46/ mode/2up.

Ulysses S. Grant Association: Mississippi State University. http://library.msstate. edu/usgrant/articles.asp#b-art.

U.S. Navy. *Official Records of the Union and Confederate Navies in the War of the Rebellion*, Series 1, vol. 22. Washington, DC: Government Printing Office, 1908.

"Vermont in the Civil War: United States Army Vermonters Who Served as General Officers, On Staff, and in Regiments from Other States." http://vermontcivilwar.or g/units/army/722.php.

Wallace, Isabel. *Life and Letters of General W.H.L. Wallace*. Carbondale: Southern Illinois Press, 2000.

Wallace, Lew. *Lew Wallace: An Autobiography*. Vol. 1. New York: Harper & Brothers, 1906.

The War of the Rebellion: A Compilation of the Official Records of the Union and Confederate Armies. Oliver Computing LLC, 2006. The Civil War CD-ROM.

Watkins, Sam R. *Co. Aytch: Maury Grays, First Tennessee Regiment; or, A Side Show of the Big Show*. First published by the author in Columbia, TN, 1882. Republished by *Chattanooga Times*, 1900. Full Books. http://www.fullbooks.com (accessed August 21, 2012).

Welch, Paul D. *Archeology at Shiloh Indian Mounds, 1899–1999*. Tuscaloosa: University of Alabama Press, 2006.

"Western Gunboat Flotilla/ Mississippi Squadron: Operations on the Mississippi, Ohio, White and Yazoo Rivers." January 1–December 31, 1862. http://www.brown waternavy.org/umiss2.htm.

Whitehead, Jane. "Picturing America." *Boston College Magazine* (Summer 2009): 14–23.

Whitman, Walt. "The Real War Will Never Get in the Books." *Prose Works*, 1892. http://www.bartleby.com/229/1101.html.

Williams, Harry T. *P.G.T. Beauregard: Napoleon in Gray*. Baton Rouge: Louisiana State University Press, 1954.

Wilson, H., comp. *Trow's New York City Directory*, Vol. 85. New York: John J. Trow, 1872. http://books.google.com/booksid= Xo0tAAAAYAAJ&pg=PA73&lpg=PA73 &dq=ALGERNON+S.+BAXTER+BRO KER

Wilson, James Grant. *General Grant's Letters to a Friend, 1861–1880*. E.B. Washburne, ed. New York and Boston: T.Y. Crowell & Co. http://archive.org/details/gengran tsfriend00ulysrich (accessed Aug. 20, 2012).

Wilson, James Grant, and John Fiske. "Algernon Sydney Baxter." In Vol. 7 of *Appleton's' Cyclopaedia of American Biography*. New York: D. Appleton, 1901. http://books.google.com/books.

Wilson, James Harrison. *The Life of John A. Rawlins*. New York: Neale Publishing, 1916.

Woodworth, Steven E., ed. *Grant's Lieutenants: From Cairo to Vicksburg*. Lawrence: University Press of Kansas, 2001.

The Works of Robert G. Ingersoll. Dresden Memorial Edition. http://www.posi tiveatheism.org/hist/ingbanq.htm#CREE DS.

Worthington, D. *The Broken Sword, or A Pictorial Page in Reconstruction*. Wilson, NC: P.D. Gold & Sons, 1901.

Wyeth, John A. *That Devil Forrest*. Baton Rouge: Louisiana State University Press, 1991.

Index